THE RETURN TO THE MYSTICAL

THE RETURN TO
THE MYSTICAL

*Ludwig Wittgenstein, Teresa of Avila
and the Christian Mystical Tradition*

PETER TYLER

continuum

Published by the Continuum International Publishing Group

The Tower Building	80 Maiden Lane
11 York Road	Suite 704
London	New York
SE1 7NX	NY 10038

www.continuumbooks.com

First published 2011

British Library Cataloguing-in-Publication Data
A catalogue record for this book is available from the British Library.

ISBN: 978-1-4411-0444-1

Typeset by Fakenham Prepress Solutions, Fakenham, Norfolk NR21 8NN
Printed and bound in India

Contents

An Explanation and
Acknowledgements

My initial interest in the subject of this book arose from a fascination and curiosity regarding two great literary figures: St. Teresa of Avila (1515 – 1582), the reforming Spanish Carmelite writer of such strikingly original poetry and prose, and Ludwig Wittgenstein (1889 – 1951), the austere and forbidding Austrian professor of logic and metaphysics who tore up and rewrote the rules of philosophy in the mid-twentieth century. As I embarked upon my doctoral thesis some ten years ago I was warned of the difficulty of taking two such original thinkers as my objects of study, and indeed I believe this is probably the first work to explore the interaction of the two figures in any depth. However, never being one to resist a challenge, I have spent the past ten years pursuing this fascinating *pas de deux*. The result is this book. So, as well as being an exposition of the 'mystical influences' which I believe went into the writing of Teresa's prose, it contains an attempt to understand the notoriously dense writings of Wittgenstein and some suggestions as to how a reading of his philosophy may help the academic study of the Christian mystical tradition. If that were not enough, I felt that as I wrote I had to delineate how I was using the word 'mystical', being aware of the huge academic controversy surrounding the term. This, alongside a genealogy of what I term the medieval *theologia mystica*, will comprise the third part of the book.

I hope that this book will remain curious to you, the reader, as the people we are dealing with are not simple writers and they often deliberately chose a style to perplex the reader, or so I argue. Their topic was perhaps the hardest that faces the human individual: how, in the face of the ineffable, can language bring about any expression that may contain any meaningful utterance, if at all? It is faced with this daunting challenge that I invite you to embark on this journey with me.

For me it has been a long *excursus* that began over twenty years ago when I first read Teresa of Avila and Ludwig Wittgenstein. However, the person to whose conversations and inspiration I am most in debt in this respect is Hymie Wyse to whom I am immensely grateful and to whom I dedicate this book. My second debt of gratitude is to my doctoral supervisors Professors Philip Sheldrake and Gerard Loughlin. Only they know how difficult it was to supervise me, and I am immensely grateful for all their kind patience and wisdom. I must not forget too some early pre-doctoral work on Wittgenstein carried out with Professor Beverley Clack in the early 1990s and I thank her for her continuing friendship. I am equally in debt to my examiners, Dr Edward Howells and Dr Chris Insole, who led me to see areas of the text that needed illumination. Apart from these key figures there have been innumerable others who have shaped the form of this book. At the risk of forgetting some I remember in particular: Dr Marije Altorf, Dr Stephen Bullivant, Dr Ivana Dolejšová, Professor Mary Grey, Professor Michael Hayes, Professor David Jones, Dr Michael Kirwan S.J., Professor Jeffrey Kripal, Professor Brian McGuire, Julienne McLean, Br Patrick Moore F.S.C., Dr Tim Noble, Professor Gerald O. Collins, Fr Paul Rowan, Dr Susan Stephenson, Dr Anthony Towey and Professor Richard Woods O.P.. During the writing of the text it was a great privilege to check certain of my interpretations with Euan Hill, one of Wittgenstein's last pupils from Cambridge. I am greatly indebted to him for his kindness and understanding. Continuum have been consistently excellent and I thank Robin Baird-Smith in particular for his inexhaustible help. As always I thank my family and friends for support during this time, especially, as ever, Gill, David, Gwynneth and Barry, Jimmy and Jenny and Ash and his family.

London
Feast of the Transfiguration
2010

Introduction: A Change of Aspect?

Much of what we are doing is a question of changing the style of thinking.[1]

(Wittgenstein LC: 28)

'Wisdom is grey.' However life and religion are full of colour.[2]

(Wittgenstein VB: 1947)

Towards the end of his life in 1949, while walking with his friend Maurice Drury around Phoenix Park in Dublin, the Austrian philosopher Ludwig Wittgenstein (1889–1951) shared the following remark:

I am not a religious man but I cannot help seeing every problem from a religious point of view.

(Rhees 1987: 79)

The curious ambiguity of the phrase with its rejection of 'religion' but appreciation of a 'religious point of view' seems to embody much of what the 'religious' meant to Wittgenstein. Since his death, and in the vast ocean of commentary and criticism that has emerged since then,

---

1   All abbreviations for Wittgenstein's works are given in the Bibliography; see note on sources at the end of this introduction.
2   *'Die Weisheit ist grau.' Das Leben aber und die Religion sind farbenreich.*

there have been attempts to either co-opt him as a closet atheist, or at least a verificationist; or, on the other hand, as an avowed and practising Christian. As will be shown in this book, neither attempt has been wholly successful and his unique blend of so many strands of nineteenth- and twentieth-century thought – idealism, logical positivism, existentialism, psychologism and linguistics – stubbornly defies simple categorization.

It is my contention in this book that it is precisely *this* ambiguity and *difficulty* within Wittgenstein's thought that makes it so helpful for investigating 'the religious point of view'. In particular, I will bring a 'Wittgensteinian point of view' to bear on a vexed and confusing subject of religion: what has been variously referred to as 'the mystical', 'mysticism' or 'the mystic'. I will argue here that this Wittgensteinian point of view can be helpful in elucidating how best to approach the concept in discussion and analysis by proposing what I term a 'Wittgensteinian methodology' for investigating the subject. In particular, I will be placing special emphasis on Wittgenstein's notion of 'aspect seeing' in a *Weltbild* (literally: 'picture of the world') as central to how I investigate the *theologia mystica*[3] in the following chapters. I will also refine this Wittgensteinian methodology by developing a threefold insight based around the move from Saying to Showing to Acting. I will then apply this Wittgensteinian methodology to interpret the rise of *theologia mystica* as a distinct method of discourse, or language game, arising from the twelfth/thirteenth-century Latin revival of the works of Dionysius in the Parisian schools. Having presented my analysis of the twelfth-century reception of the works of Dionysius I shall move on to the evolution of the 'language game', tracing its evolution from the schools and monasteries of Paris and Germany to its ultimate flowering in the convents and friaries of Renaissance Spain. I will conclude the book by returning to Wittgenstein's own life and work, and comparing it with that of probably the greatest of the 'Spanish mystics': Teresa of Avila.

3   Literally 'mystical theology'. I will use this term throughout the book to refer to what I call the 'language game' of the High Middle Ages that developed in the mystical schools influenced by the writings of Dionysius the Areopagite.

Thus, although the book begins by seeking to apply Wittgensteinian analysis to 'mystical situation', the final result is to produce a tool which can be reflected back on to Wittgenstein's writing, thus showing his own 'mystical strategies'. Ultimately, it will be argued, this helps to make sense of his own 'mystical' claims in works such as the *Tractatus Logico-Philosophicus* and perhaps throw light on the famous 'Wittgensteinian religious point of view' with which we began.

WHY WITTGENSTEIN?

At first sight, Ludwig Wittgenstein, the austere linguistic philosopher known for the rigour and spareness of his gnomic collections of philosophical reflections, does not seem to be the most promising agent for analysing the Christian mystical tradition. Yet, although as far as I am aware no such similar study has been undertaken before, it is my contention in this book that close analysis of his writings allows us to develop a linguistic tool to observe the 'mystical strategies' employed by medieval writers of the *theologia mystica*. In particular, I will concentrate in this survey on three areas that the Wittgensteinian tools provide for analysis of mystical writing:

1. Wittgenstein's tools for doing philosophy, in themselves often surprising and frequently misunderstood.
2. How the mechanisms for philosophy may be applied to spiritual and theological questions.
3. The limits of language in addressing these questions.

These considerations lead to a particular *method*. This method may be summarized in the line from the *Philosophical Investigations* (PI: 66) – '*Denk Nicht, Sondern Schau!*' 'Don't think – But look!'. While not being an anti-theoretical philosopher, Wittgenstein preferred an approach to the subject matter that 'consisted in seeing connections' rather than being interested in the 'occult identities' of metaphysics.

Of course, there will be problems if such a modern linguistic method is applied to the medieval writings of the Christian mystical tradition. Most significantly, these medieval writings were not written as philosophical texts – let alone a reaction to the prevailing philosophical critiques of the day. Unlike Wittgenstein,[4] most of the medieval writers surveyed here seem to have had an unshakeable belief in the power of God the Trinity to direct their lives. Such a clear metaphysical mandate is not so obvious in the case of Wittgenstein; his God is more a matter of conjecture. However, in the account which follows I will argue that by applying a 'Wittgensteinian' critique to these medieval writings new things can be revealed in their approach to some fundamental questions of what may be termed 'practical theology'.

CHANGING ASPECTS

What is incomprehensible is that nothing, and yet everything, has changed.

(Wittgenstein RPP2: 474)

One of the central contentions of this book will be that a key 'family resemblance' between Wittgenstein and the medieval Christian mystical writers is their shared preoccupation with 'making pictures' to stimulate a 'change of aspect' in our way of seeing and acting in the world. In this respect it will be argued that their writing must be seen as fundamentally *transformational* in character.[5]

In his final years Wittgenstein became increasingly interested in what he termed 'aspect seeing', stimulated in particular by prolonged reflection on Jastrow's famous 'Duck-Rabbit' diagram:

---

4   Wittgenstein's own beliefs remain a matter of some conjecture; we shall return to them later.
5   For more on the transformational nature of Christian spirituality see *Sources of Transformation: Revitilizing Traditions of Christian Spirituality*, ed. E.Howells and P.M. Tyler. Continuum, 2010.

In his final remarks written in the late 1940s and published posthumously as *The Last Writings on the Philosophy of Psychology* (RPP1), *Remarks on the Philosophy of Psychology* (RPP2), *Lectures on Philosophical Psychology* (LPP) and *The Philosophical Investigations* (PI) he returns continually to the figure and how an aspect is changed in our thought and life. The 'incomprehensible' matter that haunted Wittgenstein at the end of his life after he had given up his professorship in Cambridge and moved to a solitary hut in Rosro near Connemara in Ireland was how 'nothing and yet everything' is changed with the change of aspect. As he wrote in 1948 at Rosro:

> We now have a language game that is remarkably the *same* as, and remarkably *different* from the previous one. Now what follows from the expression 'Now I see...' is completely different, even though there is once again a close relationship between the language games.
>
> (RPP2: 476)

What is incomprehensible is that *nothing*, and yet *everything*, has changed, after all. That is the only way to put it. Surely *this* way is wrong: It has not changed in *one* respect, but has in another. There would be nothing strange about that. But 'Nothing has changed'

means: Although I have no right to change my report about what
I saw, since I see the same things now as before – still, I am incom-
prehensibly compelled to report completely different things, one
after the other.

(RPP2: 474)

I will argue in this book that both Wittgenstein and the medieval
authors examined elicit this 'change of aspect' by what will be referred
to as 'mystical strategies' or 'mystical performative discourse'. The aim
of their writing, I suggest, is not to leave the reader cold but to elicit
transformational change.

Wittgenstein concluded from the midst of a difficult life of struggle
and self-reflection that the aim of philosophy was to 'show the fly the
way out of the fly bottle' (PI: 309). For him philosophy could never
be an abstract, rarefied discipline; it had to have a *practical, ethical*
dimension. For him, the right seeing of true philosophy will bring about
right action. Thus, a key feature of the 'mystical strategies' described
in this book will be how the change of aspect brought about by those
strategies leads to action. It will be argued also that both Wittgenstein
and the medieval authors discussed often initiate this process by means
of disorientation and deconstruction. In this respect I will suggest that
the Wittgensteinian *Blick* (literally, 'view') shares many characteristics
with the *Blick* of what is termed the *theologia mystica*. It will be demonstrated that both achieve this objective by inventing new similes, new
ways of looking at things, turning our assumptions upside-down, using
humour, aporia and irony. Their gestures and comments will nudge us
in certain directions so that in Wittgenstein's case we can begin to 'see
the world aright' (T: 6.54) and in that of our mystical writers we will be
brought into a deeper contemplative relationship with God. Their strategies interrupt the spontaneous, unselfconscious flow of our ongoing
'mental' activity forcing us to re-evaluate our place in the world and our
attitude to it. They will use language in unusual and provocative ways
and, by the means of carefully selected images and metaphors, suggest
new ways of seeing and acting. By sometimes shocking and surprising
us, these authors will bring us back to what we knew already but were

unable to express in words. Through it we shall return to where we began and see something for the first time.

I will also argue that both understand that for there to be a real life-changing 'change of aspect' ordinary discourse must be challenged by 'apophatic' modes of speech. This will enable us to 'see the world aright' and initiate embodied ethical action in the world. For Wittgenstein the *Weltanschauung* (literally, 'view of the world') is not changed by mere verbal reasonings but by the presenting of pictures. In PI: 139 he takes the example of how we learn the meaning of the word 'cube', asking:

> What then exactly hovers before us (*vorschwebt*) when we *understand* a word? – Isn't it something like a picture? Can't it *be* a picture?[6]

Rather than presenting traditional classical arguments in treatise form, Wittgenstein realizes (as he did when he wrote the *Tractatus*) that such shifts of the *Weltanschauung* occur through presentation of *pictures* rather than systematic argument:

> His acceptance of the new picture consists in his now being inclined to regard a given case differently: that is, to compare it with this rather than that set of pictures. I have changed his way of looking at things (*Anschauungsweise geändert*).
>
> (PI: 144)

> I wanted to put this picture before your eyes, and your *acceptance* of this picture consists in your being inclined to regard a given case differently; that is, to compare it with *this* series of pictures. I have changed your *Anschauungsweise* (way of viewing).
>
> (Z: 461)

6   My translation; Anscombe in her translation gives: 'comes before our mind' (see reference in Bibliography). I have avoided this as it limits the ambiguity of the German *vorschweben*.

This is precisely the method of writing of a mystical Christian author such as Teresa of Avila. Teresa's method in many of her works, especially the *The Interior Castle/Las Moradas*,[7] is to present us with *pictures* to make her argument. As we shall see later the very opening passage of the *Moradas* presents this beautifully:

> While I was beseeching our Lord today to speak through me (*por mí*),[8] as I was unable to find a thing to say (*no atinaba a cosa que decir*)[9] or how to begin to comply with this obedience, what I will say now presented itself (*ofreció*)[10] to begin with this starting point: that we consider our soul to be like a castle, totally of diamond or very clear crystal, where there are many abodes (*aposentos*),[11] as in heaven there are many mansions. Now if we consider it carefully, sisters, the soul of a just person (*el alma del justo*)[12] is nothing else but a paradise where He says he takes his delights (*El tiene sus deleites*).[13] Well then, what do you think such an abode would be like where a King so powerful, so wise, so pure, so full of good things, takes his delight? I cannot find

7   Hereafter 'M'. All abbreviations for Teresa's works are given in the Bibliography.
8   Peers gives 'through', Kavanaugh and Rodriguez give 'for'; see Bibliography.
9   Peers gives 'I could find nothing to say', Kavanaugh and Rodriguez 'I wasn't able to think of anything to say'.
10 Peers: 'a thought occurred to me', Kavanaugh and Rodriguez 'there came to my mind'.
11 Peers: 'a rather more pretentious word than the English "room": dwelling place, abode, apartment', Kavanaugh and Rodriguez: 'Teresa uses the Spanish words *moradas, aposentos y piezas* in approximately the same sense; they refer to rooms or dwelling places within the castle... Most people today think of a mansion as a large stately home, not what Teresa had in mind with the term *moradas*. "Dwelling places" turns out to be a more precise translation of Teresa's *moradas* than is the classic "mansions" and more biblical and theological in tone.'
12 Peers: 'the soul of the righteous man', Kavanaugh and Rodriguez: 'the soul of the just person'.
13 Peers: 'He takes His delight', Kavanaugh and Rodriguez: 'He finds His delight'; see also V: 14:10 and Exc: 7, allusion to Proverbs 8:31.

anything with which to compare the great beauty and capacity of the soul; and truly our intellects will no more be able to grasp this than they can comprehend God, no matter how keen they are, for He Himself said that He created us in his own image and likeness.

(M: 1.1.1)

For both, astonishment, shock and surprise are *essential* components of the 'change of aspect' required for their writing. As Wittgenstein puts it:

Astonishment (*Staunen*) is essential to a change of aspect. *Und Staunen ist Denken* – And astonishment is thinking.

(RPP1: 565)

Faced, as will be argued, with such performative masters of 'shock and awe', certain difficulties arise for the academic researcher. As we shall see, and as has been pointed out by many commentators, neither Wittgenstein nor many of our mystical writers is concerned with developing a systematic body of theory or explanation. As Stanley Hauerwas puts it with reference to Wittgenstein:

[Wittgenstein] slowly cured me of the notion that philosophy was primarily a matter of positions, ideas, and/or theories. From Wittgenstein, and later David Burrell, I learned to understand and also do philosophy in a therapeutic mode... Moreover, Wittgenstein ended forever any attempt on my part to try to anchor theology in some general account of 'human experience', for his writings taught me that the object of the theologian's work was best located in terms of the grammar of the language used by believers.

(Hauerwas 1983: xxi)

Like Kierkegaard, whose writings greatly influenced him, Wittgenstein was not so much concerned with 'making difficult things simple' for his readers' comprehension but 'to make easy things difficult' for the sake of his reader's character (See Kierkegaard 1992: 186). Thus we look in vain in Wittgenstein and many of our 'mystical writers' for systematic complexity. Wittgenstein does his philosophy through remarks and aporia, while our medievals do their theology through image, metaphor, embodiment and playing with our affect. As we shall see, all of them want to engage us in conversation and fail insofar as their writing does not 'seize us with passion' in order to 'turn us round'.[14]

One aim of this book is to recapture the spontaneity and ruggedness of the original texts of both Wittgenstein and our Christian mystics. In the case of Wittgenstein the task of interpreting this type of approach to philosophy is made more difficult by the range of sources and collections to which his disparate *Nachlass* (literary inheritance) has been put by his executors and interpreters. As will be demonstrated in Chapter Two, before we embark on our study it is necessary to define exactly what we understand by the Wittgensteinian *corpus* and at least have a nodding acquaintance with the various schools of interpretation that have consequently grown up since his death. As we shall see there, there have often been two opposing trends – to go against Wittgenstein's own words and try to make him a systematic philosopher presenting a systematic treatise or, as is increasingly the case, to emphasize the 'Kierkegaardian' nature of his philosophy and what has been termed its therapeutic nature. Accordingly, throughout this book, although an academic argument based on the writings of our authors will be presented, it is hoped that something of their spirit of spontaneity, aporia and humour can be preserved.

A NOTE ON SOURCES AND TRANSLATION

To conclude this Introduction it may be helpful to note some aspects of the sources, translation and terminology that will be employed throughout the text.

14 Both quotes from Wittgenstein, VB: 1946; we shall return to them in the penultimate chapter.

As has already been alluded to, when studying Wittgenstein in particular, certain choices have to be made as to the sources that will be used and how they will be interpreted. This book draws on both published and unpublished material. With published work it has been usual to quote the English translation as it appears in the relevant English text. However, there have been occasions when it was felt that some phrases needed an altered translation to clarify a point that was being made; in this case the author's own translation has been indicated. In the case of unpublished *Nachlass* the full original German wording is given with the author's translation. All Wittgenstein's works have been listed as they appear in English translation with abbreviations in the Bibliography. References to Wittgenstein's manuscripts adopt the classification first used in von Wright's 1969 paper *The Wittgenstein Papers* reprinted in *Philosophical Occasions 1912–1951* (PO), pp. 480–510.

In the case of our other mystical writers a complete list of the works referred to, with abbreviations, is given in the Bibliography. Other primary and secondary sources are referenced using the usual academic conventions and full details may be found in the Bibliography.

PART ONE

A Wittgensteinian View of the Mystical

1

What is Mystical Anyway?

Sometimes an expression has to be taken out of the language and sent to the cleaners. Then it can be re-introduced into service.

(Wittgenstein VB:1940)[1]

Any book wanting to clarify the nature of 'mystical speech' in the Christian tradition has to begin by addressing the definitions of 'mystical' with which it is working. A comprehensive review of all the usages of the term in every area of academic discourse would neither be possible nor desirable; consequently this chapter will argue that our understanding of the contemporary academic discourse on 'the mystical' may best be seen as comprising two overarching tendencies: that towards evaluating 'mysticism' as a quasi-ontological, cross-credal category, what we shall refer to as 'modern mysticism', and a contemporary academic movement which seeks to concentrate primarily on the *form* of mystical discourse at the expense of any content, especially psychologistic content, what we shall refer to as 'constructivist' approaches.[2] It is the argument here that much contemporary discussion on the issue, especially in the theology and philosophy faculties, is centred around these two movements and reactions to them. By contrast, in the following chapter I shall propose a Wittgensteinian methodology that navigates the

1   'Man muß manchmal einen Ausdruck aus der Sprache herausziehen, ihn zum Reinigen geben. – und kann ihn dann wieder in den Verkehr einführen.' My translation.
2   For a good recent review of the debates see *Christian Mysticism: An Introduction to Contemporary Theoretical Approaches*, ed. L. Nelstrop, K. Magill and B. Onishi. Farnham: Ashgate, 2009.

3

impasse between these two understandings, presenting 'mystical speech' which is neither de-psychologized nor overly ontological. However, before we move to that position it is necessary to review this debate and the main movements that have shaped it, beginning with the creation of 'modern mysticism'. In this survey I will largely confine myself, in what will necessarily be a brief summary, to the archaeology of the term in the English-speaking context.[3]

Recent scholarship on the archaeology of the terms *mystical/mysticism/ mystic* has been dominated by the work of Michel de Certeau (1992), Louis Bouyer (1981) and Bernard McGinn (1991, 1994, 1998a, 2005) who have traced the prehistory and early modern history of the words *mystic, la mystique* and *mysticum*. From this research and analysis, which is by no means concluded,[4] it is argued that *mysticism* as a distinct category – that is, 'associated with distinct religious experiences' (Sheldrake 1991:39) emerges in the late sixteenth and early seventeenth centuries in the cultural and religious exchange between Golden Age Spain and France. More specifically, de Certeau favours Bordeaux as the region of 'transition (and translation) from sixteenth-century mystic Spain to seventeenth-century mystic France' (de Certeau 1992:10). For seventeenth-century France is the place 'where the mystic wave breaks' and from here we can 'move backward toward the horizon from which it came'.

De Certeau points out, when we speak of 'mystics', 'sixteenth-century authors instead said "contemplatives" or "spirituals" ' (de Certeau 1992:94). He cites traditional usage by Bernard of Clairvaux, Bonaventure and Thomas Aquinas, among others, and in the sixteenth and seventeenth centuries gives numerous instances (de Certeau 1992:95). Regarding Teresa of Avila and John of the Cross, he suggests they both prefer the term *contemplación* and, in the case of John of the

---

3   For this reason I have not explored the origins and use of the term by, *inter alia*, such notable German scholars as Heiler, Stolz and Rahner. For a perceptive account of the latter's views on *das Mystische* see Endean 2004.

4   Volumes 1–4 of McGinn's *Presence of God* series on the history of Western Christian mysticism have so far emerged, with two more volumes in preparation; see McGinn 1991, 1994, 1998a, 2005.

Cross anyway, 'uses "mystical" theology to designate the "negative" aspect of infused contemplation in reference to the apophatic tradition of Dionysius the Areopagite'. We shall return to this later, and to Teresa's use of the term 'mystical theology' suggesting other interpretations of the *theologia mystica* from our Wittgensteinian perspective.

By this time, argues de Certeau, the adjective 'mystical' takes on the aspects of the 'hidden key', the hermeneutical lodestone or alchemical secret (following Bouyer, it returns to its original Greek meaning of *mus*, hidden or closed). The hermeneutic of the esoteric is strongly enforced: 'At this point the term "mystical" becomes the proper one to qualify any object, real or ideal, the existence or signification of which eludes direct knowledge' (de Certeau 1992:96). He further suggests that the movement which brought about this specialized use of 'the mystical' also created a new 'science of extraordinary facts': mystics: *la mystique*.

THE EVOLUTION OF *MODERN MYSTICISM* IN THE EIGHTEENTH AND NINETEENTH CENTURIES

The analysis of the rise of *la mystique* as a distinct category of human learning is complemented by recent categorization of another movement – that of the 'psychologization' of mysticism that began towards the end of the nineteenth century and continues to the present day. Again, this is a large topic and takes in many branches of psychology, theology, philosophy, psychiatry and social sciences. In addition, throughout the nineteenth century we see the effects of colonialism and imperialism on Western European/American understandings of *the mystical* and what has been termed by Said (1978) as 'Orientalism'. Scholars such as Nicholas Lash (1988) and Rowan Williams (1991) see much of the modern psychologization of mysticism as arising from the influence of William James, in particular his groundbreaking *The Varieties of Religious Experience* (James 1902). However, recent work by Leigh Eric Schmidt (2003) has attempted to bridge the gap between de Certeau's work on the sixteenth and seventeenth centuries and the later work by scholars on James and beyond.[5] As with Teresa of Avila, Schmidt shows that the prevailing category in the English-speaking world up until the early decades of the eighteenth century was again 'mystical theology', especially as seen as interpretation of the Dionysian tradition. Thus, in 1656, Thomas Blount provided this definition in his *Glossographia*:

> Mystical Theology is nothing else in general but certain Rules, by the practise whereof, a vertuous Christian may attain to a nearer, a more familiar, and beyond all expression comfortable conversation with God.
>
> (Blount 1656:235)

As Schmidt points out, Blount's work contains no definitions for *mystic* or *mysticism*. The older understanding of 'mystical interpretation of scripture' (i.e. a 'hidden or internal' meaning) seems to have been retained (e.g. in Ephraim Chambers' *Cyclopeadia* of 1738); however, it is not until the mid-eighteenth century that the term 'mysticism' is employed as a substantive in its own right, and here it is mainly used in a pejorative sense to criticize the enthusiasms and 'amorous extravagancies' of 'the sects', especially Methodists and Quakers. The first usage in this way has been found by Schmidt in Henry Coventry's dialogues *Philemon to Hydapses: Or, the History of False Religion*. Here he contrasts 'the true spirit of acceptable religion' with 'the seraphic entertainments of mysticism and extasy' (Coventry 1761:56/60). Religion, rightly practised, is described as a 'liberal, manly, rational and social institution' (i.e. tolerant and full of aesthetic proportion and public decorum) and is contrasted with the 'deluded votaries of mysticism' (Coventry 1761:44). For Coventry, the great source of such mystical 'extasies' was 'disappointed love': the frustrated passion is 'transferred from mere mortals to a spiritual and divine object, and love... is sublimated into devotion' (1761:47).

---

5   De Certeau's perspectives can be criticized as too narrow to allow a full general picture (See McGinn 1991) and as leaving out developments beyond the French-speaking world, with their specific characteristics.

The 'mystics' came to be seen increasingly as a small sect or band within Christianity, much as the *alumbrados* had been seen in sixteenth- and seventeenth-century Spain, and the 'Molinists' later.[6] Thus, in the 1797 entry for the *Encyclopaedia Britannica* 'the mystics' are defined as:

> A kind of religious sect, distinguished by their professing pure, sublime and perfect devotion, with an entire disinterested love of God, free from all selfish considerations... The principles of this sect were adopted by those called *Quietists* in the seventeenth century, and under different modifications, by the Quakers and Methodists.
>
> (1797:598)

Schmidt sees the 1840s and 1850s as the point where a shift occurs in definitions of *mysticism*; from something associated with a small sect or group with esoteric characteristics it slowly defines something broader and wider with universalist and perennialist elements. Thus in the 1858 edition of the *Encyclopaedia Britannica* (eighth edition) we find the following: 'Its main characteristics are constantly the same whether they find expression in the Bagvat-Gita of the Hindu (*sic*), or in the writings of Emmanuel Swedenborg' (1858:755). This is really the beginning of the modern understanding of mysticism which is still with us today; that is, mysticism as a universal form of religious experience that finds specific expression in distinctive environments: Buddhist mysticism, Indian mysticism, Spanish mysticism, German mysticism and so on.

The other significant element that arises at this time is the 'orientalization' of mysticism. Robert Alfred Vaughan's (1823–57) two-volume collection, *Hours with the Mystics* (1856) as well as comparable publications in French and German[7] helped to popularize this notion, this

---

6   See Tyler 2005: *Alumbrados* and 2010a: *Miguel de Molinos* in *The Cambridge Dictionary of Christianity*, ed. D. Patte, Cambridge: Cambridge University Press, 2010. We shall return to this theme in Chapter Six.

7   Including works by Johan Heinroth, Joseph von Görres, Ludwig Noack, Adolph Helfferich and Victor Cousin.

being supplemented by orientalist notions of the 'mystic East' (see King 1985).

By the end of the nineteenth century authors such as Octavius Frothingham in his *Ten Great Religions* (1871–83) were able to imagine a future religion of the United States that was liberal and universal without being dogmatic, ecclesiastical, sacramental or sectarian, with *mysticism* being its binding glue (Frothingham 1891:115–132). Emerging from the Civil War period, it seemed that *mysticism* could provide a unifying influence on a fragmented country and the hope of a Universal Religion. This late nineteenth-century Transcendentalist stream combined with others to create the climate in which William James's *Varieties of Religious Experience* (1902) could fruitfully appear.

WILLIAM JAMES AND THE PSYCHOLOGIZATION OF *MODERN MYSTICISM*

William James's father, Henry James Senior, had friends among the transcendentalists, read Swedenborg and had a faith that has been characterized as 'an idiosyncratic fusion of Calvinism and republicanism' (Levinson 1981:11). For Henry Senior, 'the old Theology' was 'substantially the same in all the sects, from the old Romish down to the modern Swedenborgian'. Henry Senior also maintained a keen interest in all the new religious movements emerging in mid-nineteenth-century America and his sons' preoccupations reflected those of their father in, among others, the Shakers, Mormons, Millerites, Spiritualists, Swedenborgians and Transcendentalists (see Levinson 1981:4). As well as these groups, James's early years saw the formation in the United States of such influential movements as the Seventh Day Adventists (1860), Jehovah's Witnesses (1872) and Madam Blavatsky's Theosophical Society (1875). During his teens and early twenties young William became involved with both Epicureanism and Stoicism, and maintained an interest in all things esoteric and 'spiritualist' throughout his life. This would help to form the final shape of *The Varieties of Religious Experience*, one of the defining texts of 'modern mysticism'. published in 1902.

In his articles of 1890 and 1892 for *Scribner's Magazine* and *The Forum* reprinted in *What Psychical Research has Accomplished* (James:1897), James details his experiences in the field of psychical research. In view of the definitions of *mysticism* arising in the mid- to late nineteenth century it is not surprising, then, that James uses the word *mystical* to describe these 'psychic phenomena', i.e. 'divinations, inspirations, demoniacal possessions, apparitions, trances, ecstasies, miraculous healings and productions of disease, and occult powers possessed by peculiar individuals over persons and things in their neighbourhood' (1897:300). *Mysticism* and *Mystical Practice* are for James clearly identified with 'practices of the occult' transmitted from generation to generation by 'this mass of human beings' outside the circles of academe. Further, the 'mystical mind' is associated with the 'feminine', in contradistinction to the 'scientific-academic' mind associated with a certain 'manliness'(1897:301, 37).[8]

By these means, the modern 'transcendental' or better 'perennialist' understanding of mysticism had been born.[9] The characteristics of this type of mysticism are as follows:

- It is primarily identified in *extraordinary* states and conditions – occult and supernatural practices reveal its presence. It is preoccupied with *religious experiences.*
- It has an orientalist component.
- It is cross-credal and universal, manifesting in different religions in differing ways.

James's descriptions of the *Proceedings of the Society for Psychical Research*, of which he was one-time President, display his methodology as to how to approach these *mystical phenomena*: experiments, surveys and observations can all be used to reveal the secret truths of these phenomena.

We have, then, much of what James will say on 'mysticism' in *The Varieties* already in embryo in these texts. The other significant element

8   An eighteenth-century theme already noted above.
9   In this respect, see also Sedgewick (2004).

that will be explored in *The Varieties* is the role of the 'religious genius' in 'picking up' these far ends of the mystical spectrum and passing them on to the mass of 'ordinary believers'. Such a genius is for James someone who has an innate mental instability (see James 1902:7). Some, at least, of this appears to be autobiographical and relates to James's own struggles in his early twenties with near-suicidal depression. This 'melancholy' cast to James's character seems to have stayed with him for some time and his struggles with these suicidal urges are recounted in his later lecture of 1895 to the Harvard YMCA *Is Life Worth Living* (James 1897:32).[10]

By the time, then, that James came to deliver the 1902 Gifford Lectures in Edinburgh the main planks of his delineation of 'transcendental mysticism', or what is called here 'modern mysticism', were in place. This, I would argue, will form the cornerstone of 'modern mysticism' as it emerges in Western academic discourse: its psychologism, perennialism (influenced by orientalism) and its concentration on unusual states or experiences – its experientialism – all of which will find its way into the final version of *The Varieties* which will do so much to influence the subsequent academic climate of discussion of 'the mystical' in the English-speaking world.

Of particular relevance to our discussion here are Lectures Sixteen and Seventeen on *Mysticism*. Much of what we find there can be predicted by what has gone before. Thus, his bold assertion at the beginning of the lecture that 'personal religious experience has its root and centre in mystical states of consciousness' will make sense in the context of this metaphysic. Briefly reprising some of his original perspectives by references to the connection between *mysticism* and 'thought-transference and spirit-return', he concentrates on defining what characteristics these mystical spirit states will have. In particular, they will have the following four characteristics:

1. *Ineffability*: The handiest of the marks by which I classify a state of mind as mystical is negative. The subject of it immediately

10   Reprinted in *The Will to Believe* (James 1897).

says that it defies expression, that no adequate report of its contents can be given in words... In this peculiarity mystical states are more like states of feeling than like states of intellect. No one can make clear to another who has never had a certain feeling, in what the quality or worth of it consists.

(James 1902:380)

The mystic, moreover, has a more 'musical ear' than most of us, attuned to this silent symphony. They have gifts in a special way 'more akin to states of feeling than intellect', enabling them to engage with James's unseen order:

Lacking the heart or ear, we cannot interpret the musician or the lover justly, and are even likely to consider him weak-minded or absurd. The mystic finds that most of us accord to his experiences an equally incompetent treatment.

(James 1902:380)

James's second quality of *mysticism* is its *'noetic quality'*. In this aspect he deepens his previous distinction of the mystical states as 'states of feeling' by characterizing them also as 'states of knowledge'. They are:

States of insight into depths of truth unplumbed by the discursive intellect. They are illuminations, revelations, full of significance and importance... and as a rule they carry with them a curious sense of authority for after-time.

(James 1902:380)

Both of these characteristics, ineffability and noetic quality, relate more to the transcendental nature of the 'mystical experience', their origins in 'another world' and, therefore, their peculiar power when manifest in the mystic in this world: a power that epistemologically gives them greater certainty than 'states of feeling' or the 'discursive intellect'.

The third quality delineated by James, *transiency*, relates more to the 'experientialist' aspect of James's agenda than its 'transcendentalist' side:

3. Transciency. Mystical states cannot be sustained for long. Except in rare instances, half an hour, or at most an hour or two, seems to be the limit beyond which they fade into the light of common day.

(1902:381)

Of the four qualities this seems the most 'experientialist' of them all, clearly indicating James's understanding of *mystical states* as discreet, specific experiences.

With his description of *Passivity* James returns to his favourite subject which is never far below the surface in *Varieties*: the exploration of the paranormal and extraordinary. He refers to the 'manuals of mysticism' which prescribe 'certain voluntary operations, as by fixing the attention, or going through certain bodily performances' which will produce mystical states such as 'prophetic speech, automatic writing or alternative personality'. We immediately recall the New England circles of spiritualism that James explored and experienced as a young man: *mysticism* here defined is clearly an esoteric and exotic function. From this perspective, his reference in the next paragraph to 'professional mystics at the height of their development' does not seem so odd after all. As he also makes clear in this chapter, and again this follows from his earlier metaphysical separation of religious experience from religious institutions and organisations, the 'mystical experience' does not have to be connected with a specific *religious* institution or organization:

Single words and conjunctions of words, effects of light on land and sea, odors and musical sounds all bring it when the mind is tuned aright.

(1902:383)

For James, 'mysticism' is the secret heart of religion, the living essence that inhabits below the surface and gives life to everything else that follows. Again, of significance for much that will follow, James suggests a relation between these states and certain chemically induced positions produced by drugs such as nitrous oxide, with which he famously experimented (see James 1902:387).

The other central innovation of James's chapter on mysticism is its marshalling of examples from 'other religions' – 'Buddhists, Hindus, Mahommedans' – another feature which will be developed in much twentieth-century discussion of mysticism – mysticism as a cross-credal entity:

> This overcoming of all the usual barriers between the individual and the Absolute is the great mystic achievement. In mystic states we both become one with the Absolute and we become aware of our oneness. This is the everlasting and triumphant mystical tradition, hardly altered by differences of clime or creed. In Hinduism, in Neoplatonism, in Sufism, in Christian mysticism, in Whitmanism, we find the same recurring note.
>
> (1902:419)

In such terms, the perennialist-experientialist view of mysticism survives intact to the present day. James's work combined with that of writers in the English-speaking world such as Vaughan (1856),[11] Inge (1899)[12]

---

11 Born in 1823, the eldest son of a Congregational minister, in Worcester, Robert followed his father into the ministry, holding posts in Bath and Birmingham. His health was always delicate and his pastoral ministry seems to have been somewhat impaired. In 1855 he showed symptoms of tuberculosis and after two years living as an invalid in Bournemouth and London he died at the early age of 34 at Westbourne Park, London in 1857. Published in 1856, his *Hours with the Mystics* ran into several editions and, until the publication of Inge's *Christian Mysticism* and Underhill's *Mysticism*, remained a key influence on further thought on the subject in English-speaking countries. See *Essays and Remains*, 1, ix–cxiv.

12 Born in 1860, William Ralph Inge taught classics at Oxford from 1888 to 1905 where he was ordained priest in 1892. After some time in parish life he became Lady Margaret Professor of Divinity at Cambridge in 1907 where he continued his studies into the neo-Platonists, especially Plotinus and the English Platonic tradition. In 1911 Prime Minister Asquith made him Dean of St. Paul's in the hope of reviving the literary eminence of the

and Underhill (1910)[13] to produce the phenomenon that I am referring to here as 'modern mysticism'. Interestingly enough much academic discourse on the topic is still dominated by this approach. With reference to Inge, Vaughan and Underhill it is possible to see the following shape to their understanding of 'mysticism' within the Christian context:

1   The key narrative for their mystical hermeneutic is historical. The authors want to stress the 'unbroken thread' that links Gospel and early Christian texts with the present day. Each of the three authors varies as to the emphasis they take. Inge, for example, privileges the 'Johannine corpus' and wants to suggest that the mystical strand arises from here. We may characterize this as the 'golden thread' view of mysticism, i.e. an unbroken thread that leads directly from apostolic and post-apostolic times, through the Middle Ages, Reformation and Enlightenment to the present day.

2   Through the lens of the Dionysian corpus all four authors agree on the Platonic and neo-Platonic structure that underlies the Western mystical tradition. Inge, for example, calls Plato the 'the father of European mysticism' (1899:78) and this idea would reach broad

cathedral. Through his published essays and weekly column in the *Evening Standard* he disseminated his views on a variety of topics to a wide public audience. His rather right-wing views on state provision of health care for 'sub-men', bursaries for the children of working-class families to enter higher education and his ambivalence to Nazism (especially its race theories) made him a controversial figure. He died in Brightwell Manor, Wallingford in 1954. See Fox (1960), Grimley (2004).

13   Born in 1875 in Wolverhampton to a prosperous family, Evelyn Underhill was taught at home, Sandgate House, Folkestone and Kings College London 'ladies department' in Kensington Square. She read extensively herself and always had an enquiring nature. She married Hubert Stuart Moore in 1907 and spent the rest of her life in London writing and researching, especially on the subject of mysticism. She died in Hampstead in 1941. See Greene (1988, 1991, 2004), Cropper (1958), Armstrong (1975) and Underhill (1943).

agreement from the others. As well as Dionysius, the neo-Platonists Plotinus and Philo are given due credit for their influence.[14]

3   Experientialism such as that found in James is accepted without much critique. The roles of ecstasies, locutions and other 'super-natural' phenomena are seen by most of the authors as aspects of the Christian mystical path. Again, they vary as to the significance and role they play. Inge, in particular, is very suspicious and tends to associate them with 'Romish' understandings of mysticism.

4   'The mystic' is seen as a genuinely different and 'other' person. For James they are the 'disturbed genius', for Underhill and Inge they are able to 'tune into' the sublime waves of the infinite. Either way it makes sense to talk of people as 'mystics' with special characteristics.

Our authors, then, in their struggle to distinguish a specifically *Christian* mysticism in contradistinction to the eclectic/perennialist/essentialist milieu within which they find themselves working, create an interpretive standpoint – *Modern Mysticism* – which has the following distinctive qualities:

1   It has an ontological nature; it is *essentialist* in that its origins and development may be traced throughout history as a distinct category of human experience which reaches its culmination in Christianity.

2   It relates to *perennialist* assumptions as found in much of James and nineteenth-century views of *mysticism*. The perennialism goes with a certain degree of eclecticism.

3   Like James, all three authors stress the importance of *mystical experience* in their approaches. Although they are not as overtly psychologistic as James (except Underhill, who here shows her reliance on James), they share his emphasis on the importance of

14   See also Inge, *The Philosophy of Plotinus* (1929) and *The Platonic Tradition in English Religious Thought* (1926). For an extended discussion of the role of Plato in the 'mystical tradition' see Turner (1995).

the discrete mystical experience as carrier of much that is of importance in the tradition.

4   Perhaps more so than James, they reveal a stronger *orientalist*
element to their hermeneutic of mysticism. This may either be
viewed positively (Underhill) or negatively (Vaughan).[15]

Much of what is laid down by these four authors resurfaces in many
subsequent early twentieth-century discussions of the topic by, for
example, Otto, Butler, von Hügel, Heiler and Stace,[16] namely its essentialism, perennialism, orientalism and experientialism, and it is to the
critique of these four elements of *modern mysticism* that we turn to
next.[17]

THE CONTEMPORARY DEBATE ON MYSTICISM

The publication of the collected essays edited by Stephen Katz, *Mysticism
and Philosophical Analysis,* in 1978 marks a convenient starting point to
summarize the contemporary scholarship on mysticism. The authors of
the essays in this volume, and the subsequent *Mysticism and Religious
Traditions* (Katz 1983) and *Mysticism and Language* (Katz 1992),
especially Katz and Robert Gimello, began the process of challenging
the notion of 'mysticism' as a cross-credal entity based on the epistemological assumption of a 'pure' unmediated or uninterpreted experience.
For this group, consequently called 'contextualists' or 'constructivists',

15   Vaughan makes numerous references to India and Indian culture. See also
his *India in 1857: Historical Parallels* in Vaughan (1858) where Vaughan
writes in response to the Indian Uprising of 1857 during which his
brother-in-law was killed and his sister was involved (1858:306–10).
16   See, for example, Butler (1926), Heiler (1932), Otto (1957), Stace (1960)
and von Hügel (1908). Of these authors perhaps the most distinctive is
von Hügel, whose characterization of the 'mystical' as an 'element' in
religion would seem to avoid many of the criticisms developed against the
essentialism of modern mysticism. In contemporary writing some of von
Hügel's approach finds its way into McGinn's analyses of the topic.
17   'Modern mysticism' is, of course, still alive and well in the academy despite
constructivist challenges. We shall return to this in the final chapter.

all experience, including mystical experience, is contextually bound and only intelligible contextually.

As Gimello puts it:

Mysticism is inextricably bound up with, dependent upon, and usually subservient to the deeper beliefs and values of the traditions, cultures and historical milieux which harbour it. As it is thus intricately and intimately related to those beliefs and values, so must it vary according to them.

(Gimello 1983:63)

In his study Gimello wants to move away from a more narrowly 'experientialist' view of mysticism to one that takes account of the historicity and contextual character of the 'mystical experience': 'the deep and formative connections between it and the systems of concept, practice, discourse and institution which produce and contain it' (Gimello 1983:85). His conclusion is as follows:

Mystical experience is simply the psychosomatic enhancement of religious beliefs and values or of beliefs and values of other kinds which are held 'religiously'... mysticism has become fascinating to many of its students exactly because it has seemed to them to be an alternative to religion. It has come to be viewed as a repository of all that is best and still admirable in religion but one that is free from such no longer acceptable elements as dogma, authority, discipline, respect for tradition etc.

(Gimello 1983:85)

Gimello's critique of the creation of *modern mysticism* assumes many of the points we have raised above. Thus he comments on the relative novelty of the academic study of mysticism, citing Underhill, Inge, Leuba Maréchal, Poulain, Otto, Von Hügel and Massignon as the key figures in its development,[18] the elitism we have noted in both Underhill and James and a suspicion of institutional religion. To these three

18   See Gimello (1983:86) and Gimello (1990) cited in Herman (2000:99).

factors we may add those mentioned above: the 'orientalist' element in the creation of modern mysticism and the privileging of an extracted 'essence' of mysticism located primarily in authoritative texts.

From this constructivist critique it is therefore possible to deconstruct the notion of 'mysticism' in a writer such as James. Taking him as an example – and most of the arguments employed here may equally be used against Underhill, Vaughan and Inge – we can summarize reactions to his categories of 'mysticism' as follows.

Elitism within 'modern mysticism'

To contemporary eyes the elitism of James's texts seems quite striking. He is rather disparaging of the 'ordinary religious believer' whose 'religion has been made for him by others, communicated to him by tradition, determined to fixed forms by imitation and retained by habit' (James 1902:6). He calls this 'second-hand religious life' and feels the study of it would 'profit us little'. The imbalance such a perspective brings to his study would not be worth commenting on were it not for the fact that the investigation of religious phenomena within the psychology faculty still too often concentrates on the exotic and exceptional rather than the everyday, thus skewing results and conclusions, as is the case with James.

Anti-institutionalism

As Lash points out (1988:56), James's contrast between personal religion and institutional religion is not incidental to his argument but essential to it, especially in his characterizations of 'first-hand' and 'second-hand' religion and his general theory of 'personal experience':

Armed with the romantic image of the genius as one charged up with psychic energy from some strange source 'beyond' the public world of social institutions, James exaggerates the pattern setter's originality. Human creativity – whether religious, scientific, or aesthetic – is never absolute. The pioneer is a *product* of the culture and traditions which he or she refashions, often (admittedly) in dramatic and unexpected ways. Without the tradition, the cultural and linguistic institutions, of the people of Israel, Jesus could not have had his 'personal' experience of the mystery he called Father, in the way that he had it, nor could Paul have had his 'personal' experience of the mystery of Christ.

(Lash 1988:57)

James's dislocation of personal 'experience' from context immediately creates the problems that Lash outlines.

Pure or private experience

As already mentioned, one of the major impacts of James's analysis was to enshrine the notion of 'religious experience' at the centre of subsequent debate about religious phenomena in general and *mysticism* in particular. Such an 'experientialist' stance has been criticized on many grounds by many authors.[19]

The notion of 'pure' experience (religious or otherwise) divorced of all categories of culture, prior experience, tradition, structures, institutions and relationships is suspect. Lying behind the concept is a sense of 'experience', perhaps as 'conscious mental going on' (Swinburne 1979:244) which betrays a Cartesian metaphysic with a disembodied 'I' trying to relate to specific sensations and 'experiences'. Lash suggests:

For *human beings*, experience, at least in the vast majority of its forms, includes a great deal more than mental goings-on. For the Cartesian 'ego', on the other hand (which being itself not bodily, can only enjoy nonbodily or 'mental' experience), Swinburne's definition seems entirely appropriate: the little person inside the skull observes or notices its body's indigestion.

(Lash 1988:92)[20]

19 See in particular Lash (1988), Turner (1995), Williams (1991) and Ferrer (2002).
20 We shall return to this argument when we review Wittgenstein's systematic critique of the influence of Cartesian dualism on Western thought in Chapter Seven. See also Kerr (1986).

The Cartesian model lies at the heart of all representational paradigms of cognition envisaging human knowledge as the inner, subjective representation of an 'outer' external world (See Ferrer 2002; Rorty 1979; also Chapter Seven in this volume). As Ferrer points out, the model is particularly unsuited to the demands of transpersonal or spiritual perspectives where the distinction between knowing subject and known object are often collapsed:

> In other words, during transpersonal events, the subjective-objective structuration of phenomena suffers such drastic inversions that these categories lose their descriptive and explanatory value. In transpersonal phenomena, it became strikingly obvious, not only what is subjective can become objective, but also what is objective can become subjective.
>
> (Ferrer 2002:30)

As we shall see in the following chapter, this 'anti-Cartesian' critique of experientialism has many of its roots in Wittgenstein's approach to the self which we shall be returning to throughout the book.

The empirical agenda

James's Cartesian base also implies an empiricist approach to religious phenomena – this is underpinned by a reductionist or positivist agenda which privileges the natural sciences as a methodological ideal for all other sciences (see von Wright 1971; Sorell 1991). The problem with such an approach to the area of spiritual enquiry is that only the methods of the natural sciences may be applied (e.g. experimentation, replication, testing, verification and falsification). The critiques of Habermas (1971) and Gadamer (1990) among others have revealed the damaging effects of importing such 'scientism' into all forms of enquiry. With reference to spiritual enquiry, Rothberg (1994) comments:

> To interpret spiritual approaches through categories like 'data', 'evidence', 'verification', 'method', 'confirmation' and 'intersubjectivity' may be to enthrone these categories as somehow the hallmarks of knowledge as such, even if these categories are

expanded in meaning from their current Western usage. But might not a profound encounter with practices of spiritual inquiry lead to considering carefully the meaning of other comparable categories (e.g. *dhyana, vichara, theoria, gnosis* or *contemplatio*) and perhaps to developing understandings of the inquiry in which such spiritual categories are primary or central when we speak of knowledge? To assume that the categories of current Western epistemology are adequate for interpreting spiritual approaches is to prejudge the results of such an encounter.

(Rothberg 1994:8)

In Ferrer's words, to apply the scientific ways of verification, experimental evidence, replicability and falsifiability to spiritual phenomena 'may be equivalent to trying to test the flavor of a savory soup with a very rusty fork' (Ferrer 2002:58). Spiritual phenomena require other methodologies than the scientific for their elucidation; this is an underlying theme to this study and one to which we shall return when we consider our Wittgensteinian methodology in the following chapter.

Experientialism and the apophatic

We shall be returning to the apophatic in greater depth in the following chapters; however, in the context of our critique of modern mysticism it is worth raising an issue presented by Turner (1995) and McIntosh (1998) among others. Simply put, even if we accept the existence of discrete verifiable 'religious experiences' it may be argued that many of the writers within the so-called 'mystical tradition' may well have cautioned against the cultivation of such experiences. Here, Turner in particular is warning us when we apply modernist (empiricist, Cartesian) categories to medieval texts, especially those with an apophatic bias:[21]

Put very bluntly, the difference seemed to be this: that whereas our employment of the metaphors of 'inwardness' and 'ascent' appears to be tied in with the achievement and the cultivation of a

---

21 To give James his credit, he largely avoids the apophatic tradition and is more concerned with cataphatic events.

certain kind of experience – such as those recommended within the practice of what is called, nowadays, 'centring' or 'contemplative' prayer – the medieval employment of them was tied in with a 'critique' of such religious experiences and practices.

(Turner 1995:4)

He concludes:

Experientialism is, in short, the 'positivism' of Christian spirituality. It abhors the experiential vacuum of the apophatic, rushing to fill it with the plenum of the psychologistic. It resists the deconstructions of the negative way, holding fast to supposititious experiences of the negative. It is happy with commendations of the 'interior' so long as it can cash them out in the currency of experienced inwardness and of the practices of prayer which will achieve it.

(Turner 1995:259)

However, it should be pointed out that there is an equal danger of reading a postmodern critique of experientialism back into the tradition as much as a 'modern mystic experientialism'. In this respect the approach of the Wittgensteinian methodology presented in the following chapter aims to tread a 'middle way' between these two extremes.[22]

Supra-credal essentialism of modern mysticism

One of the defining features of *Modern Mysticism*, as we have seen, is an understanding of 'mysticism' as a cross-credal category found in all religions and none. As James puts it: 'in Hinduism, in Neoplatonism, in Sufism, in Christian mysticism, in Whitmanism, we find the same recurring note' (James 1902:252). This *essentialism* which has become a central part of modern definitions of mysticism[23] has been comprehensively challenged by Stephen Katz in his essay *Language, Epistemology*

22   I am grateful to Professor Philip Sheldrake for this observation.
23   See for example Huxley (1946), Otto (1957), Suzuki (1957), Heiler (1932), Stace (1960) and Smart (1958, 1962, 1967, 1978).

and Mysticism (Katz 1978). Katz identifies three forms of statements associated with this cross-credal mysticism:

1) All mystical experiences are the same; even their descriptions reflect an underlying similarity which transcends cultural or religious diversity.
2) All mystical experiences are the same but the mystics' reports about their experiences are culturally bound. Thus they use the available symbols of their cultural-religious milieu to describe their experience.
3) All mystical experience can be divided into a small class of 'types' which cut across cultural boundaries. Though the language used by mystics to describe their experience is culturally bound, their experience is not.

(Katz 1978:24)

Katz objects to these assumptions on several grounds. First, he disputes the idea that there are *pure* experiences of any type:

That is to say, *all* experience is processed through, organized by, and makes itself available to us in extremely complex epistemological ways. The notion of unmediated experience seems, if not self-contradictory, at best empty... the experience itself as well as the form in which it is reported is shaped by concepts which the mystic brings to, and which shape, his experience.

(Katz 1978:26)

Therefore, the Hindu will experience *Brahman*, the Buddhist *Nirvana* and the Christian *Unio Mystica* – all three of which are specific to their categories and context and cannot be interposed. He continues by criticizing notions of 'common core' mysticism such as are found in the authors cited:

What appear to be similar-sounding descriptions are not similar descriptions and do not indicate the same experience. Choosing descriptions of mystic experience out of their total context does not provide grounds for their comparability but rather severs all grounds of their intelligibility for it empties the chosen phrases, terms and descriptions of definite meaning.

(Katz 1978:47)

SUMMARY

This has, by necessity, been a somewhat dense chapter. However, it has been necessary to give a comprehensive overview of how *the mystical* has been used in academic discourse since the rise of 'modern mysticism' and its consequent critique over the past thirty years before we can proceed.

It has been argued that for the 'makers of *modern mysticism*', namely James, Inge, Vaughan and Underhill, there was a clear ontological category of *mysticism,* which was basically essentialist, experientialist, orientalist and perennialist in character, and for James this was filled out by his concept of *mystical experience*. It was further argued that these categories were adopted, largely uncritically, by the chief writers on 'mysticism' in the twentieth century, such as Otto, Stace and Zaehner, and were commonplace assumptions in scholarly discourse until the constructivist critique of Katz *et al.* in the late 1970s/early 1980s.[24]

Since Katz we have seen varying reactions to the 'deontologization' of *mysticism*. At one end Forman and the neo-perennialists have wanted to restore full ontological status to the category of *mysticism* (See Forman 1990, 1998); at the other end of the spectrum is Cupitt advocating a totally de-ontologized approach (see Cupitt 1998). In between, with McIntosh (1998), McGinn (1991), Turner (1995), Williams (1983, 1984, 1991) and Kripal (2001, 2004) we see varying levels of ontological content imported into the category.

In the following chapter we shall look at how Wittgenstein's writings offer another approach to the problem. Unlike Underhill, Vaughan,

---

24   See e.g., Zaehner 1957, 1970.

James and Inge *et al.* I shall not be looking for a cross-credal, experientialist, ontological (and possibly orientalist) category called 'mysticism'. Rather I shall be concentrating on the 'mystical form, strategy or game' using an approach which will be developed from Wittgenstein's writings while avoiding some of the emptiness of the constructivist approach.

Following Sells (1994), Cupitt and Kripal I shall argue for a *deconstructive* element to *the mystical/mysticism/mystic*. In addition, like Kripal and McIntosh, I shall explore the embodied/affective element of the mystical as manifest in the medieval writings we shall survey. Finally, recognizing the importance of Williams's and McIntosh's contributions to understanding the constructivist critique in Christian theological context I will also be concerned with developing the specifics of 'mystical speech', especially as 'incomplete speech act' in 'interpretative framework'. However, throughout, my argument will be that Wittgenstein's work offers us an approach to the mystical which avoids the pitfalls of the 'modern mystic' approach while also avoiding the loss of psychologistic content that often attends certain constructivist approaches. The use of this analysis will then be demonstrated by applying it to the medieval development of the 'language game' of *theologia mystica*.

2

Saying and Showing: A Wittgensteinian Methodology

4.121 Propositions cannot represent logical form: it is mirrored in them. What finds its reflection in language, language cannot represent. What expresses itself in language, we cannot express by means of language. Propositions show the logical form of reality. They display it. What can be shown, cannot be said.

(Wittgenstein: *Tractatus Logico-Philosophicus*)

WITTGENSTEIN'S *NACHLASS* AND THE PROBLEM OF INTERPRETATION

One of the difficulties with working with Wittgenstein's writings is that there is no general consensus as to how they should be approached. In addition, there have emerged differences of opinion as to how his literary legacy – his *Nachlass* – should be treated. While not agreeing entirely with all of Daniel Hutto's arguments in *Wittgenstein and the End of Philosophy* (Hutto 2003) I have found his division of Wittgensteinian interpretation into that of *theoretical* and *therapeutic* helpful and will adopt a version of this while surveying various interpretations of Wittgenstein's approach, especially to the philosophy of religion.

On Wittgenstein's death in 1951 his literary executors Georg von Wright, Rush Rhees and Elizabeth Anscombe believed at first that Wittgenstein's literary legacy consisted of a few notebooks that he had in his possession at the time of his death (See PO:480). However, as von Wright narrates in *The Wittgenstein Papers* (in PO:480–506) it soon transpired that there was much more material than had originally been thought. In his introduction to the *Wiener Ausgabe* (WA:1:51) Nedo gives the number of extant pages to date as 30,000. Based on von Wright's description in *The Wittgenstein Papers* and his own analysis, Stern (1996:473) and others suggest that the figure is nearer to 20,000 pages rather than 30,000. Regardless, the material of the *Nachlass* accordingly turned out to be vast. In his will Wittgenstein had requested that his executors 'shall publish as many of my unpublished writings as they should think fit' (Stern 1996:454). As he had published so little in his lifetime: the *Tractatus Logico-Philosophicus* (1922, T), a *Wörterbuch* for the children of Upper Austria (1926, WB) and a short paper for the Aristotelian Society (1929, AS) the executors did not have much to guide them in making their decisions as to what was publishable and what not. From the nearly completed *Philosophical Investigations* (1953, PI) onwards there flowed (and continues to flow) a stream of works authorized by the executors (see 'Wittgenstein's works' in the Bibiography). Although the work of the executors was punctilious and industrious they have not been entirely beyond reproach. Various attempts have been made to publish the *Nachlass* as a whole, beginning with the Cornell microfilm facsimile of 1967. Although helpful the microfilm facsimile was at times hard to read, and certain texts, such as the so-called *Geheime Tagebücher* (GT), had been deliberately covered over to spare the public possible embarrassment from his more personal reflections (we shall return to this later). Stern (1996) charts the unhappy evolution of the *Wiener Ausgabe* under Nedo which is only now just appearing. However, perhaps the fullest and most accessible of all the attempts to open up the *Nachlass* has been the Bergen Electronic Edition (2000, BEE) which was produced in 2000 by the University of Bergen in Norway. The production of these various editions of the *Nachlass* has allowed scholars to see the shortcomings of some of the editorial decisions made by the original executors (See Stern 1996; Savickey 1998; also BEE). The chief criticism is that the executors did not provide enough critical apparatus to justify their editorial decisions and it was left unclear why certain portions of the *Nachlass* were published in a certain way and not another. This has been particularly the case with collections of *Bemerkungen* published in collections such as *Culture and Value* and *Remarks on Colour*. As the editors of the Bergen Electronic Edition put it in their introduction to the Edition:

> With the aim of honouring Wittgenstein's intentions, his editors have sometimes put together selections from a range of different manuscripts. Unfortunately, Wittgenstein's intentions can rarely be established with any certainty. The instructions he wrote into his works are numerous and often contradictory. Those selections that have been made have secured Wittgenstein a place among the first rank of Western thinkers. Regrettable, however, is that his editors do not always document their decisions, thus obscuring the relationship between the publicised material and its sources.
>
> (BEE:Introduction)

Along with this lack of critical apparatus, commentators such as Stern and Savickey also see another, more insidious tendency in the editing process: that is, a tendency to 'tidy up' Wittgenstein's *Bemerkungen* to produce well-manicured and philosophically balanced 'texts'. One of my key arguments in this book is that like the mystical texts of the Christian tradition, we tidy up Wittgenstein's works at our peril. Having examined them for the past twenty years, especially through the lens of the *Nachlass* editions, it is my conviction that they can only be read aright as a radical attempt to *change our perception of philosophical problems*. Wittgenstein was not interested in producing finely polished philosophical tracts (notwithstanding the fact that he took great care and time to produce the *Bermerkungen* in an order and form he was happy with[1]) but rather he wanted his texts to 'trouble the reader' – 'I

---

1   Monk in his biography (Monk 1990:319) gives a detailed picture of how Wittgenstein went about this process: 'Wittgenstein had a peculiarly laborious method of editing his work. He began by writing remarks into small notebooks. He then selected what he considered to be the best of these remarks and wrote them out, perhaps in a different order, into larger manuscript volumes. From these he made a further selection, which he

should not like my writing to spare other people the trouble of thinking'
– as he writes in the Preface to the *Philosophical Investigations* (PI:vi).
From my point of view, when we are reading Wittgenstein the *style and
presentation* of his writings is as important as the *substance* – a tendency
we shall see repeated when we examine the mystical texts later.

READING WITTGENSTEIN: THEORY AND THERAPY

Surveying the reactions to Wittgenstein's work nearly fifty years after
his death, Rorty in his essay *Keeping Philosophy Pure* summed up the
position thus:

> Academic philosophy in our day stands to Wittgenstein as intel-
> lectual life in Germany in the first decades of the last century
> stood to Kant. Kant had changed everything, but no one was sure
> just what Kant had said – no one was sure what in Kant to take
> seriously and what to put aside.
>
> (Rorty 1982:20)

In this essay Rorty suggests that Wittgenstein's writings throw down a
gauntlet to all who read them, especially professional philosophers: the
challenge to enter the 'transcendental standpoint' of the *Tractatus* and
the further challenge of the 'twice born' to resist this temptation and
the challenge to both of the position expounded in the *Philosophical
Investigations* that transcends the need to 'explain, justify and expound'.
In tracing this distinction, which Hutto (2003) calls the 'theoretical and
the therapeutic', Rorty emphasizes the importance of the *Tractatus* for
those who have expounded Wittgenstein from the former position and
the importance of the *Investigations* for those of the latter disposition.

dictated to a typist. The resultant typescript was then used as a basis for a
further selection, sometimes by cutting it up and rearranging it – and then
the whole process was started again.' We have in the *Nachlass* examples
of work at all stages of this process.

The distinction between the emphases of the work of the 'earlier' and 'later' Wittgenstein, and this possible distinction between a theoretical and an anti-theoretical approach to his writings, has been a constant since the voluminous Wittgensteinian secondary literature began to swell. As Pears puts it (1988b:218), in these later works 'he is moving away from theorizing and towards plain description of the phenomenon of language'. Many of these commentators take as their key text the famous remark from PI:126 on the nature of philosophy:

> Philosophy simply puts everything before us, and neither explains nor deduces anything. – Since everything lies open to view there is nothing to explain. For what is hidden, for example, is of *no interest to us*.

Consequently, among the Wittgensteinian secondary literature we see a split between those commentators who see the work of the later Wittgenstein as continuing the work of the earlier Wittgenstein and those who see a new anti-theoretical shift in the post-*Tractatus* works. As suggested at the beginning of this chapter, much of this (mis)interpretation may even arise from the confusion surrounding the publication of the *Nachlass*.

To add to the confusion, a recent book, *The Third Wittgenstein: The Post-Investigations Works* (Moyal-Sharrock 2004) has argued that the parts of the *Nachlass* that have appeared charting the latter period of Wittgenstein's life, in particular *On Certainty*, suggest a *third* interpretation of Wittgenstein that transcends even the position developed in the *Investigations*.

We are thus left with four possible ways of viewing his works in the authors of the secondary literature.

The 'Two Wittgensteins': 'The standard interpretation'

Those who remain with the traditional division between the 'earlier' and the 'later' Wittgenstein and see the later works, especially the *Investigations*, as a critique of the earlier works, especially the *Tractatus*. Representative of this trend would be Peter Hacker whose work

Wittgenstein: Connections and Controversies (Hacker 2001) makes this point. Crary (2000:2) calls this position the 'standard narrative' by which Wittgensteinian interpretation is guided. By this is meant the notion that the *Tractatus* and *Investigations* are two separate works, the latter intended as a specific critique of the former. The *Tractatus* represents the culmination of the first phase of Wittgenstein's thinking (broadly up to 1918) which is essentially the delineation of the limits of meaning by the delineation of the 'logic of our language' – the form of language and the form of the world will thus reflect each other. This 'picture theory of meaning' is rejected in the post-*Tractatus* works, especially the *Investigations,* in a period which extends from about the early 1930s up to his death in 1951, at which time he was still trying to marshal his thoughts into an order with which he was happy for publication. The 'second Wittgenstein' is not so much concerned with a theory of meaning that connects the meaning of a word to a particular pattern of external reality but rather to one in which meaning is derived from the *use* of the word, often described by a concentration on *Sprachspiele* – language games. The tendency of the first phase is to lead to a notion of meaning which is truth-conditional and essentially realist, whereas that of the latter depends on a notion of meaning based around assertibility conditions and is essentially anti-realist. The classic exponents of this view are Dummett (1991), Hacker (2001) and Pears (1988b), among others.

The so-called 'new Wittgensteinians'
Those who see a theoretical union between the early and later Wittgenstein and reject any notion of a firm break between the two.

They are best represented in Crary and Read's collection *The New Wittgenstein* (Crary and Read 2000), which includes amongst others, Stanley Cavell, John McDowell, James Conant, Cora Diamond and Hilary Putnam.[2] They share with the authors of the 'standard interpretation'

---

2   Although the collection includes an essay by Peter Hacker he is dissenting from the general view of the 'New Wittgensteinians' and would prefer to place his view in that of the 'standard interpretation'.

the notion that Wittgenstein sought in his later writings to overturn the metaphysical implications of the 'picture theory' of meaning found primarily in the *Tractatus*. Where they differ from the 'standard interpretation' is in seeing this critique as being present throughout Wittgenstein's writings, even including the *Tractatus*. Crary describes this as the *therapeutic* aspect of Wittgenstein's work, a notion we will return to below. One important influence from the 'new Wittgensteinians' that has influenced my approach here is the importance they give to the *style* of his writings as much as his *substance*. As we shall see later when we compare the means of expression in Wittgenstein and in the mystical texts of our mystical authors, *how* things are said may be as important as *what* is said. Thus these interpreters get away from a notion that has often haunted the executors of the *Nachlass* that Wittgenstein's work has to be 'tidied up' in order to get at a 'real' philosophical text. Rather, the fragmentary nature of the collections of remarks, including their often contradictory authorial voices, should be understood in the 'therapeutic' tradition of philosophers such as Kierkegaard (as we have seen, an acknowledged influence on Wittgenstein) rather than the systematic treatises of, say, a Hegel or a Kant. In Crary's words, 'the dialectical structure of Wittgenstein's writing makes an internal contribution to the philosophical instruction it contains' (2000:7). For this aspect of the 'new Wittgensteinian' agenda a lot of thanks must go to Stanley Cavell who has long championed this notion of the 'confessional and therapeutic' within Wittgenstein's work (see e.g. Cavell 1976, 1979).

The Third Wittgenstein

The premise of *The Third Wittgenstein – The Post Investigations Works* (Moyal-Sharrock 2004) is to present a collection of papers that argue for the significance to the *Nachlass* of the material published post *The Philosophical Investigations*, in particular *On Certainty*. Moyal-Sharrock, the editor of the volume, believes that these works do not mark a distinctive break with the writing of the *Investigations* but rather continue Wittgenstein's thoughts in ways that are not so manifest in the *Investigations*. For reasons given above regarding the difficulty of sorting out the publication of the *Nachlass,* it would at first sight seem odd to give the *Investigations* a cohesion of thought that its unsystematic collation would not seem to merit, which is why many of the contributors to the volume want to make a distinction between Part One and Part Two of the *Investigations*. They see the former as largely as Wittgenstein hoped it would be published, while the latter is more akin to the posthumously published *Nachlass* which makes up the bulk of Moyal-Sharrock's 'Third Wittgenstein'.

In support of this view, von Wright is quoted:

> I lean, myself, towards the opinion that Part 1 of the *Investigations* is a complete work and that Wittgenstein's writings from 1946 onwards represent in certain ways departures in new directions.
>
> (von Wright 1982:136)

Thus these later works, beginning with Part Two of the *Investigations*, are seen as launching out in new directions, in particular the examination of the relationship between philosophy and psychology.[3] For Moyal-Sharrock the 'Third Wittgenstein' embraces all the works after 1946, consequently published as Part Two of the *Investigations*, *On Certainty*, *Zettel*, *Remarks on Colour* and *Last Writings on the Philosophy of Psychology*. From the point of view of the interpretation of Wittgenstein presented in this book a key interpretation from *On Certainty* has been incorporated as understood by recent scholarship. This is the work of Judith Genova, in particular *Wittgenstein: A Way of Seeing* (1995) taken up by Ivana Dolejšová in *Accounts of Hope: A Problem of Method in Postmodern Apologia* (2001). Genova's and Dolejšová's interpretation of a move in *On Certainty* from thinking to seeing to acting appears a helpful way of understanding the later Wittgenstein, as will be explained shortly.

Generally speaking, if pushed, I would ally myself with scholars such as Hutto who see a philosophical consistency throughout Wittgenstein's work. As argued at the beginning of this chapter the confusion in the manner of publication of the *Nachlass* has probably contributed to the

---

3   On this see Kerr (2008) for an excellent summary.

perception of different Wittgensteins with differing aims and intentions. This point was raised in a conversation with one of Wittgenstein's last pupils in 2006,[4] and I was told that if Wittgenstein were alive now his thoughts would have moved on while using the same methods that he consistently used throughout his life. The concerns of the late 1940s would not be his concerns today, yet his *method* would probably remain the same. Of all his later works perhaps *On Certainty* clarifies most clearly the movement that Wittgenstein had developed from saying to showing to acting and an inherent foundationalism that can, as Hutto argues, be found in his works well before 1946. In addition, as already presented in the Introduction above, the post-1946 works contain some very perceptive work on aspect-seeing which has been incorporated into this book; however, in Chapter Seven I will point to 1916 and Wittgenstein's experiences in the First World War as being decisive to a key shift in his subsequent philosophical viewpoint.

WITTGENSTEIN AND BIOGRAPHY

The unique style of Wittgenstein's writings and his challenges to straightforward academic or conventional interpretations of his work, coupled with the problems of establishing generally accepted definitions of what constitutes a Wittgensteinian 'text' have all contributed to the growth of another basis for evaluating Wittgenstein's contributions to academic discourse: namely accounts and interpretations of Wittgenstein's life, especially records of conversations with friends, students, colleagues and so on. From the early 1950s onwards these have regularly appeared. Although we seem now to be coming to the end of first-hand accounts of encounters with Wittgenstein, we still have the formidable body of literature which tries to interpret his philosophy through the events, actions and conversations that occurred in his life. Wittgenstein's often 'larger-than-life' personality, eccentricities and colourful acquaintances have all added to this tendency. From the point

4   Conversation with Euan Hill, Carshalton, November 2006.

of view of our study here, two of the most important collections of encounters are those by his former pupils Norman Malcolm (in *Ludwig Wittgenstein: A Memoir*, (Malcolm 2001), first published 1958) and Maurice Drury (in Rhees (1987), *Recollections of Wittgenstein*). In both we find Wittgenstein talking candidly about religion in a way that is not often so evident in his written remarks. These conversations, especially with Drury, have helped complete the picture of Wittgenstein's views on such matters and to extend the conversation beyond the written texts. This process has been extended by the two excellent biographies of Wittgenstein produced in the late 1980s/1990s: Brian McGuinness's *Wittgenstein – A Life* (McGuinness 1988) which covers the period up to 1921, and Ray Monk's *Ludwig Wittgenstein: The Duty of Genius* (Monk 1990), the first biography of the complete life of Wittgenstein. Again, much extra-textual material has helped to give us a better overview of Wittgenstein's life and work, and in particular how the two were often seamlessly interconnected. As we shall see later however, the problem of the availability of *Nachlass* material has also influenced these two projects and the publication of, for example, the *Geheime Tagebücher 1914–1916* in 1992 (GT) has brought more material to light. We shall return to this in our final chapters.

WITTGENSTEIN AS THERAPIST

Following from the above, it is therefore legitimate to ask the question: 'Was Wittgenstein a *therapist* as much as a *theoretician* or *logician*?'

As stated above, one of the first writers to emphasize the 'therapeutic' within Wittgenstein's writing was Stanley Cavell (1976, 1979). By the time Alice Crary's collection *The New Wittgenstein* (Crary and Read 2000) came out it seemed as though the notion had influenced a whole generation of Wittgensteinian scholars. The authors collected there, Crary suggested, shared an interpretation of Wittgenstein's work as (1) a unified whole, and (2) broadly 'therapeutic' in nature. The first point has already been discussed above. The second emphasizes the shift in recent Wittgensteinian scholarship away from the understanding of his work as largely *theoretical* (or, in Rorty's words, largely concerned with the reactions and concerns of fellow 'professional philosophers') to an understanding which is built around seeing his work as contributing to individual existential development, or as Hosseini calls it in a recent work, 'the development of wisdom' (Hosseini 2007). For Crary this 'therapeutic aim' is largely around helping us to see the 'sources of philosophical confusion' we hold by replacing a need for a metaphysical view of language to a concern with the observation of the running of language as a means to solving philosophical confusion. Thus, for Cavell, the aim of Wittgenstein's philosophy is to bring us back from metaphysical speculation to the everyday discourse of 'forms of life' (*Lebensformen*) where language has its natural home. Whereas Cavell *et al.* are primarily concerned with the purely philosophical consequences of a reading of Wittgenstein's work, other contemporary authors have gone further and ascribed to Wittgenstein a therapeutic agenda that goes beyond the purely philosophical. In this respect there has been a growing movement to connect Wittgenstein's writings with psycho-therapeutic literature, beginning of course with his fellow Viennese theorist, Sigmund Freud (1856–1939).[5]

Although Wittgenstein's remarks about Freud are scattered throughout the *Nachlass*, especially the collection of remarks published as *Culture and Value* and the conversations with Rhees in 1942 published as the *Conversations on Freud* in *Lectures and Conversations on Aesthetics, Psychology and Religious Belief* (LC:41–52), the first systematic survey of the relationship between the two authors was Jacques Bouveresse's 1995 work *Wittgenstein Reads Freud: The Myth of the Unconscious* (Bouveresse 1995).[6] Bouveresse's work, like others who have followed him, such as Levy (1996), concentrates more on Wittgensteinian critiques of Freudian notions of unconscious, ego, superego and the general Freudian 'mechanics of the mind' rather than

5   Wittgenstein famously once remarked of his fellow countryman: 'It takes one Viennese to know another!'
6   See also Frank Cioffi's 'Wittgenstein's Freud' (Cioffi 1969) and McGuinness's 'Freud and Wittgenstein' (McGuinness 2002).

notions of philosophy as therapy per se. More helpful for my mystical investigations here has been Peterman's (1992) *Philosophy as Therapy* which has taken Cavell's ideas of the therapeutic in Wittgenstein and extended them beyond the philosophical to the ethical. Its emphasis on the movement from *theoria* to *praxis* in Wittgenstein's writings seems to be of fundamental importance for a balanced interpretation of his work, as we shall see later. In this respect the notion of the significance of the *confessional* has been an important theme in many therapeutic interpretations of his work and one that will play a role here.[7] Finally, it is worth noting that the later Wittgenstein saw the value of Freud's work not as a pseudo-scientist but in the function of Freudian analysis as 'aspect-changing':

> When a dream is interpreted we might say that it is fitted into a context in which it ceases to be puzzling. In a sense the dreamer re-dreams his dream in surroundings such that *its aspect changes...*
>
>   In considering what a dream is, it is important to consider what happens to it, the way its aspect changes when it is brought into relation with other things remembered, for instance.
>
> (LC:45–46)

It is to this that we turn next as we develop our own Wittgensteinian methodology for the study of the Christian mystical tradition. This methodology will be based primarily on the notion of the *Übersichtliche Blick/Darstellung* ('Clear Overview') and the importance Wittgenstein gives to a distinction between *Weltanschauung* and *Weltbild* if his approach to philosophy is to be understood aright. Accordingly, we shall turn now to consider the following areas: the tools for doing philosophy and how the mechanisms for philosophy can be applied to spiritual and theological questions in the *Übersichtliche Blick*.

---

7   See also *Wittgenstein's Confessions* (Thompson 2000).

THE TOOLS FOR DOING PHILOSOPHY

As argued at the beginning of this chapter, Wittgenstein's approach to philosophy is notoriously dense and obtuse; indeed, it could be argued that much of his philosophical method was about *attacking* philosophical method (See Fann 1969; Genova 1995; Kallenberg 2001; Peterman 1992; Rorty 1982; Sass 2001). 'With the eye of a practiced marksman,' writes Genova, 'he hit his target squarely, rather than rarely, challenging philosophy's emulation of science, especially the latter's penchant for theory and faith in progress' (Genova 1995:xiii). His famous 'anti-philosophical' stance, however, is not the whole story, since, as he assures us himself, his aims were also deeply philosophical. An anti-method it may have been, but Wittgenstein still considered himself to be a philosopher going about the work of philosophy:

> I know that my method is right. My father was a business man, and I am a business man: I want my philosophy to be business-like, to get something done, to get something settled.
>
> (Rhees 1981:125)

There is clearly 'method behind the madness'; indeed, as we have seen already, much of Wittgenstein's intentional aim seems to have been to re-envisage the aims, goals and techniques of philosophy itself; his style itself being part of that revolution. Style, or how something is said, determines for Wittgenstein what is said:

> In philosophy it is not enough to learn in every case *what* is to be said about a subject, but also *how* one must speak about it. We are always having to begin by learning the method of tackling it.
>
> (RC III:43)

As Genova states:

> Nowhere in the zillion remarks patiently recorded in his notebooks can one find an explicit declaration of his aims and intentions.

Instead, cryptic and hostile sayings pepper the text... In part, he is reluctant to propound and declare like a scientist or prophet. Instead, sarcasm seems a better teacher than sincerity for would-be lovers of wisdom. The results, however, are few clues and even fewer descriptions of his new way of doing philosophy.

(Genova 1995:xv)

We want very much to 'pin Wittgenstein down' but this is precisely what he *does not want us to do*, and he makes it as hard as he possibly can for someone who wants to do this – a difficult challenge for the author who tries to assess his contribution to the Christian mystical tradition! Many times over the past several years there has been the desire to abandon the project, yet ultimately, the challenge of putting Wittgenstein's anti-method or anti-philosophy into philosophical and theological categories proved irresistible and the result is this book. As Genova comments on the phrase from *Remarks on Frazer's Golden Bough*: 'The crush of thoughts that do not get out because they all try to push forward and are wedged in the door' (RFGB:3), saying, 'After suffering the squeeze for twenty years, I came to the conclusion that there is no one, final presentation of his thought, but a variety of arrangements, some more perspicuous than others' (Genova 1995:xvii):

One is always in danger of saying too much or too little. As with poetry, wrenching the thoughts from their embodiment invariably does them damage. One produces theory, the phenomenon Wittgenstein dreaded most, instead of change, the only thing that mattered to him.

(Genova 1995:xvi)

It is on this challenging cusp between avoiding theoretical pronouncements and enunciating Wittgenstein's (and the mystical) agenda for change that this book hovers. For Wittgenstein, I argue here, was clearly not intending to view philosophy *sub specie aeterni* (T:6.45), i.e. to create an overriding view of the world, or indeed a 'school' or 'Fach' in his name (see Rorty 1982). Rather, the task of Wittgenstein's approach is to cultivate what he calls the *Übersichtliche Blick*, the aim of this *Blick* being, as we have already seen, to cultivate a 'change of aspect' in our way of seeing the world. Let us look more deeply then at what he meant by the cultivation of this *Blick*.

'A WAY OF SEEING'/DIE ÜBERSICHTLICHE BLICK: THE LIMITS OF SAYING AND SHOWING

How hard I find it to see what is right in front of my eyes!

(Wittgenstein VB:1940)

In his lectures of 1930 Wittgenstein defines the task of philosophy as one of attempting to 'be rid of a particular kind of puzzlement. This "philosophic" puzzlement is one of the intellect not of instinct' (CLL:21). From this time onward he sees philosophy as possessing a clear method, or as he describes it in the *Philosophical Investigations* and the *Remarks on Frazer's Golden Bough* (RFGB), *eine Übersichtliche Blick* – a 'clear overview' or, as it is often translated, a 'perspicuous view'. For Wittgenstein, what we are doing in philosophy is 'tidying up' our notions of the world, making clear what may be said about the world. From the 1930s onward Wittgenstein begins to talk increasingly about *die Übersichtliche Darstellung* as a way of 'doing philosophy': literally, a 'way of seeing'. Thus in the *Remarks on Frazer's Golden Bough*, written in 1931, he contemplates Frazer's approach to certain anthropological events and how far such an *Übersichtliche Darstellung* can critique reflections such as Frazer's. He states his own position as one which has the form: 'Here one can only *describe* and say: this is what human life is like' (RFGB:121), contrasting it with what he sees as Frazer's approach:

'And so the chorus points to a secret law' one feels like saying to Frazer's collection of facts. I *can* represent this law, this idea, by means of an evolutionary hypothesis, or also, analogously to the schema of a plant, by means of the schema of a religious ceremony, but also by means of the arrangement of its factual content alone, in an *Übersichtliche Darstellung*.

(RFGB:133)

This 'perspicuous view' is: 'of fundamental importance' to Wittgenstein's approach and he describes it as that which 'brings about the understanding which consists precisely in the fact that we "see the connections". Hence the importance of finding *Zwischengliedern* ("connecting links")' (PI:133). These *Zwischengliedern* 'do nothing but direct the attention to the similarity, the relatedness of the *facts*'.

By the time Wittgenstein begins writing the text which will ultimately become the *Philosophical Investigations* (unpublished at the time of his death) the position of the *Übersichtliche Darstellung* has become clearer and more refined. Thus we find the following key passage which develops the earlier idea of the *Remarks*:

A main source of our misunderstandings is that we do not *übersehen* (oversee) the use of our words. – Our Grammar is lacking an *Übersichtlichkeit* (overview). – The *Übersichtliche Darstellung* produces the understanding which allows us to 'see connections'. Hence the importance of finding and inventing *Zwischengliedern*.

The concept of the *Übersichtliche Darstellung* is of fundamental significance for us. It designates our *Darstellungsform* (viewpoint), the way we see things. (Is this a *Weltanschauung*?).

(PI:122)

He follows this with important clarifications that point to the nature of the *Übersichtliche Darstellung*:

A philosophical problem has the form: 'I don't know my way about'.

(PI:123)

Philosophy may in no way interfere with the actual use of language; it can in the end only describe it. For it cannot give it any foundation either.

It leaves everything as it is.

(PI:124)

Philosophy simply puts everything before us, and neither explains nor deduces anything. – Since everything lies open to view there is nothing to explain.

(PI:126)

Wittgenstein therefore proposes a methodology, based on the *Übersichtliche Darstellung*, where we simply put 'everything before us'. We observe the 'language games' or our context while not concerning ourselves with 'hidden things' 'behind the language'. This is nothing new to Wittgenstein but already in germinal form in the earlier *Tractatus*: the notion that language does not so much *say* as *show* (see quote at the head of this chapter). This is a crucial distinction for Wittgenstein and the notion from which the later *Übersichtliche Darstellung* arises.

He is concerned that the *Übersichtliche Darstellung* is not another competing *Weltanschauung* with others in the post-enlightenment/ scientific world (Hence the phrase 'Is this a *Weltanschauung*?'). The point is clarified in the remarks from *Vermischte Bemerkungen*:

Clarity, perspicuity (*Durchsichtigkeit*) are an end in themselves. I am not interested in constructing a building, so much as having a clear view (*durchsichtig*) before me of the foundations of possible buildings. My goal, then, is different from the scientist and so my think-way is to be distinguished.

(VB:459)[8]

---

8   Written as a draft foreword to *Philosophische Bemerkungen* in 1930. See also *Zettel* 464: 'The pedigree of psychological phenomena: I strive not for exactitude but *Übersichtlichkeit*.'

We have before us the clear view of possible buildings rather than constructing another building: conflicting *Weltanschauungen* may be held before the *Übersichtliche Darstellung*.

In his last writing *On Certainty*, written as he lay dying in Cambridge, he clarifies the concept by contrasting a *Weltanschauung* with a *Weltbild*. In contrast to the *Weltanschauung*, which sees itself as *the* way of seeing, the *Weltbild* is *a* way of seeing:

> It (the *Weltanschauung*) takes itself too seriously, as the ultimate explanation and foundation of our convictions. In contrast, the concept of a *Weltbild* completely avoids the knowledge game.
>
> (Genova 1995:50)

There are certain propositions that are not open to doubt (OC:341); they 'make themselves manifest' but cannot be subject to sceptical deconstruction – 'if I want the door to turn the hinges must stay put' (OC:343). These beliefs form a system that is not a knowledge system but 'an ungrounded way of acting' (Genova 1995:51). In investigating language we cannot, as it were, 'step outside language'; our investigation of language takes place within the 'stream of life' – and language itself. This is the implication of Wittgenstein's proposal of the *Weltbild*. To develop one of Wittgenstein's metaphors we can only, as it were, make repairs on the engine while the engine is running, or at least we can only see how the engine works if we investigate when it runs – when it idles we cannot make sense of it. The feeling that we can 'step outside language' and only then make sense of it, is fallacious and ultimately misleading – *this* is the 'picture that once held us captive' (PI:115) and led us to seek an 'Archimedean point' from which we could survey language from outside, a false assumption:

> 'But *this* is how it is –' I say to myself over and over again. I feel as though, if only I could fix my gaze absolutely sharply on this fact, get it in focus, I must grasp the essence of the matter...
>
> A *picture* held us captive. And we could not get outside it,

for it lay in our language and language seemed to repeat it to us
inexorably.

(PI:113, 115)

In formulating and developing the notion of the *Weltbild* Wittgenstein
was influenced by his reading of Oswald Spengler's work of 1923, *Der
Untergang des Abendlandes/The Downfall of the West* (Spengler 1923).
In a note among the *Vermischte Bemerkungen* he remarks, *inter alia*,
that Spengler (as well as Russell, Hertz, Schopenhauer, Boltzmann, Frege,
Kraus, Loos, Weininger and Sraffa) have influenced him (VB:1931) and
Drury notes that in the early 1930s Wittgenstein was recommending
that he read the work.[9] Although rather sprawling and baroque,
Spengler's classification, based on Goethe, does contain germs that will
later develop into Wittgenstein's *Weltanschauung/Weltbild* distinction.
Among other things Spengler points out a difference between theorizing
that 'atomizes' our perspective on the world and theorizing that takes
a broader picture:

> The tendency of human thought (which is always causally disposed)
> to reduce the image of Nature to the simplest possible quantitative
> form-units that can be got by causal reasoning, measuring and
> counting – in a word, mechanical differentiation – leads neces-
> sarily in Classical, Western and every other possible physics, to an
> atomic theory.
>
> (Spengler 1926:384)

This 'atomizing', scientistic tendency is contrasted with the '*Formgefühl
und Weltgefühl des Erkennenden*' – 'The Form-feel and World-feel of
the knower' (Spengler 1923 I:494):

---

9   See Rhees 1981:128. However, Wittgenstein also adds in his conversation:
     'I don't trust Spengler about details. He is too often inaccurate. I once
     wrote that if Spengler had had the courage to write a very short book, it
     could have been a great one.'

The thinker, in imagining that he can cut out the factor of Life, forgets that knowing is related to the known as direction is to extension and that it is only through the living quality of direction that what is felt extends into distance and depth and becomes space.

(Spengler 1926 I:387)

From Spengler, then, Wittgenstein clearly takes the notion of 'seeing a whole' and 'forming connections' to make that whole. This is brought out in a passage from *Logik, Sprache, Philosophie*, the work on which Wittgenstein collaborated with Waismann:

Our thought here matches with certain views of Goethe's which he expressed in the *Metamorphosis of Plants*. We are in the habit, whenever we perceive similarities, of seeking some common origin for them. The urge to follow such phenomena back to their origin in the past expresses itself in a certain style of thinking...

We are collating one form of language with its environment, or transforming it in imagination so as to gain a view of the whole of space in which the structure of our language has its being.

(Waismann 1965:80)

The *Übersichtliche Darstellung*, then, as Wittgenstein comes to formulate it in his later philosophy, is influenced by a Spenglerian/Goetherian 'taking an overview', what we characterized earlier as the 'change of aspect' that allows us to 'see the world aright'. In creating his own philosophical synthesis Wittgenstein was also indebted to the writings of the nineteenth-century physicist, Heinrich Hertz (1857–1894). Writing about the 'mysterious' natures of electricity and force, Hertz compared this mystification with the clarity with which we can speak of gold and velocity, saying:

I fancy that the difference must lie in this. With the terms 'velocity' and 'gold' we connect a large number of relations to other terms; and between all these relations we find no contradictions which offend us. We are therefore satisfied and ask no further questions. But we have accumulated around the terms 'force' and 'electricity' more relations than can be completely reconciled amongst themselves. We have an obscure feeling of this and want to have things cleared up. Our confused wish finds expression in the confused question as to the nature of force and electricity. But the answer which we want is not really an answer to this question. It is not by finding out more and fresh relations and connections that it can be answered; *but by removing the contradictions existing between those already known,* and thus perhaps reducing their number. When these painful contradictions are removed, the question as to the nature of force will not have been answered; but our minds, no longer vexed, will cease to ask illegitimate questions.

(Hertz 1956:7)

Applying the practice of the *Übersichtliche Darstellung,* then, to our 'mystical investigations', here we observe a process of *watching* or *seeing* the 'Form of Life' (*Lebensform*) through the 'language games' (*Sprachspiele*) that are employed. Our job is not to make mystical interpretations of certain *Weltanschauungen* but to present 'everything as it is'. The ontological questions no longer concern us. When Wittgenstein's approach is applied to the spiritual realm, its application is neatly summarized by Drury's remarks concerning *The Tractatus*:

For me, from the very first, and ever since, and still now, certain sentences from the *Tractatus Logico-Philosophicus* stuck in my mind like arrows, and have determined the direction of my thinking. They are these:

1. 'Everything that can be put into words can be put clearly'
2. 'Philosophy will signify what cannot be said by presenting clearly what can be said'
3. 'There are, indeed, things which cannot be put into words. They make themselves manifest. They are mystical'.

(Drury 1973:iv)

I refer to this passage for two reasons. First, Drury seems to neatly sum up much of Wittgenstein's method for approaching philosophy, and second, he delineated the relationship between (1) the need to speak clearly – the *Übersichtliche Blick* of the philosopher, and (2) how this relates to the 'unsayable' and the 'mystical'. By delineating what can be said clearly we also delineate what cannot be said but can be shown. This, I argue following Wittgenstein, is the role of the philosopher who investigates the 'mystical' and is central to Wittgenstein's own view of 'the mystical', and to which we shall return in the final chapter.

We see then how Wittgenstein's philosophy 'leaves everything as it is'. Its aim, in his words, is 'to present everything before us' so that we can have a grasp of the *Weltbild* rather than the *Weltanschauung*. Following Wittgenstein's death there was a tendency to emphasize the importance of analysis of the *Sprachspiel* or 'language game' as the major outcome from the *Übersichtliche Blick*. Yet, the argument presented here has suggested a rather wider concept of Wittgenstein's *Weltblick*, one that encompasses the *Sprachspiel* but that goes beyond this to analyse the whole nature of the speech/action interface that underlies human communication. For Wittgenstein, we have argued, the philosophical *Blick* is not simply about a dry analysis of 'language games' (as is often interpreted by contemporary scholars) but a wider, all-embracing understanding of the act of human communication. Thus the 'view' advocated here leaves behind the hard ontological realism of what I referred to as 'modern mysticism' in the previous chapter as well as the empty anti-realism of constructivists such as Katz and Cupitt. Rather, the Wittgensteinian approach advocated here concentrates the mystic 'speech act' in its overall communicative intent; that is, through *showing* as well as *saying*. This leads to the notion we will explore in later chapters of the 'performative discourse of mystical speech'.

THE MOVE FROM THINKING TO SEEING: 'METHODOLOGICAL NON-FOUNDATIONALISM'

A consequence of the adoption of the *Übersichtliche Darstellung* is a move throughout Wittgenstein's later work from 'thinking' to 'seeing' (or, as we may put it, from 'saying' to 'showing') to finally, in the last works such as *On Certainty*, a 'way of acting'. The 'change of aspect' that accompanies the *Übersichtliche Darstellung* will also, by implication, lead to a change of life and action – the fly will be led out of the fly-bottle. As he wrote in 1931:

> A present day teacher of philosophy doesn't select food for his pupil with the aim of flattering his taste, but with the aim of changing it.
>
> (VB:1931)

As is argued throughout this book, at its roots, Wittgenstein's philosophy, like the Christian mystical theology, is basically *transformational*.

In the *Philosophical Investigations* we are exhorted to '*Denk nicht, sondern schau! –* Don't think, only look!' (PI:66). We take our material – the 'language games' – and we observe 'similarities, relationships' and 'anything common at all'. The aim of philosophy, for the later Wittgenstein, is:

> The uncovering of one or another piece of plain nonsense and of bumps that the understanding has got by running its head against the limits of language. These bumps make us see the value of discovery.
>
> (PI:119)

Understanding is no longer a 'mental process' (PI:154):

> Try not to think of understanding as a 'mental process' at all. – For *that* is the expression that confuses you. But ask yourself: in what sort of case, in what kind of circumstances, do we say, 'Now, I know how to go on'.

His philosophy 'simply puts everything before us, and neither explains nor deduces anything. – Since everything lies open to view there is nothing to explain. For what is hidden, for example, is of no interest to us' (PI:126).[10]

We saw in the previous chapter how elements of such an approach have been adopted by commentators on mysticism such as Sells (1994) and Kripal (2001) in reference to the mystical discourse, teasing out the 'mystical games' of deconstruction, subversion and the libidinal. However, in both writers there seems to be an ambiguity about the 'ontological content' 'behind' the discourse. In the case of Sells, there is 'reference' to an apophatic 'event' behind the apophatic text. Kripal is ambiguous here and seems to be closest to the 'ontological agnosticism' being advocated in this book, although he does not state it in those terms. From Wittgenstein's analysis we see that the meaning of a discourse is derived not only from the language itself but from its context in the 'stream of life': 'words have meaning only in the stream of life' (RPP1:913).[11] *Pace* Cupitt (1998) and other anti-realists, with such a conception it is hard to image a language game that does not 'have contact with reality', i.e. the 'stream of life'. As Wittgenstein puts it in *On Certainty*: 'The human frame of reference, that includes the capability of experience and of judgment, is seen as constitutive for our relation to reality' (OC:80.81).[12] The truth of certain empirical propositions cannot be tested; however, our understanding of a proposition can be. Applied to mystical discourse, the 'truth' of these statements cannot be 'tested' (*pace* James and other psychologistic and experientialist approaches) by verification, but they *can be understood* nevertheless: 'The truth of certain empirical propositions (like "I am in pain") belongs to our frame of reference' (OC:83) and therefore 'the

---

10 Cf. PI:435: 'For nothing is concealed... for nothing is hidden.'

11 See also T:4.031: ' this proposition represents such and such a situation.'

12 See also LPE:143. One of the arguments of this book is that Wittgenstein's methodology implies an ambivalence towards the ontological commitments of his approach; he is not radically *dis-ontological* as implied by Cupitt and Phillips, nor does his approach suggest the 'hard' realism of, say, Teresa of Avila. We can perhaps suggest that he opens an ontological door which Teresa, for one, is free to pass through. I am indebted to Chris Insole for help in elucidating this point.

truth of my statements is the test of my understanding of these state-ments. That is to say: if I make certain false statements, it becomes uncertain whether I understand them' (OC:80.81). The 'human frame of reference' (judgement and experience) is necessary for our relation to reality. To think of a 'language game' entirely unhinged from 'reality', which seems to be the direction of Cupitt's analysis, is neither desirable nor helpful; our 'frame of reference' allows for the 'truth' of a particular discourse. Mystical discourse does not necessarily have to be reduced to empirical statements requiring empirical verification; the understanding of the discourse within its framework brings meaning. In Dolejšová's words:

> No sharp distinguishing line can be drawn between what is consti-tutive for our frame of reference and what is a product of it, what is the capability of experience and of judgment, and what are their expressions. Both are expressed in propositions, and there is no better way of expressing them. Both propositions are part of a kind of 'mythology'.
>
> (Dolejšová 2001:269)

To illustrate this point Wittgenstein uses the famous metaphor of the riverbed of 'hardened empirical propositions' allowing other fluid propositions to flow in (OC:95–97).

From Wittgenstein's analysis we are presented with another epistemo-logical alternative which avoids many of the problems we encountered in the previous chapter. We are presented with a 'methodological non-foundationalism' (Dolejšová 2001:270) which arises from the frame of reference of our (mystical) speech. Wittgenstein presents three moments to the communicative act: knowing, believing and acting. Within these there is a 'hierarchy of certainty': 'in the beginning is the deed', acts come first, which provide the credibility of belief upon which our knowledge is based. In our analysis of the mystical discourse (games) in the remainder of this book we will not be looking for a certain extra-linguistic category ('mysticism'/'mystical experience', etc.) that grounds the discourse and gives it certainty (the question 'Was

so-and-so a mystic or not?' is therefore misleading) but the certainty
that arises from the knower's *knowledge* in the discourse itself. The
certainty arises from the discourse: 'The truth of my statements is the
test of my understanding of these statements... If I make false statements, it becomes uncertain whether I understand them' (OC:80, 81).
It is possible to have a 'mystical orientation' without a fixed belief
system 'behind it' (whether this is explicitly ontological in the case of
Underhill and Inge, or explicitly disontological in the case of Katz and
Cupitt). The meaning of the mystical statement arises from its use by
the agent, or as Wittgenstein states in the *Philosophical Investigations*:
'the meaning of a word is its use in the language' (PI:43). The certainty
of mystical discourse is not something to be derived but something
from whence we start. Consequently, our emphasis here, using our
Wittgensteinian perspective, will be on the *form* of mystical language
game or what I will refer to as *performative discourse*.

Wittgenstein's analysis releases the fly of mystical analysis from the
mystical fly-bottle. We are no longer concerned with finding ghostly
('occult', see Z:605, 606) 'entities' or categories that lie 'behind'
mystical discourse ('And so the chorus points to a secret law' [RFGB:
133]). Mystical discourse possesses meaning *qua* mystical discourse; its
language games are embedded in a practice or 'way of life' that enables
reference to occur. Rather, our aim is to pursue 'a more active kind of
practical understanding' in accord with the general thrust of this book
which is towards a *practical* philosophical theology:

> An understanding that will allow us to 'go on' in an activity in a
> socially concerted and unconfused manner... Instead of seeking
> something hidden, something that will explain a circumstance to
> us, intellectually and passively, (Wittgenstein) provides us with a
> more active kind of practical understanding.
>
> (Shotter 1997:9)

In summary, it is proposed here that 'mystical discourse' be understood as a means of 'changing aspect' through the *Übersichtliche
Darstellung*. This then frees us up to 'see the world aright' which will

have implications for how we live in a practical way. In short, we could summarize our position by suggesting that *the meaning of mystical speech is found through transformative act.* We turn now to how this is done through the move from seeing to acting.

FROM SEEING TO ACTING: PERFORMATIVE DISCOURSES AND STRATEGIES OF ELUCIDATION

Worte sind Taten – Words are deeds.

(Wittgenstein VB:c. 1945)

Language is not a representational structure but a presentational act.

(Genova 1995:117)

By the time of the last writings, especially *On Certainty*, Wittgenstein is supplementing the 'way of seeing' with a 'way of acting':

> Giving grounds, however, justifying the evidence, comes to an end; – but the end is not certain propositions striking us immediately as true, i.e. it is not a kind of *seeing* on our part, it is our *acting*, which lies at the bottom of the language game.

(OC:204)

The frame of reference of the mystical discourse in the 'way of life' is essential:

> What has to be accepted, the given, is – so one could say – *forms of life.*

(PI:226)

We have moved 'out of the head' to find understanding and meaning in the wider arena of *games*. Our aim is not to 'refine or complete the system of rules for the use of our words in unheard-of ways' (PI:133), there is not one 'philosophical method' but 'methods, like different therapies' (*gleichsam verschiedene Therapien*). As we saw earlier, this analogy with therapy is telling, and relates clearly to the 'mystical strategies' of the writers we are investigating here. As we shall see in the remainder of this book, our mystical writers are usually not so much concerned with enunciating metaphysical theories of theology as with providing a *practical way of acting* which will help a distressed person find peace and solace. Likewise, Wittgenstein is concerned to move the reader from thinking to seeing and finally acting. The reading of his philosophy, as has been empha-sized all along, is not a passive act but must be an active engagement that challenges the reader to engage with the work at all levels; a strategy, as we shall see, which he shares with our mystical writers. As in psychotherapy, both Wittgenstein and the mystical writers involve us in observing the foundations of possible buildings rather than trying to build one building – the *Weltbild* rather than the *Weltanschauung* (See also Tyler 1999). Like a successful therapist, they do not provide clever interpretations and inter-ventions but allow the clarity of insight (*Übersichtliche Darstellung*) to be turned on the 'foundations of possible buildings'.

This post-enlightenment way of knowing (therapeutic discourse – to which we could also add mystical discourse) requires a more interactive and immediate medium or frame of reference than either thinking or seeing provide. Action is the closest activity available to language and such activity will be tempered by a necessary vein of humility arising from the lack of an overriding *Weltanschauug*; in this humility is a necessary component of the overall 'mystical strategy' (see below).

For both Wittgenstein and our mystical writers discussed in this book, *change* and *transformation* are paramount. They entice us, excite us, goad and puzzle us. *They are not meant to leave us alone.* They pose us problems (Wittgenstein's thought games, the mystical writers' word pictures and challenges) which cannot be ignored. By their nature they 'subvert'; if they do not subvert they have failed in their task. If we play their games with them they reorientate our perceptions of reality, ourselves and our place in the world: they are primarily purveyors of *performative discourses* that 'show' rather than 'say'. In Genova's words these discourses are 'elucidations':

Elucidations are in a class of their own, not quite poem, aphorism or logical equation, they resist categorization... They instruct by example, by showing rather than saying.

(Genova 1995:108)

As Wittgenstein states in his preface to the *Tractatus,* there is what is presented on the written page and what is unwritten, and often 'this second part is the important one' (LPE:143).[13] Thus,

Instead of helping us 'find' something already existing but supposedly hidden behind appearances, (Wittgenstein's) methods help us grasp something new, as yet unseen, in the emerging articulation of our speech entwined activities.

(Shotter 1996:16)

Accordingly, when in the following chapters we turn to the *Sprachspiel* of the *theologia mystica* we shall identify these *Spiele* as *Performative Discourses for Changing Aspects.* They are discourses out of which action arises and which cannot be viewed without their concomitant context of action.

LINGUISTIC STATEGIES: HOW THE MIDWIFE UNDERTAKES HER WORK

Anything your reader can do for himself leave to him.

(Wittgenstein VB:1948)

As we noted above, one of Wittgenstein's main aims was to let his reader 'do their own work'. He was primarily concerned for his students to 'do their own thinking'. Euan Hill in 2006 referred to it as 'bootstrapping' from computational theory, i.e. you just give enough program for the

---

13   Cf. The Tractatus 4.1212: 'What *can* be shown, *cannot* be said.'

computer itself to go on developing the program.[14] Thus we find in his writings a variety of subversive or 'prompting' strategies to enable him to do this to his reader. He is not going to bamboozle us or dazzle us with layers of sophisticated theory; rather he will challenge us to wake up and start thinking for ourselves.

Wittgenstein clearly states that he does not want to spare his readers the trouble of 'thinking for themselves' (PI:viii). He says of his later philosophy:

> I do philosophy now like an old woman who is always mislaying something and having to look for it again: now her spectacles, now her key.
>
> (OC:532)

Genova comments:

> Dressed as an old woman (a guise used often by philosophers, e.g. Diotima) instead of the conquering hero, Wittgenstein pads about his conceptual domain seeking what he mislaid, namely, the pictures that free one from the fly-bottle... Its goal is pure performance in that once it completes its job, to change the way of seeing, it ought to self-destruct. Words ought to dissolve into the attitudes and actions from which they came. They are, in the strictest sense of the word, 'deeds'.
>
> (Genova 1995:129)

Or further, we may say that he disguises himself like Socrates's midwife the better to give birth to individual and independent thought in the listener or reader. As Kallenberg has stressed, he wants to inspire in the reader the same 'passion of subjectivity' as his mentor, Kierkegaard, had in himself.

In such a way of 'doing philosophy' our normal conventions of philosophy and conceptual discourse dissolve. No longer the systematic

14   Conversation in Carshalton, March 2006.

introduction, exposition and conclusion – these are the requirements of the *Weltanschauung*; the *Weltbild* has differing requirements. His comments appear as a sequence of numbered remarks, sometimes apparently randomly thrown together, yet as we have already seen, we know that he took great time and trouble arranging and rearranging their sequence so that the discourse would have the desired performative effect on the person who engaged with it:

> They point or gesture towards ends that are somewhat alien to our current preoccupations. In fact they are written in the form of 'striking similes' and 'arresting moments' – they have a 'poetic quality' their function is to change our 'way of looking at things' (PI:144).
>
> (Shotter 1997:1)

For Wittgenstein our words become tools, instruments to challenge and wake us up; he refers to them as 'the levers in the cabin of a locomotive' or 'tools in a toolbox'. Throughout his writings he uses them carefully, and develops and traces his strategic elucidations with care and caution. Shotter (1997:14) isolates four 'linguistic strategies' adopted by Wittgenstein:

1. To arrest or interrupt ('to deconstruct') the spontaneous, unselfconscious flow of our ongoing 'mental' activity. These strategies provoke us into examining whether there is 'more to it' than we expected. We are shocked into 'standing back'.
2. To use certain 'instructive forms of language' that provoke us to give 'prominence to distinctions which our ordinary forms of language easily made us overlook' (PI:132). They are 'instructive gestures' which point and show.
3. To suggest new ways of thinking through the use of carefully selected images, similes and metaphors which can help the process giving 'first form to such sensed but otherwise unnoticed distinctions, thus to make reflective contemplation of their nature possible'.
4. To use the comparison of different 'language games' to present 'an order in our knowledge of the use of language: an order with a

particular end in view; one of many possible orders; not the order'
(PI:132).

His similes, his playful use of metaphors, are there to 'show' rather than
'say'. They recall us to our right relationship to our language, our selves
and those around us. In terms of mystical discourse, we can talk about
a play that reminds us of our right relationship with the triune God.
Just as the chiropractor hits our bones at certain angles to bring the
correct alignment back to the body, so Wittgenstein, and our 'mystical
strategists', hit our mental, emotional and spiritual bones at different
angles to bring our thought, emotions and spiritual seeing back into
right alignment. As part of this subversive linguistic toolkit, Genova
(1995:130) isolates four 'subversive stategies' used by Wittgenstein:

1. Talking to himself
2. Contradicting himself
3. Avoiding arguments and conclusions
4. Refusing orientating structures.

When we come to investigate the linguistic strategies, or performative
discourse, of the *theologia mystica* we shall return to these strategies.
For now it is necessary to conclude this chapter with a summary of the
argument developed so far.

SUMMARY

Our analysis of the Wittgensteinian performative discourse in this
chapter has opened up a possibility of exploring the mystical 'language
games' or 'strategies' while remaining 'ontologically agnostic'. Certain
key aspects of the Wittgensteinian methodology have been isolated
which will be adopted in the remainder of this book.

I began by emphasizing the adoption of a *Weltbild* (rather than
a *Weltanschauung*) based on an *Übersichtliche Darstellung*. It was
then argued that Wittgenstein sees a change of *Weltbild* as necessary

to 'change our aspect' or 'way of looking at the world'. Ultimately, I argued, this will inevitably lead to a change of life or action. Drawing upon Wittgenstein's writings I emphasized the importance of *action and performance* to his understanding of discourse. I suggested that similar strategies may be found in mystical discourse and proposed to search for this *performative discourse* in the *theologia mystica* of the Western medieval Christian tradition. In investigating these writings in Part Two from this Wittgensteinian perspective the following points will be borne in mind:

1. I shall not be seeking to find quasi-ontological 'mystical entities' in the texts. I will choose not to adopt this essentialist methodology (the position of 'modern mysticism' elaborated in the previous chapter). Following the arguments presented above, I shall be observing the *Weltbild* of the discourse.
2. Although I shall not adopt an essentialist approach to mystical discourse I shall not, conversely, see that discourse as a cold constructivist narrative. I will analyse the discourse from its performative or participatory perspective; that is to say, appreciating the *transformational* aspect of mystical discourse and how it leads, in a Wittgensteinian sense, from saying to showing to acting. I will be concerned with the whole communicative intent of mystical speech as transformative act.
3. It was argued above how Wittgenstein delineates a philosophical method that concentrates as much on *how* something is said as much as *what* is said. Therefore, in applying his methods to the mystical writings of the Christian tradition I will concentrate as much on *how* they say something as on *what* is said.
4. In this chapter a move in Wittgenstein from *thinking to seeing to acting* has been isolated. I will show in the following chapters how such a move helps elucidate the 'mystical strategies' of the *theologia mystica* to produce a similar move from thinking about God to experiencing God through what is termed embodiment or affectivity. As well as the 'deconstructive strategy' mentioned above, it forms, I will suggest, the second strategy of the *theologia mystica*.

Having argued against using the essentialism of 'modern mysticism' and the cold linguistic analysis of constructivism to approach the writings of the mystical tradition, I conclude with the proposal for analysing mystical writings from a third perspective based on the Wittgensteinian approach outlined in this chapter. Namely, what I propose to call *the performative discourse of theologia mystica*. It is to this that we turn now in Part Two of this book.

PART TWO

The Evolution of the Theologia Mystica

3

The Origins of the Theologia Mystica: *Dionysius the Areopagite*

Theological tradition has a dual aspect, the ineffable and mysterious on the one hand, the open and more evident on the other.
The one resorts to symbolism and involves initiation. The other is
philosophical and employs the method of demonstration. The one
uses persuasion and imposes the truthfulness of what is asserted.
The other acts by means of a mystery which cannot be taught.

(Dionysius Ep:9.1, Dion:638)

The remainder of this book will concentrate on applying the
Wittgensteinian approach developed in the previous chapter to the
'mystical strategies' of the medieval Christian mystical tradition.
However, before we turn to those writings themselves it is necessary to
clarify one final term which we have already introduced and which will
be used from now on – namely that of *theologia mystica*.

In the previous chapter a Wittgensteinian approach was presented
which sees the mystical text through the *Weltbild* of an *Übersichtliche
Blick* that concentrates on the performative aspects of the discourse.
At the beginning of Chapter 1 we saw how commentators such as de
Certeau emphasized the origins of *la mystique* as a distinctive area
of humanistic study and that out of this 'modern mysticism' would
eventually arise. In this chapter I will suggest that there is a distinctive
pre-modern tradition of what I term the 'performative discourse of
theologia mystica' that arises from interpretations of the Dionysian
texts in the Parisian schools of the twelfth and thirteenth centuries

and thence spreads throughout Europe, reaching sixteenth-century Spanish writers such as Teresa of Avila via the texts of Francisco de Osuna (whom Teresa terms 'her master'), Bernardino de Laredo and Jean Gerson. By applying the Wittgensteinian *Blick* developed in the previous chapter, this chapter will concentrate on the language game of *theologia mystica* and highlight two 'performative discourses' that will be explored. In tracing this 'mystical lineage' from Dionysius to the Spanish school via Gallus, Gerson, Laredo and de Osuna I am aware that I will not be mentioning large areas of the tradition. The aim of this book is not to cover every aspect of the medieval tradition of *theologia mystica* but rather to demonstrate how one strand of its influence can be traced. Whether such a complete overview would be possible or desirable is questionable. However, perhaps the nearest one scholar has come to completing such an overview is Bernard McGinn in his five-volume *Presence of God* (See Chapter One of this volume, and references in bibliography). It is neither my intention nor desire to emulate that massive undertaking.

THE CREATION OF THE MEDIEVAL DIONYSIAN TRADITION: THE *CORPUS DIONYSIACUM*

Key to understanding the tradition of *theologia mystica* are the writings variously alluded to as the *Dionysian Corpus*. These writings evolved through one thousand years of interpretation and translation to assume, by the late medieval period, a unique position in the West's understanding of theological exegesis, becoming identified with the tradition of *theologia mystica*.

The four works and epistles (Ep) of the *Corpus Dionysiacum*: the *Mystical Theology* (MT), *Celestial Hierarchy* (CH), *Ecclesiastical Hierarchy* (EH) and *Divine Names* (DN) make their first entry in Western intellectual life through the Greek manuscipt presented to Louis the Pious, the Frankish king, by the Eastern emperor, Michael the

Stammerer, in 827.[1] Attributed to the Areopagite who appears in Acts 17:34 the works retained semi-canonical status throughout most of the Middle Ages until Erasmus and Lorenzo Valla began to question the attribution in the early sixteenth century. Their doubts were reflected by Luther who used Erasmus's phrase *'Dionyisus ille quisquis fuerit'* (*'Dionysius, whoever he was'*) in his *Babylonian Captivity of the Church* of 1520.[2] Despite this, the apostolic authority of Dionysius continued to be defended into modern times, however, scholarly work in the nineteenth century by Stiglmayr (1895) and Koch (1895) demonstrated conclusively the link between Dionysius and the neo-platonic circle around Proclus, one of the last heads of Plato's Academy in Athens, the Academy itself being closed in 529 by the Emperor Justinian. Accordingly, it looks as though our author could not have been writing before the mid-fifth century and most likely dates from the turn of the fifth and sixth centuries. In the words of Andrew Louth:

Denys the Areopagite, the Athenian convert, stands at the point where Christ and Plato meet. The pseudonym expressed the

---

1   The most recent scholarly edition of the original Greek texts is the *Corpus Dionysiacum* edited by Suchla, Heil and Ritter (1990). In this book we shall be largely concerned with the twelfth-century interpretations of the text that formed the tradition of *theologia mystica* in the West. Accordingly we shall concentrate on the Latin versions of the text found in *Dionysiaca* (1937–1950), *Patrologia Latina* (1844), Harrington (2004) and McEvoy (2003). For English translations we shall draw on *Pseudo-Dionysius: The Complete Works* translated by Luibheid (1987), *Dionysius the Areopagite on the Divine Names and Mystical Theology* and *Denis Hid Divinity* edited by McCann (1924). For an up-to-date summary of contemporary academic debates on the Areopagite see S. Coakley and C. Stang, *Re-Thinking Dionysius the Areopagite* (2009). For more on the reception of the Dionysian corpus and its Syrian and Greek roots see Louth, *The Reception of Dionysius up to Maximus the Confessor* and *The Earliest Syriac Reception of Dionysius* by Perczel in Coakley and Stang (2009).
2   *Luthers Werke,* Weimar Edition 6:562. See also Malysz, *Luther and Dionysius: Beyond Mere Negations* in Coakley and Stang 2009.

author's belief that the truths that Plato grasped belong to Christ,
and are not abandoned by embracing faith in Christ.

(Louth 1989:11)[3]

Whoever the real author was (and perhaps we shall never know), the
texts represent a fascinating insight into the world of late paganism
and emerging Christianity, suggesting, as Louth indicates, an interplay
between the two forces.

Early on, *scholia* were written to the texts by John of Scythopolis and
Maximus the Confessor,[4] the former possibly in close contact with the
original author.[5] The Dionysian texts are first cited in an ecclesiastical
forum at the Council of Constantinople in 532, although the *scholia*
were already closely associated with the documents by this time.

As already mentioned, the documents really entered the Western
tradition with the gift of a codex from Michael the Stammerer to Louis
the Pious in 827.[6] Louis gave the work to Hilduin, Abbot of St. Denis
in Paris, to translate into Latin; he went further in identifying the
author of the texts with St. Denis, the bishop and martyr of Paris in his
hagiographical *Passio sanctissimi Dionysii* (See Chevallier 1957:319).
Compounded with the identification with Dionysius, the first bishop
of Athens (first by Eusebius), the texts now assumed an authority that
would be unassailable throughout the Middle Ages (see Sells 1994:34).

3   The main works drawn upon for this study of Dionysius are as follows.
     The article in the *Dictionnaire de spiritualité (DS)*, 'Denys L'Aréopagite:
     Doctrine' 3:244–86 by René Roques and his 1954 work *L'univers
     dionysien*. Rorem, *Pseudo-Dionysius. A Commentary on the Texts and
     an Introduction to their Influence* (1993), Louth, *Denys the Areopagite*
     (1989), McGinn, *The Foundations of Mysticism* (1991), Knowles (1975)
     and the commentaries and articles found in the texts by Luibheid,
     Harrington, McEvoy and Walsh mentioned in the previous footnote. See
     also Coakley and Stang (2009) and Golitzin (2003).
4   See von Balthasar, *Herrlichkeit: einer theologische Ästhetik, II. Fächer der
     Stile, 1. Klerikale Stile (1962)* and Rorem and Lamoreaux (1998).
5   See Saffrey (1979), Suchla (1980) and Louth (2009).
6   Although they were known to Gregory the Great who refers to them in
     Homily 34 on the Gospels (see Louth 1989:121).

Hilduin's translation (H), made between 832 and 835, was the first of a long line of Latin translations of the text.[7] Théry, who rediscovered and edited it, believed it to be the collaborative work of three people. This would accord with medieval practices of translation as found later in centres of scholarly translation such as Toledo in Spain. In both cases one party would read out the manuscript which would then be orally translated from Greek to Latin by a second party, and finally written down by a third party. The result is highly erratic and has been called unreadable (Harrington 2004:1); he employs up to sixteen different translations for some Greek words and there seems to be little understanding of the text being translated.[8] The text was soon superseded by that of Eriugena (810–77) made some thirty years later around 862 on the command of Charles the Bald, Louis's son.

John 'The Scot' Eriugena was a philosophical theologian in his own right, the translation of the *Corpus* being followed by at least three significant works in the area: the *Periphyseon* or *De Divisione naturae* of the 860s, the *Commentary* on Dionysius's *Celestial Hierarchy* and the *Homily and Commentary* on St. John's Gospel.[9] The importance of Eriugena's translation of Dionysius was its ability to have greater intelligibility than Hilduin's while retaining a lot of the unusual language and terminology of the original Greek. Later translations may have been more accessible but Eriugena retained something of the wildness and rough edge of the original. For example, whenever Eriugena comes across a Greek word with the ὑπερ- prefix he simply creates a new word with a *super*-prefix; thus, ὑπέρθεε becomes *superdeus* which we could render in English as *over-god* or *hyper-god*. Thus retaining the 'roughness' of the mystical text which we have already identified as part of its nature as 'performative discourse'. As with Wittgenstein

---

7   Unless otherwise stated, our main source for the Latin translations is *Dionysiaca*. The Hilduin translation was rediscovered and edited by Gabriel Théry in 1932 and reprinted in *Études dionysiennes*, vol. 1 (Paris, Vrin), 101–42 using the manuscript of the BN 15645. It is reproduced in *Dionysiaca*.

8   See also Delaporte (2006).

9   See DS 3:250, McGinn 1994:80–118 and Rorem 2009.

it is notable that scholarly approaches to the Dionysian texts have been divided between those who want to 'tidy them up' to produce a coherent theoretical whole, and those who want them to retain their 'rough edges' and concomitant 'oddness'.[10]

When Eriugena's translation was sent to Rome for approval the reaction of the papal librarian, Anastasius, to this seemingly miraculous manifestation of cultural genius from the far-flung outposts of 'civilization' was summarized in his letter accompanying the manuscript:

> It is also cause for wonder by what means that uncultivated foreigner (*vir ille barbarus*), placed on the borders of the world... could grasp such matters with his intellect and translate them into another tongue: I mean John the Irishman, a man who I know by hearsay is in all things holy. But herein was the working of that creative Spirit who made this man as fervent as he was eloquent... For love was the master who taught this man what he accomplished for the instruction and edification of many.[11]

While marvelling at the work he also lamented the shortfalls in Eriugena's approach. Part of Anastasius's response to the translation was to complement it with translations of the *scholia* to the *corpus* which had been attached to it from its earliest appearance and associated with John of Scythopolis and Maximus the Confessor (see Harrington 2004:16–18).[12] In not having to rely on the same (impaired) document as Eriugena held at Saint Denis, Anastasius was also able to correct some aspects of Eriugena's translation as well as adding some scholia of his own.[13]

---

10   As McGinn points out (1994:80 *passim*), Eriugena holds three distinct cultural streams in his writing: the Latin, Celtic and Greek. The result is a unique synthesis that was to play a significant role in the future development of the *theologia mystica* tradition.

11   In PL 122:1025, translation Mary Brennan *Materials for the Biography of Johannes Scottus Eriugena* in *Studia Medievali* 3a serie 27 (1986):431.

12   On the methodology of Anastasius's translation see Neil (1998).

13   eg PG 4:417.6 *Ardentibus: Ardentes quod interpres posuit Graecus on*

This process of annotation and correction, usually in the addition of marginalia, would continue for the next three centuries so that by the time the Latin West re-engaged with the documents in the 'twelfth-century Renaissance' they were already heavily annotated from 700 years of commentary. In Harrington's words:

> The thirteenth-century reader came to the text of the *Mystical Theology* with much of the interpretative work already done for him, finding difficult metaphors and foreign concepts set within a more familiar Latin framework.
>
> (Harrington 2004:27)

Central to the twelfth-century revival of interest in Dionysius was Paris, especially its emerging university and the still influential Abbey of Saint-Denis (see Haskins 1957; Knowles 1962; Morris 1972).[14] The group of writers and commentators associated with the Abbey of St. Victor in Paris took particular interest in the Dionysian *corpus*. The abbey grew with the schools of Paris and was open to the new theological developments of the university, and from its inception it was concerned with questions on the relationship between the *intellectus*

---

imbutos seu initiatos – id est on conscecratos – habet. Er notandum quod alios indoctos dicat et alios non imbutos/'Firebrands': Where the Translator puts 'firebrands' the Greek has 'unimbued' or 'unitiated' – that is, 'unhallowed'. Note that Dionysius calls some 'untaught' and others 'unimbued' (Harrington 2004:63).

14 The Abbey was founded by William of Champeaux, a master of the schools of Paris, and described by Abelard as 'the first dialectician of his age', founding the abbey after retiring from the schools in 1108. He set up a small community at the site of an old hermitage on the left bank of the Seine just beyond the walls of Paris. Almost, it seems, by accident, a community grew up around William who departed in 1113 to be made Bishop of Chalons. His disciple, Gilduin, was elected first abbot of the community in the same year and under his leadership the abbey grew and flourished. Following the *Rule of St. Augustine*, the community was at the forefront of clerical renewal through prayer, study and liturgy.

and *affectus*.[15] The distinctive Victorine tradition established there combined 'a vigorous program of Bible study, serious and creative theological investigation and disciplined pursuit of contemplation all set in the context of a community orientated towards liturgical regularity and shared experience' (Zinn 1979:3). The abbey continued to flourish throughout the twelfth and thirteenth centuries, surviving until the French Revolution when it was destroyed.

From the point of view of our study, the chief development which would shape future interpretations of the Dionysian texts, and indeed the shaping of the tradition of *theologia mystica* itself in the late Middle Ages, was this very combination of *intellectus* and *affectus* in the understanding of the texts.

Of the first generation of Victorines, the most celebrated was Hugh of St. Victor (1096–1141); probably born in Saxony, he moved to St. Victor around 1115 and was elected abbot of the foundation in 1133.[16] Hugh's *Commentary* on Dionysius's *Celestial Hierarchy* was incorporated into the commentaries on the Dionysian corpus circulating in Paris and became part of the standard Dionysian edition until the late medieval period (See Harrington 2004:3).

Recent scholarship has highlighted the complexity of the nature of the *corpus Dionysiacum* as it was taught at the university and disseminated throughout Europe.[17] To prepare his 2004 edition of the Paris text of the *Theologia Mystica*, Harrington uses two main manuscripts: MS. *Paris, Bibliotheque nationale, lat. 17341(C)* and *lat. 1619 (D)* (Harrington 2004:34), both dating from the thirteenth century and held by the Dominican convent of Saint-Jacques and the University of Paris respectively. The contents of these manuscripts

15 Literally 'intellect' and 'affect'.
16 A prolific writer he combined theology, biblical exegesis, contemplation, philosophy, rhetoric and knowledge of the original biblical languages. He seems to have had knowledge of both Greek and Hebrew and evidently happy to consult contemporary Jewish authorities on the Jewish sense of the scriptures (see Turner 1995a:265; Rorem 2009).
17 See especially Dondaine (1953) and the editions of Harrington and McEvoy already cited.

reveal how the dionysian 'midrash' had developed by this time. As well as the Latin translations of Hilduin and Eriugena there are Hilduin's preface to the whole *corpus*,[18] Anastasius's letter to Charles the Bald of 23 March 875 as well as some of his *scholia*, verses of Eriugena and Eriugena's letter to Charles introducing his translation. Finally there are the contributions of the Victorines: Hugh of St. Victor's prologue and commentary, the commentary of John Sarracenus and the paraphrase of Thomas Gallus.

The Victorines were at the forefront of the reintroduction and re-examination of the corpus, introducing innovations that have been referred to as the interpretation of 'affective Dionysianism' (See Rorem 1993:216; McGinn 1998c:84). It is precisely this late medieval 'affective Dionysianism' that will produce the *theologia mystica* on which we are concentrating here (for more on this see the following chapters).

Sarracenus produced his version of the *corpus* in 1166–1167, the first full translation since Eriugena, some 300 years earlier. As Dondaine points out (1953:64), Sarracenus used the glosses of Anastasius and Hugh of St. Victor to perfect and advance his own translation.[19] Generally, as we shall see, Sarracenus in his translation (S) smoothes out some of the inconsistencies and hard edges in Eriugena to present a more flowing Latin text. In particular, he avoided the strange Greek-Latin hybrid words that Eriugena often produced from his straightforward transliterations of Greek terms. Thus he renders $\theta \varepsilon o \sigma o \phi \iota \alpha \varsigma$ in MT as *divina sapientia* (lit. divine wisdom) rather than Eriugena's *theosophia*

---

18 This may be found in PL:106.
19 We know next to nothing of Sarracenus himself, it even being unclear whether he was actually a brother of St. Victor (See Solignac 1988:353). We know that he was translator of St. Denys under Abbot Odon between 1167 and 1169 and while John of Salisbury was in exile in France between 1164 and 1170. Solignac suggests he may have acquired his *nomme de plume* 'Saracen' during a sojourn in the Middle East during the second crusade (1147–1149); this may also have been an occasion for him to have access to the Greek manuscripts of Dionysius while in the Byzantine territories. The letters of John of Salisbury (see PL 199:143–144) suggest that he was working in Poitiers after his time under Abbot Odon, possibly one of the 'magister scholarum' of the cathedral school.

(lit. theosophy). However, he does retain the *super-* terms introduced by Hilduin and Eriugena: ὑπέρθεε changes gender from *superdeus* to *superdea* in MT presumably in reference to the holy *Sapientia*; however the text remains ambiguous with the reference to *trinitas*.

To complete our references to the twelfth/thirteenth-century translators of Dionysius and the creation of the tradition of *theologia mystica* we need to finally mention Thomas Gallus and Robert Grosseteste.

The work of Gabriel Théry in the mid-twentieth century recovered the importance of Thomas Gallus (also known as Thomas of St. Victor and Vercellensis) in the interpretive tradition of the *Corpus Dionysiaca*.[20] In regard to the *corpus*, Gallus's lasting achievement may be seen as the introduction of the affective Victorine tradition into the tradition of Dionysian interpretation. Drawing mainly on the translation of Sarracenus, he continued the tradition of glosses on the corpus, producing glosses on the whole Dionysian body, completed in 1233. McEvoy's recent edition of the *Glosses of Gallus* on the *Mystical Theology* contains much previously unedited material of these *Glosses* (he refers to it as the *Expocisio* – McEvoy 2003:5). We shall refer to this below.

Following the *Glosses*, Gallus completed an *Extractio* of the whole corpus in 1238. In McEvoy's words, 'The *Extractio* constitutes a literary genre all of its own... It was, one might say, just the thing required by the busy university minds of his age, who were eager for doctrinal

---

20   Born in France sometime in the late twelfth century (hence 'Gallus', in Italy he was referred to as 'Thomas Parisiensis') we know that he was a canon of St. Victor and was a professor of theology at the University of Paris. In 1219, on the invitation of Cardinal Guala Bicchieri, Thomas and two other canons travelled from Paris to Vercelli in Northern Italy (Bicchieri's native town) to found an abbey and hospital. Thomas was subsequently elected prior in 1224 and abbot in 1226. Most of the next seventeen years were spent at Vercelli apart from a lengthy visit to England in 1238 (where he had discussions with Grosseteste, another translator of the Dionysian *corpus*). He was finally deposed as abbot in 1243 as a casualty of the thirteenth-century conflict between the Guelphs and Ghibelines. He may have been reinstated at the abbey before his death where his remains lie to this day.

understanding but were largely untroubled by any kind of philological or antiquarian curiosity' (McEvoy 2003:5). The result is a curious document that 'translates' the Dionysian corpus into the Latin world of the thirteenth century and would have considerable influence over the next centuries.[21] This was finally followed by a full *Explanacio* of the whole corpus produced between 1241 and 1243, the date of his exile from Vercelli. This has not received a full modern critical edition despite the pioneering work of Théry.[22]

What are the distinctive qualities of Gallus's work? As stated above, Gallus is at the beginning of the second wave of Dionysian reception in the West following the first wave headed by Eriugena in the ninth century. Here, as has been pointed out (see especially Rorem 1993:214–219, and 2009; McGinn 1998c), the *affective* interpretation of Dionysius begins to surface. Influenced by Augustine (as passed down from Richard and Hugh of St. Victor), Gallus also incorporated the influences of the newly formed Cistercian movement, especially in Bernard's inspiration found in the Song of Songs.[23] We shall return to this in the following chapter.

The final commentator and translator we shall refer to in this survey is the Englishman Robert Grosseteste, Bishop of Lincoln (*c.* 1168–1253). As the University of Paris and its scholastic culture was growing throughout the twelfth and thirteenth centuries so too the University at Oxford was developing, where Grosseteste's contribution was significant (See McEvoy 2000). Callus's work in the twentieth

---

21 Reprinted in Dion 1:710–712.

22 Although much is to be found in J. Walsh's doctoral dissertation on Gallus (Walsh 1957).

23 Although Leclercq suggests that the Dionysian corpus played only a minor role in the Cistercian reforms of the twelfth century. David Bell notes (1978:265) that Thomas the Cistercian in his *Commentary on the Song of Songs* 'does not seem to care for Pseudo-Dionysius... It is interesting to note the conspicuous lack of Dionysian ideas and terminology in Thomas's works... Thomas, like Bernard, remains Latin.' The same, Leclercq claims, may be said of Bruno and the founders of the Carthusian order, although our analysis of Hugh of Balma in Chapter 4 would suggest its later importance to the order.

century argued for a date of 1240 to 1243 for Grosseteste's translation (Callus 1947) which is now largely accepted (McEvoy 2003:56). Using the translations of Eriugena and Sarracenus, he used his own knowledge of Greek to further refine their work. Significantly, there is a uniformity of Latin word assignment, so that each Greek term tends to receive a constant Latin translation. As with our other authors, his translation was accompanied by a commentary and glosses. We shall use the translation found in *Dionysiaca*: R.[24]

Like Gallus, Grosseteste places importance on the 'affective' interpretation of the Areopagite. However, of the two, Grosseteste had the better knowledge of Greek and this shows in his deeper understanding of the Greek inflections of the original text; in this respect his translations sometimes refer back to the awkward 'Greek-Latinisms' of Eriugena.

Following Dondaine (1953), we can see that by the thirteenth century the University of Paris had amalgamated Eriugena's translation and commentary on Dionysius, as well as sections of the *Periphyseos*, with Sarracenus's and Anastasius's translations and the commentaries of Hugh of St. Victor and Sarracenus to produce a Dionysian omnibus for use in the university. The translation and commentary of Thomas Gallus added a new dimension to the Dionysian *corpus* by its emphasis on the affective and the emphasis on the 'ray of darkness' and 'cloud of unknowing'. Dionysius's mystical union with God is now made through love (*affectus*) rather than intelligence. It is this thread of interpretation of the Dionysian *corpus* made by subsequent writers that creates what we term the *theologia mystica*.[25]

In subsequent printings of the Dionysian *corpus* into the early

---

24   As McEvoy points out, the two commentators, Gallus and Grosseteste, as well as sharing the same intellectual resources and milieu were also companions and addressed questions to one another, and it seems likely they may have met in 1238 during Gallus's visit to the church of Chesterton.

25   With reference to the affective interpretation of Dionysius by Gallus, Rorem memorably comments that 'the Dionysian darkness becomes Solomon's lovesick night' (Rorem 1993:218).

modern periods the work of Gallus and Grosseteste was combined with that of the other authors mentioned. Thus, the Strassbourg printing of the corpus of 1502 (Salisbury 1502) contains the Grosseteste ('Lincolniensis') and Sarracenus translations and commentary together with the *Extractio* of Gallus. As McEvoy comments:

> It cannot be too much emphasised that the entire later inter-
> pretation of the *Mystical Theology* was deflected into the path
> it actually followed through the combined influence of Thomas
> Gallus and Robert Grosseteste. These earliest Latin commen-
> tators provided the context within which not only the mystical
> theology of monastery and university but also the actual spiritual
> experience of countless souls was to be formed.
>
> (McEvoy 2003:128)

THE MYSTICAL STRATEGIES OF DIONYSIUS

Having clarified what is meant by the 'Dionysian *corpus*' I shall now use the Wittgensteinian approach identified in the previous chapter to look at the Latin Dionysian texts from this perspective. I shall not be looking for 'occult entities' but rather examining the *Sprachspiele,* arguing for a 'mystical strategy' or 'performative discourse' within these writings. In doing so I will be concentrating on Dionysius's performative strategies as laying down the basic form of the *theologia mystica* as it will be inherited and used up to the sixteenth century. Since I am particularly concerned here with examining the development of the tradition of *theologia mystica* in the Western tradition between the twelfth and sixteenth centuries I shall concentrate mainly on the Latin texts of Dionysius available to Western writers in this area, i.e. the translations of Eriugena, Sarracenus, Grosseteste and Gallus as outlined above.

In his striking essay on Dionysius in *Herrlichkeit: Eine theolo-gische Ästhetik* (1962) von Balthasar emphasizes the unique nature of Dionysius's writing and how for him *style* is an essential element in understanding his process:

With Denys we have a unique case in theology, indeed in all intellectual history. A man of the foremost rank and of prodigious
power hid his identity not only from centuries of credulity but
also from the critical acumen of the modern period, and precisely
through that concealment exercised his influence. That for our
modern, and above all German, scholarly world is unforgiveable.
After their tank-formations have laid waste his garden, there is for
them not a blade of grass left: all that remains is PSEUDO-, written
in bold letters, and underlined with many marks of contempt.

(von Balthasar 1984:144)

Von Balthasar reminds us of the special nature of the mystical text,
and this *Ur*-text of the Western tradition in particular.[26] The attempt,
since Koch and Stiglmayr, to discover the 'real' Areopagite is not only
ill-founded but also missing the point of the texts themselves and the
role they have played in the Western tradition: 'All these untenable
hypotheses are signs of a certain spiritual "colour blindness" which
prevents them, for all their individual scholarship (which Stiglmayr, Pera,
Honigmann and the rest doubtless have), from grasping the general flow
of the Areopagitic handwriting' (von Balthasar 1984:146).[27] Within

26   For more on the antique role of the pseudonym see Stang's perceptive
     essay *Dionysius, Paul and the Significance of the Pseudonym* in S. Coakley
     and C. Stang (2009) where he concludes: 'we should understand this
     pseudonymous endeavour as resting on the conviction that historical
     time can be collapsed such that the apostolic past and the present enjoy
     "contemporaneity," and that writing is a means by which to collapse that
     distance, such that the author in the present comes to understand himself
     as an "extension" of the personality of the ancient authority' (20–21).
     For the possible importance of the esoteric nature of the text see Perczel
     2009:35.

27   'Is one telling the Syrian monk in 500AD anything new', von Balthasar
     asks, 'if one proves to him that he was not converted by the speech on
     the Areopagus in 50AD? Or does not the whole phenomenon exist on an
     utterly different level?' This 'utterly different level' which contrasts a post-
     Cartesian scientism with an alternative hermeneutic lies at the heart of our
     book. For Balthasar, Dionysius's 'identification of his task with a situation

the fun that von Balthasar is clearly having with the 'pseudo-nature' of Dionysius, there is also the concealed truth he is picking up, namely that as a *mystical strategist* the author of the Dionysian *Corpus* understands that he must adopt special strategies to get his readers 'to do their own work'. These are the foundations of the subversive or 'mystical strategies' of the *theologia mystica*.

As did his teacher Hierotheus, von Balthasar argues, so Dionysius also engaged in a method of what we might term 'indirect transmission' to get his message across. The text is indeed *performative* rather than *informative*:

> Hierotheus is the surpassing genius, his work 'is like a kind of second sacred scripture which discloses itself immediately to those who are divinely inspired', his 'vision, self-witnessed, of the spiritual revelations' and his 'synoptic manner of teaching' presupposes a spiritual power that stands (*presbytikē*) closer to God (cf. DN III.2).
>
> (von Balthasar 1984:150)

Von Balthasar in this commentary limits himself to 'unfolding his teacher's "synoptic" statements' (1984:157). The 'object' of the discourse, that is, our engagement with the material, can only be 'grasped' by a 'circling movement' where we are 'mutually implicated' in the method (see Ep. 8).[28]

> in space and time immediately next to John and Paul clearly corresponds for him to a necessity which, had he not heeded it, would have meant a rank insincerity and failure to respond to truth' (149). 'One does not *see* who Denys *is*, if one cannot see this identification as a context for his veracity.' 'And,' he concludes, 'one can only rejoice over the fact that he succeeded in vanishing behind the Areopagite for a millennium, and that now afterwards, in the age of opening of graves, he has been brought out, he stubbornly hides his face, I suppose, for ever.'

28 See also Louth 2009:62: 'The most striking feature of Dionysius' interpretation of the Divine Liturgy is perhaps his emphasis on movement, the movement of the hierarch out from the sanctuary, around the Church, and back again into the sanctuary, symbolizing the circular movement,

The moment of Dionysius is a moment of 'celebration' – it is a festival or dance (cf. CH:7.4, Ep. 8):

> The style strides along so consciously loaded, draped with so many sacred garments, that it makes any haste impossible and compels us not only to follow him in his train of thought but also to join with him in his mood of celebration.[29]
>
> (von Balthasar 1984:172)

Theology, as Dionysius 'hymns' it, is as much 'initiation' as 'discourse'. This is the 'indirect initiation' of Hierotheus, reflecting the *myesthai* of the classical initiation into the Dionysian cult (see DN:1.8, 3.1, 3.2; CH:2.5, 1.5, where the whole of Christianity is described as a 'mystery religion'). As von Balthasar points out, even the term *thiasōtēs* – that of the participant in the cult of Dionysius – is used by Dionysius in CH:2.1, 3.2 and EH:1.1. Dionysius, following Plato and his Neo-Platonic interpreters, makes a contrast between the rational philosophy that persuades by dialectic and the means of *logos* and reason, and this latter kind of 'initiation' that is formulated through the *mythos* (Louth 1989:25), cf. Ep. 9:

> The tradition of the theologians is twofold, on the one hand ineffable and mystical, on the other manifest and more knowable; on the one hand symbolic and presupposing initiation, on the other philosophical and capable of proof – and the ineffable is interwoven with what can be uttered. The one persuades and contains within itself the truth of what it says, the other effects and establishes the soul with God by initiations that do not teach anything.
>
> (Ep:9, Dion:1105)[30]

expressed in Neoplatonic language of rest, procession and return, that underlies the whole of reality.'

29   Cf. Wittgenstein's deliberate 'slowing the reader down' by the style of his writing, in Chapter Seven of this volume.

30   Louth also draws the parallel with Aristotle's distinction within the Eleusian mysteries, that the initiate does not *learn (mathein)* anything but *experiences or suffers (pathein)* something (Aristotle, *De Philosophia frag* 15).

We have returned again to the Wittgensteinian world of 'saying' and 'showing'. Theology in these texts does not so much 'say' as 'show' – this is the purpose of the discourse. This latter method, the method of *pathein*, suffering is the one explicitly used by Dionysius's master Hierotheus:

> Whatever he learned directly from the sacred writers, whatever his own perspicacious and laborious research of the scriptures uncovered for him, or whatever was made known to him through that more mysterious inspiration, not only learning (*mathein*) but also experiencing (*pathein*) the divine things. For he had a 'sympathy' with such matters, if I may express it this way, and he was perfected in a mysterious union with them and in a faith in them which was independent of any teaching.
>
> (DN:2.9)

Just as for the ancients in their Dionysian initiation, so his contemporary Christians ' "cannot grasp the breadth and length, the height and depth" of the revelation of Jesus Christ' (DN:2.9, cf. Paul Ep:3).

Louth suggests that Hierotheus is being described as 'some kind of experiential mystic' which immediately leads him into a fruitless discussion on the nature of 'mystical experience' such as we analysed in Chapter One. A discussion which is fruitless and ultimately inconclusive precisely for the reasons we have already stated: 'whether it is the individual experience of the mystic (maybe of some ecstatic kind) that is involved is not so clear' (1989:25). Von Balthasar avoids this danger by concentrating on the discourse rather than any supposed original 'experience' and thus avoiding any supposed scientistic links to a post-Cartesian 'mystical phenomenology' (the 'occult entities' of Wittgenstein).[31] As stated above, no one can 'prove' whether Hierotheus, Dionysius, or anyone else for that matter, was or was not a 'mystic' or had 'mystical experience'. What we can do (and do here) is concentrate on the *performative role* of the discourse and its relation

---

31 I am grateful to Professor Gerard Loughlin for clarifying this point.

to the 'initiation' described by Dionysius, Hierotheus and von Balthasar (following Plato, Aristotle and St. Paul). We shall see how this will later feed into the affective interpretation of Dionysius.

How then is this initiation enacted? How does Dionysius, the initiator of *theologia mystica*, initiate?

Dionysius begins the *Divine Names* by stating that what he is about to set down must, by necessity, transcend the 'realm of discourse or of intellect' (DN:1.1). The 'hidden divinity' cannot be set down by means of 'words or conceptions'. The heart of this revelation lying in the 'sacred oracles' or 'scripture' (DN:1.4). He talks of a 'divine enlightenment' 'into which we have been initiated by the hidden tradition of our inspired teachers', 'a tradition at one with scripture'.

If such 'divine names' transcend all conception and words, how can we speak of them? For 'the union of divinised minds with the Light beyond all deity occurs in the cessation of all intelligent activity' (DN:1.5). Drawing from scripture, the names are primarily *praised*. God the Trinity, for Dionysius, cannot be expressed in words, only approached through 'aporias of unknowing' (see Sells 1994). Thus Dionysius introduces his *hyper-* terms in DN:2.4 ('supra-essential subsistence, supra-divine divinity, supra-excellent goodness, supremely individual identity') which will be reproduced at the beginning of the *Mystical Theology*. For God, for Dionysius, is 'beyond every assertion and denial', since in the following chapters of the *Divine Names*, Dionysius does not try to *describe* the divine reality but rather plays with various models and pictures of the divine. As has been pointed out (See McGinn 1991), his first choice of names reflects the Neo-Platonic structures with which he works: good, light, beautiful, *eros*, ecstasy and zeal.

It is perfectly possible, following the suggestion of Endre von Ivánka in his *Plato Christianus* (1964), to see the structure of the *Divine Names* as reflecting Neo-Platonic treatises on the Good (cf. *The Republic* Books 4–6), the 'neoplatonic triad' of Being-Life-Wisdom and the Constantian Triad of Wisdom-Power-Peace.[32] As McGinn points

---

32 Von Balthasar presents his own schema based on the neo-Platonic emanation and return of God (1984:189).

out (1991:161), the theological heart of the text seems to be how the utterly unknowable God manifests himself in creation in order that all creation may return to this unknowable source. On the level of thought – *intellectus* – the divine is utterly unknowable. This is the point of the aporia, the incomprehensibility, heralded by *the strategy of deconstruction and unknowing* leading to the necessary transformation required by the texts. When we look at the other writers of the tradition of *theologia mystica* we shall see how they accomplish this strategy of deconstruction by disorientation, contradiction, aporia and the humility of unknowing.

Despite his Neo-Platonic credentials, Dionysius is primarily a Christian author (as writers such as von Balthasar and Golitzin make abundantly clear) and these processes take place within a specifically Christian engagement, in particular the Divine Liturgy and the message of the Scriptures (referred to by Dionysius as the 'divine oracles'). The *theologia mystica* is born within this context and it would be misguided to try to divorce it from this milieu (*pace* attempts by some of the authors covered earlier trying to create a cross-credal, perennialist 'mysticism'). If, according to Dionysius, *knowledge* of the Divine is not possible, how do we access the 'supra-real'?

Here, Dionysius relies on the other key strategy of the *theologia mystica* which will be explored here – *the strategy of affectivity/embodiment*. In DN:4 Dionysius introduces his discussion of *eros* and the erotic and how *eros* connects us to the deity. In McGinn's words:

> The Dionysian program is a cosmic one in which the divine Eros refracts itself into the multiple theophanies of the universe, which in turn erotically strive to pass beyond their multiplicity back into simple unity.
>
> (1991:161)

All movement in the hierarchy of creation, for Dionysius, comes from above and is 'fundamentally erotic'. Not only do all things strive erotically for the Beautiful and the Good (DN:4), but the Deity itself is *Eros*: 'Divine *Eros* is the Good of the Good for the sake of the Good'

(DN:4.10, McGinn's translation). Using the Proclean procession of *monē* (remaining), *proodos* (proceeding) and *epistrophē* (reverting), God in God's being as *eros* is able to proceed out to all creation and remain in the Godhead at the same time:

> It must be said that the very cause of the universe in the beautiful, good superabundance of his benign *eros* for all is carried outside of himself in the loving care he has for everything. He is, as it were, beguiled by goodness, by *agape* and by *eros* and is enticed away from his dwelling place and comes to abide within all things, and he does so by virtue of his supernatural and ecstatic capacity to remain, nevertheless, within himself.
>
> (DN:4.13, translation McGinn)

Thus, the 'sympathetic' initiation described above is also an *erotic* initiation. *Eros* is the occasion for the 'special experience of knowing' (*pathein*) in contrast to the 'knowing by mental effort' (*mathein*).[33] It is the arena of Hierothus's initiation:

> By some more divine inspiration, not only learning the things of God but experiencing them, and through this sympathy with them, if we may say this, having been consummated in initiation into mystical union and faith in them which cannot be taught.
>
> (DN:2.9, translation McGinn)

Or to put it in our terms above, it is a knowing which involves the libidinal or *affectus* as much as the *intellectus*. Within Dionysius's

---

33 The *sympatheia*, as McGinn following Rorem (1982) points out, is a key term in late Neo-Platonism in making the connection between the different levels of the 'theurgy' possible: '*sympathy* for Dionysius is not so much an ontological bond by which material things are manipulated to acquire an access to the upper world as it is an affinity for "reading" the inner meaning of the hierarchies as manifestations of the Thearchy.' (McGinn 1991:172). Hence Dionysius's adoption of the phrase 'so as to speak' to suggest he is adapting a term from the Neo-Platonic school.

mystical game the strategy of deconstruction is complemented by the strategy of embodied, erotic affectivity – in effect a strategy of *ecstasy*.

'What cannot be demonstrated' by the Church, McGinn suggests, is according to Dionysius, 'made present both on the material level of symbols used by scripture and in liturgy and also by extension, on the conceptual or intellectual level, where the negation of names and eventually the removal of both affirmation and negation bring the soul to union with the divine mystery' (1991:173). This union is the *erotic union* engendered by *eros* through the *affectus* and the libido. This is the ex-stasis, the ecstasy: 'Through ecstasy we pass beyond the human condition and become divinised' (McGinn 1991:179), an ecstatic union so memorably captured in the writings of the Spanish mystical writers to which we shall return later.

Letter Nine of Dionysius describes God as a drunken lover 'standing outside all good things, being the suprafullness of all these things' (Ep:9.5), the model here being St. Paul, Dionysius's ecstatic teacher and erotic initiator:

> This is why the great Paul, swept along by his yearning for God and seized of its ecstatic power, had this inspired word to say: 'It is no longer I who live, but Christ who lives in me' (Gal 2:20). Paul was truly a lover and, as he says, he was beside himself for God (2 Cor:5.13), possessing not his own life but the life of the One for whom he yearned (in *eros*), as exceptionally beloved.
>
> (DN:4.13, translation McGinn)[34]

Following Roques (DS:2.1908–1910), McGinn sees Dionysius's concept of union as being based on the transcendentalization of knowing into unknowing and yearning *eros* into ecstatic possession. Thus, the two

---

34 See also Stang 2009:17–18: 'Paul is "possessed" by his yearning and "participates" in its ecstatic power, such that he comes to live the life of his Beloved... Ecstasy must answer ecstasy according to Dionysius. Thus the self that would suffer union with God must learn how to yearn to such an extent that it suffers ecstasy, becomes literally beside itself for God.'

processes we have identified as key to the 'mystical strategy' of the *theologia mystica* are intimately connected. As we shall see, Dionysius's exposition of *the unknowing-affective strategy* allows later Christian writers to mine the erotic side, especially through the medium of the exposition of the Song of Songs.[35]

As McGinn points out, Dionysius here is standing in an already established Christian tradition of equating the *agape* of the New Testament with the *eros* of the Platonic tradition, beginning, he suggests, with Origen's *Commentary on the Song of Songs*:

> The power of love is none other than that which leads the soul from earth to the lofty heights of heaven, and... the highest beatitude can only be attained under the stimulus of love's desire.
> (Prol:63.9–11 in McGinn 1991:120)

McGinn's exposition of this topic is of a special clarity. However, his device of dividing eros into what he calls EROS I when referred to the Deity and eros ii when referring to the creature seems to defuse the potentially subversive nature of the erotic language which, as we suggest here, is one of the key reasons for adopting it in the mystical strategy. McGinn, as with so many commentators on mystical texts, finds it hard to resist the desire to 'tidy up' and 'smooth over' problems, subversions and other difficulties in the texts which, I argue, are deliberately placed there to 'work on' the reader.

Thus, turning our Wittgensteinian lens on the *Sprachspiele* of the Dionysian texts, especially in their twelfth-century interpretations, we can identify two 'mystical strategies' of *unknowing/deconstruction* and *embodiment/affect*. The unknowing aspect delineates the limits of human knowledge of God; the affective allows the entry into union with the divine through the libidinal and affective. The two processes occur side by side and necessarily complement each other. This insight was particularly seen by Thomas Gallus and developed by him, and would continue throughout the subsequent history of the 'mystical tradition'

35 On this, see especially Turner (1995a).

through the use made of Dionysius by Gallus himself, Hugh of Balma, Gerson, De Osuna, Laredo and eventually the sixteenth-century Spanish mystical writers such as Teresa of Avila and John of the Cross.

SUMMARY OF DIONYSIUS: THE MYSTICAL STRATEGIES OF THE *THEOLOGIA MYSTICA*

In summary, then, we may characterize the *mystical strategies* of Dionysius as fitting into a wider perspective (*Weltbild*) that by necessity embraces the strategies of deconstruction and embodiment.

The overall orientation is summarized by von Balthasar thus:

According to Denys the essence of each being is itself ecstatic towards God (something that so little threatens its individuality that this movement itself determines it at its deepest level); indeed, that this ecstasy of creaturely *eros* is itself an imitation of the ecstatic divine *eros* which out of love goes out of itself into the multiplicity of the world; that therefore mystical experience represents a philosophical and theological realization of that which *is*.

(von Balthasar 1984:205)

The mystical strategies we have proposed, therefore, are of the *essence* of Dionysius's *theologia mystica*. Theology, or the reading of *mystical theology*, is by its nature a matter of *initiation* into the erotic mystery of creation. Like the Dionysian rites, this is a secret initiation that must be hidden from scorn and derision of the unitiated: 'If the profane were to see or listen to these rites of ours I think they would laugh heartily and pity us for our misguidedness' (EH:7.3.1):

Which to the man in the street appear quite extraordinary (*multis monstruosas* [E], *prodigiales locutiones* [S]). Among uninstructed souls the fathers of unspeakable wisdom (*secretae sapientiae patres* [S]) give an impression of outstanding absurdity when, with secret and daring riddles (S: *per quaedem occulta quidem et praesumpta*

aenigmata), they make known that truth which is divine, mysterious, and, so far as the profane are concerned, inaccessible (S:
manifestant divinam et mysticam et inviam immundis veritatem).

(Ep:9:1)[36]

In the *Divine Names*, Dionysius exhorts Timothy, his addressee, to
'guard these things in accordance with divine command and you must
never speak nor divulge divine things to the unitiated' (DN:1.8) – 'Let
such things be kept away from the mockery and the laughter of the
unitiated' (S: *et ipsa ab indoctorum risibus et delusionibus aufer-
entes*). Thus, Dionysius distinguishes the 'knowing' that comes from
disputation and the 'exoteric sciences' of theology from the 'knowing'
that comes from the 'mystical initiation'. Both, as we have seen, are
considered essential for good theological practice:

> Theological tradition has a dual aspect, the ineffable and myste-
> rious on the one hand (S: *hanc quidem secretam et mysticam*),
> the open and more evident on the other (S: *illam apparentem et
> notiorem*). The one resorts to symbolism and involves initiation
> (E: *eam quidem symbolicam et perfectivam*). The other is philo-
> sophical and employs the method of demonstration (E: *hanc vero
> philosophicam et approbativam*). The one uses persuasion and
> imposes the truthfulness of what is asserted. The other acts by
> means of a mystery which cannot be taught.
>
> (Ep:9.1, Dion:638)

This is the 'divine enlightenment' (S: *deifica lumina*, Gk: θεουρνιχά
φώϊα) into which, according to Dionysius, we have been 'initiated
by the hidden tradition (*occulta traditio*) of our inspired teachers – a
tradition at one with scripture' (DN:1.4).

Thus, for Dionysius, when we 'say anything about God... we set
down the truth not in the plausible words of human wisdom but in the
demonstration of the power guided by the Spirit (1 Cor:2.4)' (DN:1.1).
For there is a 'power by which, in a manner surpassing speech and

36 See also Perczel (2009:35).

knowledge, we reach a union superior to anything available to us by way of our own abilities or activities in the realm of discourse or of intellect' (DN:1.1).[37] This is why 'we must not resort to words or conceptions concerning that hidden divinity (S: *occulta Deitate*) which transcends being, apart from what sacred scriptures (S: *ex sacris eloquiis*) have divinely revealed' (DN:1.1).

For Dionysius the process of 'initation' is beyond the 'rational processes'. As we saw above, Dionysius will often resort to the strategy of aporia through his ὑπερ- words to make this point:

> Mind beyond mind, word beyond speech, it is gathered up by no discourse, by no intuition, by no name, it exists as no other being (S: *et intellectus non intelligibilis et verbum non dicible et irrationabilitas et non-inteligibilitas*) (R: *unintelligibilitas et innominabilitas, secundum nihil existentium existens*).
>
> (DN:1)[38]

As argued above, Dionysius deliberately dances around the nature of the mystical 'initiation' or 'knowledge'. It *cannot* be disclosed in the text, by its very nature: it is not to be learnt from theological disputation in the faculty of reason and intellect. How then is it communicated? As we have seen, Dionysius gives us enough clues as to where to look for this knowledge. His own teacher, Hierotheus, has been initated and in his description of this Dionysius points out the direction in which we must look:

> Whatever he learned directly from the sacred writers, whatever his own perspicacious and laborious research of the scriptures uncovered for him, or whatever was made known to him through that most mysterious inspiration, not only learning but also

---

37 S: *secundum quam ineffabilibus et ignotis* [R: *incognitos*] *ineffabiliter et ignote* [R: *incognite*] *conjungimur secundum meliorem nostrae rationabilis et intellectualis virtutis et operationis unitonem.*

38 See also DN:2.3: over-good, over-divine, over-existent, over-living, over-wise (S: *superbonum, superdeum, supersubstantiale, supervivens, supersapiens*).

experiencing the divine things (S: *non solum discens sed et patiens divina*, E: *non solum discens sed et affectus divina*, P: *verum etiam iis animo affectus et permotus*, Gk: χαί παθών τά θεϊα). For he had 'sympathy' (S: *compassione*, E: *coaffectione*, Gk: συμπαθείας) with such matters, if I may express it that way, and he was perfected in a mysterious union with them and in a faith in them which was independent of any education.

(DN:2.9)

As we have seen above, this *sympatheia* is the *erotic* initiation of Dionysius (DN:4.10). The *eros* as 'Good seeking Good for the sake of the Good' (S: *est divinus amor bonus boni propter bonum*) and, following the essential understanding of the human person as *persona ecstatica*, *eros* brings us to our essential ecstatic being: 'Eros brings ecstasy so that the lover belongs not to self but to the beloved' (S: *Est autem faciens exstasim divinus amor*). For Dionysius, God himself is enticed by *eros* 'from his transcendent dwelling place and comes to abide within all things, and he does so by virtue of his supernatural and ecstatic capacity to remain, nevertheless, within himself' (DN:4.13).

From the above we can see that Dionysius presents a synthesis of two strategies: deconstruction/unknowing and embodiment/affect, in one overarching survey of the *erotic-ecstatic* nature of the human person. As von Balthasar points out, his text beguiles and plays with us as he stretches us beyond our intellectual and rational limits to make connection with the divine through the play of *pathē* – emotions and affect (Eriugena's *affectus*). The argument here has been that this vision of the ecstatic union and return of the self to God, this affective-deconstructive strategy, is a key aspect of the medieval tradition of *theologia mystica*.

This affective-deconstructive strategy (Dionysius's *stulta sapientia*: DN 7:1, Gk μωράν σοφία – which is '*alogos*' and '*anous*') seems to be fundamental to the tradition of *theologia mystica* and it is this, it is argued, that is at the heart of the 'mystical strategies' of the Western medieval tradition of mystical theology.

We turn next to the evolution of these strategies as they develop after the twelfth century.

4

The Medieval Flowering of the Theologia Mystica

Love takes hold of the beloved and creates ecstasy, and this
is called rapture because of the manner in which the mind is
lifted up.

(Jean Gerson GMT:1.36.1)

In the previous chapter we mapped the application of the Dionysian
programme as a Wittgensteinian 'language game'. In this chapter we
trace the evolution of this language game in medieval development of
theologia mystica with particular reference to three works: the Victorine
work of Thomas Gallus, that of the Carthusian Hugh of Balma and its
exposition by the Chancellor of the University of Paris, Jean Gerson.

DEVELOPMENT OF THE UNKNOWING-AFFECTIVE
STRATEGY UNDER THOMAS GALLUS

As we saw earlier, much recent work in recovering the nature of the
medieval Dionysian tradition has led to a reassessment of the Victorine
influence, in particular that of Thomas Gallus, Abbot of Vercelli. As I
suggested before, one of the key innovations of Gallus's interpretation
was the admission of the 'affective' interpretation of the Dionysian
corpus. As Rorem states, 'there is no reference whatsoever' (Rorem
1993:216) to the role of love in the Dionysian ascent in the West before
Gallus. From the thirteenth century onwards the commentators begin to

introduce the affective into the mystical ascent (See McGinn 1989:68). The key question from this time, in Rorem's words, becomes:

> How did the Areopagite's clear emphasis upon union with the unknown God through knowing and unknowing relate to the Western emphasis upon union with the loving God through love, as seen earlier in Augustine, Gregory the Great and Bernard, especially in their exegesis of the Song of Songs?
>
> (Rorem 1993:216)

This tension between the apophatic knowledge of Dionysius and the affective stream of the Latin West led to various interpretations of the relationship between the *affectus* and the *intellectus* and the development of the so-called 'affective Dionysianism' first presented by Thomas Gallus.[1] Gallus, working within the Victorine tradition, allows the affective to mould his understanding of the Dionysian treatises. For example, he follows Hugh of St. Victor when he takes the 'fire' of the Seraphim ('heat makers' – *calefacientes* – in Eriugena's translation: McGinn 1998:84) in Dionysius's *Celestial Hierarchy* (CH 7.1) to refer to the 'fire of love'.[2] 'Love surpasses knowledge and is greater than *intelligentia*. For one loves more than one understands and love enters in and draws near where knowledge remains outside.' In Rorem's words, 'Where knowledge stops on the threshold in ignorance (unknowing), love can still advance and approach' (Rorem 1993:217; see also Rorem 2009:78).

Hugh of St. Victor's interpretation of Dionysius was adopted and strengthened by Gallus's approach. Thus, for example, at the end of Chapter 1 of the 'Mystical Theology' Dionysius suggests that Moses, breaking free of all that can be perceived by body or mind, plunges 'away from what sees and is seen, and plunges into the truly

---

1   See McGinn 1998:79; Rorem 1993:216.
2   *Dilectio supereminet scientiae, et major est intelligentia. Plus enim diligitur, quam intelligitur, et intrat dilectio, et approprinquat, ubi scientia foris est.* PL 175:1038D, *Commentarium in Caelestem Hierarchiam* 6.7.

mysterious darkness of unknowing. Here, renouncing all that the mind may conceive, wrapped entirely in the intangible and the invisible, he belongs completely to him who is beyond everything' (MT:1, Luibheid 1987:137). For Gallus this becomes:

> Separated from all things and from oneself, as it were, one is united to the intellectually unknown God *through a uniting of love which effects true knowledge* by means of a knowledge much better than intellectual knowledge, and, because intellectual knowledge is left behind, one knows God above intellect and mind.[3]

Although previous Christian writers had emphasized the role of love in the movement to God, this Victorine interpretation understands the priority of love through new ways. It is precisely these new accents that are taken up by the later writers under discussion.[4]

As we have seen, the discussion of *eros* in Chapter Four of the *Divine Names* may have played an important role in the affective turn of the thirteenth century: 'Because God is *eros*, the universe that is his manifestation must also be erotic, with the Divine Eros serving as both the object of its love and in participated form, the power by which it moves towards its goal' (McGinn 1998:81). For Dionysius, the *eros* is not to be feared, 'nor be upset by what anyone has to say about these two names

---

3   *Et ab omnibus et quasi a se ipso segregatur, et per unitionem dilectionis quae effective est verae cognitionis unitur Deo intellectualiter ignoto, cognitione multo meliori quam sit cognitio intellectualis, et in eo quod intellectualem cognitionem derelinquit super intellectum et mentem deum cognoscit. Dion* 1:710. See McGinn 1989:81.

4   However, see Coolman (2009) where he demonstrates the subtlety of Gallus's approach in his aspects of 'descending love' and 'ascending intellect'. For Coolman, Gallus's 'merging of the Song's spousal imagery with the Dionysian ascent allows the Victorine to introduce a Christological dimension precisely where it seems absent in the *Mystical Theology* – at the very highest point of ascent, where the soul is united to God' (Coolman 2009:94). From the perspective of my argument here I think Coolman's analysis brings out the subtleties to which the affective-deconstructive affective Dionysianism will be used by Gallus and his heirs.

(*eros* and *agape*), for, in my opinion, the sacred writers regard *eros* and *agape* as having one and the same meaning' (DN:4, Luibheid:81.709B). This eros brings 'extasis' 'so that the lover belongs not to self but to the beloved' (DN:4, Luibheid:82.712A). God is not only the *eros*, but the object of *eros*: 'So they call him the beloved and the yearned-for since he is beautiful and good, and, again, they call him yearning and love because he is the power moving and lifting all things up to himself' (DN:4, Luibheid:712C). In this new tradition, then, yearning desire is central to spiritual transformation.[5]

For Gallus, as the soul ascends to God there comes a point where it is cut off from the *intellectus*: love rejects the lower forms of knowing in its ascent. Gallus (McGinn 1998:85) makes use of *excessus mentis, ecstasies* and *raptus* in his descriptions of the soul's journey to God. 'Love is of such power,' Gallus says, 'that not only does it place one outside oneself in relation to God, but (if we can say it) it draws God outside himself to the human person, as it were, so that the Infinite may unite things that are distant.'[6] *Dilectio* is greater than *intellectus* and one loves more than one understands.

Gallus's paraphrase of the Dionysian *corpus* in his *Extract* (1238) and commentary (*The Explanations*:1242), which harmonized the Dionysian apophatic way with the affective path of, for example, the Song of Songs, was immediately popular so that the semi-official *corpus* of Dionysian writing that we have seen circulating by the end of the thirteenth century comprised the translations of Eriugena and Sarracenus, the commentaries of Hugh of St. Victor and Eriugena, and the paraphrase of Gallus. Thus this 'affective Dionysianism' will be taken up by later authors and commentators on the tradition so that by the time of the Tegernsee controversy of the fifteenth century and

5   Coolman (2009) emphasizes the 'circling' motion of the *intellectus* and *affectus* in Gallus's *Commentary on the Song of Songs* to produce 'an unceasing *circulation circa Deo*'; see also footnote 28 on p.77 above.

6   From the *Explanatio* on DN 4.14 cited in Javelet 1962:99: *Tante autem virtutis est deleccio ut non tantum hominem extra se ad Deum, sed, si fas est dicere, quasi Deum extra se trahit ad hominem, ut infinitum distantes uniat.*

Vincent of Aggsbach's commentary on Hugh of Balma it has become common currency.[7]

THE *VIAE SION LUGENT:*[8] ORIGINS AND AUTHORSHIP OF THE TEXT

A key work that illustrates the transmission of this affective Dionysianism is Hugh of Balma's *Viae Sion Lugent*. The text adopts the twelfth-century innovations of the Victorines, especially in the importation of the affective into the Dionysian tradition, as well as building on it to develop a very experiential understanding of the role of the *affectus* in the search for God. Although the text does not use the *eros* by name it makes use of the affective schema of Gallus to make its point. Balma's text is also worthy of study, since it acts as one of the important means of transmission of the tradition of *theologia mystica* to the sixteenth-century Spanish mystical writers. This occurs through two main routes: the direct translation into Spanish as the *Sol de Contemplativos* of 1514, and its influence on Gerson, Francisco de Osuna and Laredo who would later, we know, influence writers such as St. Teresa of Avila.

The manuscript referred to throughout the late medieval/renaissance period as the *De Mystica Theologia, De Triplici Via* or *Viae Sion lugent* and attributed variously to Hugues of Balma/Palma, Hugues of Dorche, Henry of Balma/Dorche and even St. Bonaventure has recently received sufficient scholarly attention to enable a critical edition to be produced by Ruello for the *Éditions du Cerf* (Balma 1995). A century of scholarly

7   See especially Martin (1997:24) on this point, and how this new sense of *theologia mystica* would in many cases replace the older *contemplatio*.

8   Although, as we shall see, the text is often referred to and printed as the *Theologia Mystica* of Hugh of Balma we shall use the title of *Viae Sion Lugent* in this book to avoid confusion with the *Mystica Theologia* of Dionysius. However, it should be noted that just as the author of the Dionysian corpus employed uncertain narrative voice, so too the exposition of the *theologia mystica* implies a similar authorial confusion; hereafter VSL.

attention has still not resolved the exact identity of the author; however, the suggestion made that the French name Hugues de Balma de Dorche is the nearest we can get to the complete name of the author seems the most plausible (see Dubourg 1927; Stoelen 1969; Guinan 1994 *inter alia*),[9] Hugues being Prior of the charterhouse of Meyriat.[10] The documents of the charterhouse, conserved in the archives of Ain, contain numerous manuscripts of Hugue's treatise, many of them carrying his name, it being remembered that it was common practice (and still is) for Carthusians to present their manuscripts anonymously.[11]

Pierre Dubourg's attempt to create a critical edition in the 1930s resulted in a census of seventy-one complete and twenty-one partial manuscripts of the text scattered around Europe and beyond, of which Ruello used fifty-nine to produce his critical text; the oldest from the fourteenth century but most from the fifteenth century (Martin 1997:60). The 1495 Strassbourg edition of the *Collected Works of Bonaventure* not only included the *Viae Sion Lugent* but modified certain references to the Carthusian order in order to refer to the Franciscan order. This

9 There are records that the de Balmey family, to which Hugh, the supposed author of the treatise belonged, also held the lands of Dorche up until the latter half of the thirteenth century (Guinan 1994:51).

10 Variously called Meyriac, Majorevi or Meyriae, subsequently destroyed during the French Revolution.

11 As Guigue de Pont's *De Contemplatione* makes reference to the *Viae Sion Lugent*, Ruello gives the VSL a date of composition not later than 29 October 1297 – the death date of Guigue de Pont. References in the text to Albert the Great's *Commentary on the Sentences* (1244–1249), Grosseteste (d. 1255), Bonaventure (d. 1273) and Thomas Aquinas (d.1272) place the work in the later half of the thirteenth century. The reference to the *Nicomachean Ethics* of Aristotle, first popularized in 1272 by Aquinas, seems to suggest a date after 1272. Ruello therefore suggests a date of composition between 1272 and 1297. As well as Hugh, the manuscript has been ascribed to Bonaventure (appearing in collections of Bonaventure's works right up to, but not including, the Quaracchi edition of 1882), a fictional Franciscan 'Henry of Balma', a Carthusian Hugh of Palma and a Henry, of Kalkar, a Carthusian of Cologne who was born in 1328. I shall use the English 'Hugh of Balma' when referring to the author throughout this book.

followed throughout the fifteenth century in editions, although the practice was challenged in the 1588 Vatican edition edited by Lamata. The first Spanish translation appeared in Toledo in 1514 under the title *Sol de contemplativos* followed by editions in Seville (1543), Medina (1553) and Alcalá (1558). Rather than use the series of texts related to the first Franciscan Strassbourg edition ('A': see Martin 1997:61) both Ruello in his critical edition and Martin in his English translation use a third set of texts which circulated in the early fifteenth century 'in the Austrian-Bavarian circles where all the "Hugh of Balma scholars" seem to have been concentrated'.

The context of the work suggests a reaction to the scholastic learning, or rather a placing of the 'mystical learning' in the context of 'scholastic learning'. It is therefore ideally situated for an investigation of the evolution of the strategies of the *theologia mystica* in the late medieval period.

AFFECTUS AND *INTELLECTUS* IN HUGH OF BALMA

From the point of view of our genealogy of the *theologia mystica*, Hugh's text is important as it condenses the views on the *intellectus* and *affectus* presented, implicity and explicitly, in Gallus's interpretation of Dionysius, and refines their use and scope. The first four paragraphs of the Prologue of the *Viae* present a picture of the discourse that will follow. In an economy of words Hugh brings us the picture that he will present; it is not so much an argument as a *showing* or *Weltbild*. It 'sets everything before us', showing the 'foundations of possible buildings'.

He paints two contrasting images, much as would a medieval wall painter. On the one side is the 'human curiosity' or 'useless science' (*'Relicta humana curiositate scientiae inutilis argumentorum et opinionum captiva'* VSL:3), the knowledge of 'philosophers, scholars and secular masters' (VSL:4), searching after new curiosities, proofs and ideas contained within the covers of 'sheepskin quartos' (VSL:2). Furthermore, 'these sciences absorb the human spirit and possess it totally, inspired by the devil, so that the true wisdom (*vera sapientia*) no

longer has a place'(VSL:1). This 'mortal philosophy' is to be found in
Plato and Aristotle.

In contrast to this mortal philosophy we have the other picture –
that of the *vera sapientia*, the 'true knowledge' that will be expounded
in the following pages. The first type of knowledge has held people
captive (here Hugh gives us a reference to Ecclesiastes 1:13[12]) which
is why 'the roads to Sion mourn' – *Viae Sion lugent* – the title of the
manuscript. Crucially, this first type of knowledge does not allow the
'flaming affections of love' (*per flammigeras amoris adfectiones*) to
reach the Creator. The second type of knowledge, the *vera sapientia*, or
as he refers to it later, the *mystica theologia* (VSL:2), is the knowledge
that arises from this flaming affection of love which inflames the affect
(*affectus*) and enlightens the intellect (*intellectus*) (VSL:3). These 'fiery
aspirations of love' raise the soul to God and true knowledge: 'Very
rapidly, quicker than can be thought, without any prior or concomitant
cogitatio, whenever she pleases, hundreds or thousands of times both
day and night, the soul is drawn to possess God alone through countless
yearning desires' (VSL:5).

These 'flaming desires' are the engine by which this wisdom is
achieved – it is an affective and performative wisdom. This is acquired
by 'practice of the purgative and illuminative ways'. 'Thus, through
practice in the purgative and illuminative ways and under the inward
instruction and direction of God alone, the soul learns experientially
what no mortal science or eloquence can unlock.' It is not acquired
through discourse but by *practice*. As with the later Wittgenstein, acting
preceeds seeing and thinking:

> This wisdom requires first that one perceive truth experientially
> within oneself… This wisdom is to be distinguished from all other

12 'With the help of wisdom I have been at pains to study all that is done
   under heaven; oh, what a weary task God has given mankind to labour
   at! I have seen everything that is done under the sun, and what vanity it
   all is, what chasing of the wind!… Much wisdom, much grief. The more
   knowledge, the more sorrow.'

sciences in that it has to be put to use within oneself before its
words can be understood – *practice precedes theory* (*et practica
ibi praecedit theoricam*).

(VSL:9)

Solus amor, love alone, is the vehicle that provides this knowledge
– 'Neither *ratio* understands or *intellectus* sees, rather, as it is said:
"*Gustate et videte* – Taste and See".'

In this 'affective knowledge' experience precedes theoretical understanding – acting precedes thinking and believing. For Hugh, within
his medieval Christian context, this wisdom proceeds from the Trinity
'an encompassing and deifying diffusion coming from the entire Trinity
on high to faithful Christians, suffusing loving spirits with heavenly
dew' (VSL:U1). 'The wisdom we are concerned with here is a surging
up through flaming affections of unitive love beyond all functions of
understanding, in order to be established at the highest summit of
affectivity' (VSL:U3). This 'kindled *affectus*' raises the spirit in a surge
(VSL:U9) which purified affect can then 'tame' the body and senses.
To acquire this knowledge 'industrious efforts' are required (VSL:U58)
which occur on four planes: 'the human spirit, the body, time and place'
(VSL:U58).

From Dionysius, Hugh reminds us that this knowledge is a hidden
(*occulto*) and anagogical knowledge handed down from Paul to
Dionysius, and hence presumably, through reading this text, to us. The
text performs its hidden task on us quoting the *De Mystica Theologia* of
Dionysius, Ch.1.1–2: 'See to it too that no untutored person learns these
things.' The condition for the 'loving upsurge – *consurrectio*' (VSL:U83)
required in this performative discourse is unknowing or apophasis
(*ignorantia*), which leads to affective change:

This *consurrectio*, which is said to occur through unknowing, is
nothing other than being moved directly through the ardour of
love, without any creaturely image, any leading knowledge or any
accompanying movement of *intelligentia* – it is solely a movement

of the *affectus* and in its actual practice the speculative knowledge
(*speculative cognitio*) knows nothing.

(VSL:U83)

Once again we have the now familiar affective-deconstructive mystical
strategy inherited from Dionysius. In the Prologue the two sorts of
wisdom were placed side by side, now in his commentary on Dionysius
Hugh goes further to agree with Dionysius on the need for a *stulta
sapientia* – a 'foolish wisdom' which is necessary before the wisdom
of the affect can take place, i.e. the apophatic or deconstructive move
mentioned above. He quotes Chapter Seven of Dionysius's *Divine
Names* in VSL:U86 to make this point:

'We praise this irrational, useless and foolish wisdom exceed-
ingly, saying that it is the cause of all mind and reason and every
wisdom and prudence. From it arises every counsel, knowledge
and prudence and in it lie hidden all treasures of wisdom and the
science of God'... It is a wisdom that no understanding can grasp
at all.

Walking around his topic Hugh returns to the practical conditions
required to enter this *Weltbild*. The 'truest and most certain knowledge'
comes when the *affectus* precedes the *intellectus*[13] which leads to a
paradox: the wisdom is 'in full view' of 'all worldly philosophers and
doctors' but is also 'hidden' (*occulta*) or 'mystical' (*mystica*) 'because
few people dispose themselves to receive it and it hides within the heart
where neither pen nor word can fully unravel its complexities' (VSL:U88).
It is worth noting the sense of 'mystical' here; it is not an aspect of an
ontological 'mysticism' as we saw in the modern definition in Chapter
One; neither is it an 'occult' knowledge that is deliberately hidden. In
fact it is not an entity at all, but rather a disposition of the self, especially

13 See also here Martin's comments on the importance of the affective inter-
    pretation of Dionysius that Hugh receives from Thomas Gallus (Martin
    1997:39); also Walsh (1957) and Ruello (1981).

the *affectus*. In Wittgensteinian terms it is not a *Weltanschauung* but a *Weltbild*. In other words, Hugh, I believe, is describing a similar process of knowing-by-seeing/acting that is presented in the later Wittgenstein. This is a clear case of a mystical *strategy of elucidation* using all the elements mentioned above: the erotic/libidinal/affective (The burning flame of the affect) and the deconstructive (*per ignorantiam*). In this state 'the *affectus* rules', 'commanding the radical abandonment (*derelinqui*) of the senses and the intellect' (VSL:U89). The wisdom is 'located totally in ardent yearning' and for Hugh, quoting Thomas Gallus's commentary on the *Mystical Theology*, this yearning finds its 'principal *affectio*' in the highest part of the soul, the *synderesis*, 'which alone can be united to the Holy Spirit'. This holy unknowing through love is accessible to the 'simple old woman or rustic shepherd' (*simplex vetula vel rusticus pascualis*) as much, or in many cases more, than the learned philosopher or wise man.[14]

Reviewing the *Viae* as a whole one is struck by the power with which Hugh uses the two mystical strategies of deconstruction and affectivity to make his points. As Martin points out, it is important not to engage in a too *linear* interpretation of Hugh's text (as with other 'mystical texts'). Such interpretations (he cites Walach in this respect) fundamentally distort the subtlety of Hugh's approach and his nuanced understanding of the nature of the relationship between affective/aspirative prayer and *intellectus/cogitatio* (Martin 1997:28–29):[15]

> Hugh's language of ascent is nearly always dynamic, rarely static. He is forever talking about being moved into God, being impelled into God, a staccato drumbeat of *movetur, consurgere, consurrectio, motio*. Since we have no real equivalent in English, it is difficult for modern English-speaking readers to grasp that even the word 'affective' is based on a past participle that describes

---

14 This mention of the simple old woman and shepherd/fool will be a constant refrain through Gerson, de Osuna, Laredo and eventually Teresa.

15 A 'circling motion' that we have already noticed in Dionysius and Gallus. See footnote 5 on p.92.

something that has happened: One is affected, one is moved, swayed, impacted by something.

(Martin 1997:37)

Although Hugh is aware of the scholastic disputes and debates of his time, Martin detects the possibility that he may at times be subtly mocking the scholastic method. Rather, his text relies on an 'anagogical (upthrusting, uplifting) hermeneutic' (Martin 1997:40). 'He does not offer a compelling demonstrative logic; rather he relies on a wide range of human realities that move a person's affective inclinations'. It is clear from the above analysis that Hugh does use the subversive linguistic strategies that recur throughout our investigation of the 'mystical strategy'. In this respect he is clearly influenced by the Dionysian tradition and is employing the affective-deconstructive strategy in his text that we identified from Dionysius's twelfth-century Parisian interpreters (and it is of course no surprise that he quotes extensively from Gallus throughout the text). Relating this to our Wittgensteinian epistemology from Chapter Two, we can see how the two strands in Hugh – the Dionysian tradition of the apophatic and Victorine tradition of the affective (as transmitted to Hugh through Gallus) – correspond to Wittgenstein's own strategies that we will revisit in the final chapter of this book.

By examining Hugh in this way it is possible to see how the essentially erotico/affective and deconstructive/unknowing strategies within Dionysius's texts have been developed and refined in their passage through the late Middle Ages. By the fifteenth century the strategies were well embedded within the Western theological tradition and referred to as the *theologia mystica*. We conclude this chapter by looking at one of the great exponents of the discourse: the Chancellor of the University of Paris, Jean Gerson.

JEAN GERSON

Unlike Gallus and Hugh of Balma, of whom we know very little, Gerson's life is well documented and accounted for. If he is known at all today, Gerson is most often cited as one of the main architects of resolving the split in the medieval church between two, and later three Popes: the so-called 'Great Schism' of 1378 to 1417. As an advocate of 'conciliar' policy Gerson is seen as a leading exponent of a non-monarchical view of ecclesiology that stresses the power of councils to determine Christian doctrine, even over the heads of popes and patriarchs (see Morrall 1960). During a lifetime of academic research the Chancellor was particularly concerned with reconciling the *affectus* and *intellectus* among his students, or as he calls it the *theologia mystica* and the *theologia speculativa*, and to this end wrote two treatises on the *theologia mystica* which both started as lectures to his Paris students: the first Speculative Treatise (*Theologia Mystica Speculativa*) presented in autumn 1402 and the second Practical Treatise (*Theologia Mystica Practica*) given five years later in 1407.[16] Although a noted intellectual, Gerson had trouble reconciling his academic life of the mind with his affective life of prayer. It seems that the tradition of the *theologia mystica* which he embraced[17] enabled the troubled Chancellor to find some peace in his life (which he communicated to his students). After many tumultuous years the tired Chancellor was finally able to spend his last ten years in Lyon, teaching children catechetics and embracing the meditative life he had so long yearned for.[18]

In the *Tractatus Primus Speculativus* of the *De Mystica Theologia*, the Chancellor begins by asking: 'whether it is better to have knowledge of God through penitent *affectus* or investigative *intellectus*?'(GMT:1, Prol. 1).[19] After much discussion Gerson makes it quite clear that he will

16 Once again note the importance of Paris for the evolution of the *theologia mystica*.

17 As well as the Victorines, he quotes Balma as a work that should be read by all students and devotes a lengthy part of the treatises to commentary on Dionysius.

18 Gerson is one of the first theologians to write directly in colloquial French so that all the faithful can understand his teaching. His insistence on 'everyday manners of talking' will be something we shall see that he has in common with Teresa of Avila (Chapter Six).

19 My translation: *an cognitio Dei melius per penitentem affectum quam per intellectum investigantem habeatur.*

employ the now familiar unknowing and affective mystical strategies within his discourse. Thus in Section 27 he declares:

> Thus we see that it is correct to say that as *contemplatio* is in the cognitive power of the intelligence, the *mistica theologia* dwells in the corresponding affective power.
>
> (GMT:1.27.7)[20]

Therefore 'knowledge of God through mystical theology is better acquired through a penitent *affectus* than an investigative *intellectus*' (GMT:1.28.1). In this passage Gerson contrasts a *theologia mystica* that depends upon strategies of unknowing and affectivity to the cognitive or speculative knowledge acquired through the *theologia speculativa*. Clearly Gerson's strategy differs from Dionysius's in his emphasis on the purification of the *affectus* 'through the fervour of penance in compunction, contrition and prayer' (GMT:1.28.2), for Gerson makes fine distinctions between the 'purified *affectus*' and the 'sordid i.e. unpurified *affectus*' (*sordidis affectibus*) corrupted by the 'sensual habits of adolescence' (*qui corruptos adhuc habent sensus ab adolescentia*). For Gerson the *eros* of *affectus* is not an unqualified force for the good as it was in the original text of Dionysius; it may be tainted by the 'sordid *affectus*' of youth.[21]

He rests with Hugh of Balma's definition of the *theologia mystica* as '*extensio animi in Deum per amoris desiderium*': 'The extension of the *animus* in God through the desire of love' supplemented by the definitions: '*sursum ductiva in Deum, per amorem fervidum et purum*','a raising movement in God, through fervent and pure love' (GMT:1.28.5) and '*cognitio experimentalis habita de Deo per amoris unitive complexum*', 'cognition experienced of God through the embrace

---

20 *Et cognoscamus quoniam, appropriate loquendo, sicut contemplatio est in vi cognitive intelligentie, sic in vi affective correspondente reponitur mistica theologia.*

21 Gerson seemed to have a problem with the sexual lives of his penitents. See *On the Art of Hearing Confessions* translated in McGuire 1998.

of unitive love' and, following Dionysius DN.7: '*Theologia mystica est irrationalis et amens, et stulta sapientia, excedens laudantes*'/ 'The mystical theology is irrational and beyond mind and foolish wisdom, exceeding all praise.' He later returns to this in GMT:1.43.2, '*mistica theologia est cognitio experimentalis habita de Deo per coniunctionem affectus spiritualis cum eodum*': '*theologia mystica* is an experimental cognition of God through the union of the spiritual *affectus* with him' – 'as the blessed Dionysius states this takes place through ecstatic love'.

Therefore, for Gerson, the *theologia speculativa* resides in the *potentia intellectiva* while the *theologia mystica* resides in the *potentia affectiva*. Speculative theology uses 'reasoning in conformity with philosophical disciplines' (GMT:1.30.2). *Theologia mystica*, on the other hand, needs no such 'school of the intellect' (*scola intellectus*). It is acquired through the 'school of the affect' (*scola affectus)* and (following Gerson's importance attached to the purfication of the affect) through the exercise of the 'moral virtues' that 'dispose the soul to purgation' (GMT:1.30.3). This is acquired through the 'school of religion' (*scola religionis*) or 'school of love' (*scola amoris*). The acquisition of the *theologia mystica* does not therefore require great knowledge or extensive study of books but may be acquired by 'any of the faithful, even if she be an insignificant woman or someone who is illiterate' (*a quolibet fideli, etiam si sit muliercula vel ydiota*) (GMT:1.30.5).[22] Concurring with St. Bernard, Gerson suggests that speculative theology can never be complete without mystical theology but the contrary can be the case: we must all acquire this 'affectivity' to reach right relationship with God. At this point, as with Dionysius, Gerson employs the strategy of concealment, for the 'language of mystical theology' is 'to be hidden from many who are clerics or learned or are called wise in philosophy or theology' (GMT:1.31:1) lest they 'tear apart with the teeth of dogs what they do not understand'. As he states at the end of section 42: 'To explain these matters an endless succession of words could be added, but for experts these few words will suffice, for the inexpert no words will ever suffice for full comprehension' (GMT:1.42.9). It is an 'irrational and mindless

22 See footnote 14 above.

wisdom' (*'irrationalis et amens sapientia'* 1.43:3) going beyond reason and mind and translating into the *affectus*.

We are once again in the place of the Wittgensteinian *Blick* at the interface of 'saying and showing', and we find this symbiotic relationship between the unknowing of intellect ('they all agree that they have come to know that they know nothing' [GMT:1.34.3]) and the 'wisdom' of the *affectus*. The *affectus*, once purified, possesses all the passionate force of Dionysius's ecstatic *eros*: 'Love takes hold of the beloved and creates ecstasy, and this is called rapture because of the manner in which the mind is lifted up' (GMT:1.36.1) and again, 'love ravishes, unites and fulfills' (GMT:1.35.3). In conclusion, for Gerson, 'the school of prayer (*scola orandi*) is more praiseworthy, other things being equal, than the school of learning/letters (*scola litteras*)'.

As we shall see in the following chapter, Gerson's high medieval formulation of the *theologia mystica* was to form the basis of how the discipline was taught throughout Christian Europe right up to the eve of the early sixteenth-century Reformation. We shall explore how the work would influence the sixteenth-century Spanish writers via the influence of the Franciscan friars Francisco de Osuna and Bernardino de Laredo. In so doing the 'performative discourse' of the *theologia mystica* would reach its apogee in the flowering of the Spanish mystical tradition.

5

The Emergence of the Spanish School: Mystical Theology as 'Recollection'

> The understanding cannot set eyes on God because of the radiance emanating from his countenance when he descends from his mountain of glory to communicate with us in this vale of tears wherein we live.
>
> (Francisco de Osuna TA:21.6)

We have seen so far how the 'unknowing-affective mystical strategy' of Dionysius spread through the medieval world via three major streams: the Victorine influence, the Parisian school around Gerson and the Carthusian school around Hugh of Balma. The main thrust of this book has been to trace how this strategy of *theologia mystica* reaches the sixteenth-century Spanish school manifested in particular in the writings of Teresa of Avila. In doing this, as stated already, I am aware of whole areas of development of the medieval *theologia mystica* that have not been covered, most notably the Rhineland school centred around Meister Eckhart, Suso and Tauler. As with Aquinas's writing on the *theologia mystica* I refer the interested reader to the references of other parallel studies in the previous chapters.

Returning in the meantime to early sixteenth-century Spain we find ourselves at a unique moment in the development of the *theologia mystica*. Spain itself, following the political and strategic union of the two crowns of Aragon and Castille under Ferdinand and Isabella and the conquest of the kingdom of Granada in 1492, was seeking at this moment to find a voice for a new unified form of Christian expression. Under the reforming Cardinal Francisco Ximenes de Cisneros (d. 1517), himself a Franciscan friar, the tools were found for the construction of this language precisely in the medieval tradition of *theologia mystica* that we have analysed in this book. The imposition of the ideals of reform by Cardinal Cisneros upon the Spanish hierarchy in 1494 was to lay the foundations for the great flowering of the Spanish mystical tradition in the sixteenth century. The ideals of the 'observants' in living simple rules (often returning to 'primitive rules'), concentration on the prayer of the heart and a life of devotion and humility was especially prevalent within the Franciscan, Dominican, Augustinian, Benedictine and Hieronymite orders.

Teresa herself mentions two specific authors by name who influenced her: Fray Francisco de Osuna and Fray Bernardino de Laredo, both Franciscan and both promoted by Cardinal Cisneros.[1] As we shall see in this chapter both of them also rely heavily on the tradition of *theologia mystica* from all the sources outlined in the previous chapter. Before we turn to each of them separately it is necessary to say a little about the context of Spanish *recogimiento* or 'recollection'.

RECOGIMIENTO: ITS ORIGINS AND BACKGROUND

In his monumental study of '*la mistica española*' between 1500 and 1700 (Andrés Martín 1975) Melquíades Andrés Martín stresses the continuity within the Spanish mystical tradition and its origins in the reform movements at the end of the fifteenth century, especially the tension between *conventualismo* and *observantismo*.[2] These movements were often contradictory and unclear, and Andrés notes:

---

1   See *The Book of the Life/El Libro de la Vida*: 4.23; also the following chapter.
2   Two conflicting movements originating in the Franciscan order and influencing subsequent reform movements on the Iberian Peninsula.

This reform movement oscillated between the study of theology, revivified by the Dominicans, and a certain anti-intellectualism, which would initially invoke a certain anti-verbosity, within the Franciscans and Augustinians, and much later affective prayer (*oración afectiva*) which placed more value on experience and love over study and intellect.

(Andrés Martín 1975:2)

Of particular importance to this nascent movement at the beginning of the sixteenth century were the reforms initiated within the Franciscan movement. I have already mentioned that to aid this reform Cisneros permitted the publication in Castilian of numerous medieval books on 'spirituality' including many of those representing the tradition of *theologia mystica* outlined above, beginning with the Seville edition of the *Obras de Bonaventura* of 1497 followed by the *Incendium Amoris* and *Liber meditationum* from the presses of Montserrat. Subsequently we find editions of Augustine, Bernard and Richard of St. Victor rapidly being produced. The *Ejercitatorio de la Vida Espiritual* of García de Cisneros of 1500 (which was to have such an impact on the young Ignatius Loyola) and, finally, the *Viae Lugent Sion* of Hugh of Balma published in Toledo as the *Sol de Contemplativos* (1514).

One strand that is very apparent in this whole nascent Spanish movement which Andrés terms 'the *recogimiento* movement' is 'the meditation that seeks love and knowledge of God through the will called the "affective prayer" (*oración afectiva*)' (Andrés Martín 1975:27): a clear manifestation of the *affective* influence from the tradition of *theologia mystica*. Indeed, Andrés cites in particular the influence of Hugh of Balma's *Viae* and Bonaventura's *Itinerario* in this respect which delineate the process as 'an action characteristic of the will in order to know God when the action of the intellect is suspended' (Andrés Martín 1975:27). Such a process is cited in Mombaer's *Rosetum* of 1494 (XIX Prologue) where it is called *meditación afectiva*.[3] Descriptions of *meditación afectiva* are also found in the works of Juan Wessel Gansfort

---

3   Mombaer, *Rosario de Ejercicios Espirituales y de santas meditaciones.*

(*Escala Meditatoria*, 1483), Gómez García (*Carro de dos Vidas*, 1500)
and García de Cisneros (*Ejercitatorio de la Vida Espiritual*, 1500)
which would be later taken up by Alonso de Madrid (*Arte de Servir
Dios*, 1521), Francisco de Osuna (*Tercer Abecedario/Third Spiritual
Alphabet*, 1527 – hereafter TA), Bernabé de Palma (*Via Spiritus*, 1531)
and Bernardino de Laredo (*Subida de Monte Sion/Ascent of Mount
Sion*, 1st edn 1535 – hereafter AM) in the first great flowering of
Franciscan mystical writing (See Gomis 1948).

When does the term *recogimiento* first make its appearance among
these mystical strategists? According to Andrés we cannot be sure
about the exact date of its origins. We can say with certainty that a
form of prayer entitled *recogimiento* was being practised by groups of
Franciscans at the beginning of the sixteenth century. When Osuna and
Laredo talk of the prayer in 1527 and 1529 they say that it has been
practised for between twenty and fifty years (TA 21:4). This would
mean that the prayer had been practised from at least 1480. Andrés
preferences the Franciscan hermitages of La Salceda (and possibly
earlier in San Pedro de Arlanza), associated in particular with the
reforms of Villacreces (d. 1422), as its place of origin.[4] Both Cardinals
Cisneros (1527) and Francisco de Quiñones (1523 – later Minister
General of the Franciscan Order) would be custodians of the shrine
of La Salceda, signifying its importance for the possible spread of
recogimiento. Whatever its origins, it was in these Franciscan *conventos*
and hermitages that it became widely practised at the turn of the fifteenth
and sixteenth centuries. Eventually the practitioners of *recogimiento*
would 'form a circle at the heart of Spain' (Andrés Martín 1975:46): La
Salceda, El Castañar, Cifuentes, Torrelaguna, Escalona, Alcalá, Ocaña,
Toledo, Oropesa and the *Descalzas Reales* of Madrid, as well as circles
of *recogimiento* in Andalusia, Extremadura and Catalonia/Valencia.

As to the first occurrence of the term in a published work, Andrés
cites García de Cisneros's 1500 *Ejercitatorio* as possibly the first
occurrence:

4   See also the Prologue of de Osuna *Sanctuarium Biblicum*, 1533; on
     Salceda and its connections to the *alumbrados* see Márquez 1972:109.

Recollect (*recógate*) often from low things to high, from temporal to eternal, from exterior to interior, from vain things to those that endure.

(Andrés Martín 1975:39)[5]

Although Andrés would like to see a clear distinction between the prayer of the *recogidos* and that of the *alumbrados*[6] it is unlikely that such a clear distinction existed. According to Andrés the separation proper between *recogidos* and *alumbrados* begins in 1523 in Pastrana between Francisco de Ortiz (*recogido*) and Pedro Ruiz de Alcaraz (*alumbrado*). Whether such a clear distinction existed between the two forms of prayer remains a moot point.

The *recogidos*, as Andrés calls this movement, thus have certain central characteristics in common (Andrés Martín 1975:55):

- the universal call to Christian perfection
- the validation of external works, rites and ceremonies
- the importance of interiority
- following Christ in his humanity and divinity
- relation of the active and contemplative lives and relative importance of the latter
- annihilation and quietude
- importance of '*consolaciones*' and '*gustos*'[7]
- the role of love
- the role of the will
- love without previous knowledge
- knowledge of affect.

Much of this we shall recognize later in Teresa's own 'mystical strategies'. The movement of *recogimiento* thus places the heart and the *oración*

5   *Recógate muchas veces de las cosas bajas a las altas; de las temporales a las eternales, de las exteriores a las interiors; de las vanas a las que siempre han de duran.*

6   A form of spiritual life declared heretical by the Inquisition in the early sixteenth century. We shall return to it in Chapter Six; in the meantime see Tyler (2005) 'Alumbrados'.

7   Literally 'consolations' and 'tastes/delights'; see Chapter Six.

afectiva at the centre of its concerns. An *oración*, I suggest, that is directly formed from the late medieval schools of affective Dionysianism whose characteristics we have already surveyed. It emphasizes the importance of the 'unknowing' as well as the affectivity of embodiment:

> The mysticism of the *recogimiento* is one that pertains to the whole of the person: person and spirit, memory, will and understanding. It does not divide the body and the soul, interior or exterior, not deprecating the latter as had been the case with the *alumbrados* and the Erasmians.[8]
>
> (Andrés Martín 1975:13)

This is nowhere better expressed than in the First Letter of de Osuna's *Tercer Abecedario*:

> Always walking together – the Person and the Spirit...
> The meaning of our letter is that wherever you go carry your thought (*pensamiento*) along with you, for no one should go divided in themselves. Do not allow the body to travel one path and the heart another.
>
> (TA 1.1, 1.2)[9]

Recogmiento, then, according to Andrés Martín, is primarily a way of '*contemplativa afectiva*' centred on love '*sin pensar nada*' ('Without thinking of anything') without any necessary prevenient or concomitant understanding. Although, at various times in his work, Andrés Martín seeks to present a systematic presentation of *recogimiento* (notably in his introduction and conclusion), as with the 'modern mysticism' we investigated in Chapter One, I would argue that his proposal suffers from the same ontological problems. Although the terms *recogimiento* and *recogidos* are useful we will continue working with the concept

8   Followers of Erasmus; see Márquez (1980).
9   My translation: *Anden siempre juntamente la Person y Espíritu: El sentido de nuestra letra sera que doquiera que vayas lleves tu pensamiento contigo y no ande cada uno por su parte divididos; así que el cuerpo ande en una parte y el corazón e otra.*

of 'mystical strategy' rather than looking for what I argue are fictive 'mystical' (or 'recognitive') entities – for the reasons given previously.

DE OSUNA AND THE *THIRD SPIRITUAL ALPHABET*

What little we know of Osuna's life and background is largely due to the painstaking researchs of Père Fidèle de Ros in the 1930s (Ros 1936).[10] After studies it appears that Osuna lived at the *recolectorio* of La Salceda, so important in the Observant reform and under the special patronage of Cisneros. Here Osuna explored *recogimiento*, probably in contact with *alumbrado* groups until 1523, which was eventually described in the *Tercer Abecedario Espiritual/ Third Spiritual Alphabet*, one of a series of six 'Alphabets',[11] published between 1527 and 1554 (after his death).[12]

10 I will draw here on the following sources: Andrés (1976, 1982), López Santidrián (1998), Ros (1936), Allison Peers (1930) and Giles (1981). It seems that he was born around 1492 in Osuna in Andalusia where his family had been in service to the counts of Ureña. We know two facts about his childhood from his own references in the *Abecedarios*: that he was present at the capture of Tripoli by Navarro in 1510 and that he undertook the pilgrimage to Santiago de Compostella sometime between 1510 and 1513. Andrés (1982) speculates whether he belonged to a *converso* family but Santidrián (1998) believes the family were probably 'old Christians'. Comparing his life as a Franciscan at Salamanca with that of his contemporaries, Ros speculates that he may have entered the Friars Minor of the Regular Observance around 1513 and then have studied for a minimum of eight years humanities, philosophy and theology, the latter at Cisneros's newly founded University of Alcalá.

11 The 'Spiritual Alphabet' was a characteristic pedagogical tool during this period. Osuna would certainly have been familiar with the *Alphabetum divini amoris* attributed to Gerson until the eighteenth century and customarily reprinted in his collected works. Other precursors of Osuna include the *Suma de los ejemplos por ABC* by Clemente Sánchez de Vercial (d. 1426) and *Parvum alphabetum monachi in scola Dei* of Thomas á Kempis.

12 Apart from the Spiritual Alphabets, other significant works include: *Gracioso Convite (1530), Norte de los estados (1531),* and two collections of Latin sermons: *Sanctuarium Biblicum (1533) and Pars Meridionalis*

One of the key elements of de Osuna's structure in the *Tercer Abcedario* is the division made in Chapter Six between the *theologia speculativa* and the *theologia mystica*. For de Osuna the *theologia speculativa*:

> Uses reasoning, argumentation, discourse and probability, as do the other sciences. It is called scholastic theology, which means it is of learned people (*letrados*) and if someone wishes to excel in it, he needs the learning tools required to excel in any science: a good mind, continual exercise, books, time, attentiveness, and a learned teacher to study under.
>
> (TA 6.2)[13]

The other *theologia*, the *theologia mystica*, differs from other sciences or learning as it is a 'hidden' (*escondida*) theology that is totally unlike any other branch of learning. It is pursued not through learning, books and teachers but through 'pious love and exercising moral virtues'. No book can teach it, including this one:

> I do not presume to teach it here, as no mortal can, for Christ alone reserves the teaching only for himself, in secret and in the hearts in which this hidden theology dwells as divine science and something much more excellent than the other theology (known as speculative).
>
> (TA 6.2)

We are back in the world of Wittgenstein's *Tractatus* that we explored earlier in this book: the world of 'saying and showing' where the book can indicate something but cannot say it:

(1533) as well as the Latin works: *Missus Est (1535), Pars Orientalis (1535), Pars Occidentalis (1536)* and *Trilogium evangelicum (1536)*.

13   *Usa de rezones y argumentos y discursos y probabilidades según las otras ciencias; y de aquí es que se llama teología escolástica y de letrados, la cual, si alguno quiere alcanzar, ha menester buen ingenio y continuo ejercicio y libros y tiempo, y velar, trabajar teniendo enseñado maestro, lo cual también es menester para cualquiera de las otras ciencias* (my translation).

> I wanted to write that my work consists of two parts: of the one
> which is here, and of everything which I have not written. And
> precisely this second part is the important one.
>
> (Wittgenstein LF:90)

Both Wittgenstein and de Osuna, I suggest, are 'delineating a world from
within'. They are both presented with the challenge of presenting in words
something that cannot be said in words; therefore they must use words to
'show' rather than 'say'. For Wittgenstein, the twentieth-century logician,
this will be a question of using logic to reveal the limits of logic; for de
Osuna, the sixteenth-century friar, the book will take us to the 'feet of
Christ' at which point Christ alone can reveal God's love in the secrecy of
our hearts: a classic strategy, I have argued, for the *theologia mystica* (and
already shown in Dionysius's, Balma's, Gallus's and Gerson's 'showing'
described in the previous chapters). This 'hidden theology' will work on
the affect and the heart (*el corazón*) to transform the reader.

In this same chapter (TA:6.2) de Osuna refers to the source from which
he receives the *theologia mystica*: Gerson's *De Mistica Theologia*, which
he quotes frequently and with which he was clearly very familiar. The
other important text on the *theologia mystica* that he quotes is Hugh of
Balma's *Viae Sion Lugent* (translated into Spanish in Toledo as the *Sol
de Contemplativas*). As we saw in the previous chapter, both Gerson and
Hugh use the 'strategies' of the *theologia mystica* to develop their approach
to this 'theology of showing'. Yet although de Osuna is clearly influenced
by the deconstruction of the Dionysian school (see e.g. TA:21.5) this is
not the deconstruction of a writer such as Eckhart or Tauler. Rather de
Osuna, like Gerson, is an heir to what we have already called the 'affective
Dionysianism', since, like Gerson and Gallus before him, he emphasizes the
libidinal, sensual aspect of the Dionysian unknowing. This is no austere
and rarified unknowing but something altogether more sensual:

> (The *theologia mystica*) is also called the art of love (*arte de amor*)
> because only through love is it realised, and in it love is multiplied
> more than in any other art or instruction.
>
> (TA:6.2)

The Dionysian unknowing is not about 'thinking of nothing' (TA:21.5) but developing the 'savour for the things of God'.

If we apply the Wittgensteinian *Blick* to the language games of de Osuna we see that he is employing the two now familiar 'language games', or what we can better term 'performative discourses', of the tradition of affective Dionysianism: unknowing and affectivity/embodiment. For de Osuna, this affective-deconstructive strategy is repackaged as the Spanish mystical concept of *recogimiento*. For, in the hands of de Osuna, *recogimiento* becomes, I suggest, nothing less than the combination of these two strategies within the wider context of Spanish spiritual developments at the time. In addition, when we examine de Osuna's influence on Teresa, we see that *recogimiento* means for her too the combination of these two strategies of eluciation. Both strategies are deployed to present the move from 'saying to showing to acting' as elaborated in Chapter Two.

As de Osuna puts it in Chapter 21 of the *Tercer Abecedario* when explaining the nature of *recogimiento*:

> There are words and works in the spiritual as well as the material. Spiritual words are the thoughts and reasonings we form in the heart and interior works are the most intense, living attention to God alone... Therefore, Our Lord does not respond in this matter with words but with works, seeing that the recollected only pay attention to them.
>
> (TA 21.6)

As we have seen in his text de Osuna is careful to relate his system to the *Corpus Dionysiacum* and its interpretation, especially through the Victorines (in particular Richard of St. Victor) and Gerson, as well as the writings of Gregory Nazianzan, Bernard and Bonaventure. Of these he continually refers back to the *Corpus Dionysiacum*:

> That you may not be able to understand Saint Dionysius does not mean he cannot be understood at all, for Gerson and many other holy theologians have comprehended him and offered advice and

caution against the wiles of the devil who strives the harder to deceive us the more we penetrate sublime matters.

(TA:21:5)

One of the most frequently cited authors by de Osuna is Gerson,[14] whose *Mystica Theologia* was one of the central manuals on the *theologia mystica* curriculum at the Universities of Salamanca and Alcalá. Gerson acts as the crucial link between the medieval exegesis of the Dionysian mystical strategy and the Spanish Fransciscan writings on *recogimiento* and *teología mística* of the early sixteenth century. Accordingly, where we see the distinction in de Osuna between *theologia speculativa* and *theologia mystica* (which has such an influence on Teresa) this is a clear reflection of Gerson. Thus, as we have seen, when de Osuna distinguishes his 'mystical theology' from the 'speculative theology' he uses terms clearly borrowed from (amongst others) Gerson:

This [theology] has two forms: one is called 'speculative' or 'investigative', which is the same thing, the other is called 'hidden', which is treated of here and which gives the title to this third alphabet. I do not presume to teach it here, as no mortal can, for Christ alone reserves this teaching only for himself, in secret and in the hearts in which this hidden theology dwells as divine science and something much more excellent than the other theology of which I spoke first... This theology [the mystical theology] is said to be more perfect and better than the first, so says Gerson, as the first serves as an introduction leading to the second.

(TA:6.2)[15]

14 Others include Gregory the Great, Augustine, Ambrose, Jerome, Basil, Gregory of Nyssa and Nazianzen as well as the Victorines, Thomas Aquinas, Bernard and Bonaventure.

15 *La cual aún es en dos maneras: una se llama especulativa o escudriñadora, que es el mismo, y otra escondida, que es la que se trata o a la que se intitula este tercero alfabeto; no que en él presuma yo enseñarla, pues*

The teaching must remain hidden as, for de Osuna, Christ alone is
the teacher; Osuna cannot present it directly, it can only be presented
through *indirect transmission*. The first (speculative) theology makes
use of the *intellectus* and reason to prepare the ground for the second,
affective, mystical theology precisely as it had done for Gerson. Again
we see the affective-deconstructive strategy of the *theologia mystica*.
By the process of unknowing we move into the affective.[16] Central to
de Osuna's affective mystical theology is the notion of 'taste' of God
rather than knowledge. In this passage he plays on the word *saber*
('know') and *sabor* ('taste') much as we will see later in Teresa of
Avila. In de Osuna's words, the 'mystical theology' is a *sabroso saber*
– literally, a 'tasty knowledge'. De Osuna then goes on to develop this
in his notion of the spiritual *gustos*, or 'taste/delight' of God, a key
term later taken up by Teresa. He concludes the section by stating:
'This exercise is known as profundity with respect to the depth and
darkness (*oscuridad*) of the devotion for it originates in the depths of
man's heart, which are dark because human understanding has been
deprived of light.'

The notion of the *gustos* and *sabroso saber* of the *theologia mystica*
is taken up in Chapter 12 of the Alphabet: '*No entiendo, mas gustando,*

> *ninguno de los mortales la enseñó, porque Christo guardó para sí este*
> *oficio de enseñar en secreto a los corazones en que viviese aquesta teología*
> *escondida como ciencia divina y mucho más excelente que la otra teología*
> *de que hablamos primer… Esta teología se dice más perfecta o mejor que*
> *la primera, según dice Gersón, porque de la primera como de un principio*
> *se servir.*

16   See, for example, the passage cited earlier from Chapter Six of the
     Tercer Abecedario: 'The first theology, called speculative, has recourse to
     reasoning, argumentation, discourse and probability, as do other sciences.
     It is called scholastic theology, which means it is of learned people and if
     someone wishes to excel in it, he needs the learning tools of any science: a
     good mind, continual exercise, books, attentiveness, and a learned teacher
     to study under. The hidden theology we are describing, however, is not
     attained by those tools as much as through pious love and exercising
     moral virtues to prepare and purge the soul' (TA:6.2).

penses alcanzar reposo' ('Not by thinking, but more by tasting, think to attain rest'). The title itself reveals how de Osuna makes a connection between the two 'mystical strategies' of unknowing and embodiment. Early on in the treatise he had spoken of the importance of desire in the search for God (TA:4.3, 11.5) and in Chapter 12 he explicitly connects this with the unknowing and emphasizes the role that the *gustos* play in this. He begins with the classic statement of unknowing which we have already explored:

> Even though the understanding may discover and analyse numerous sublime matters, there is good reason for you to believe that complete, fulfilling repose is not to be found through functions of the intellect and that ultimately the least part of what we do not know exceeds everything we do know.
>
> (TA:12.1)

Knowledge, for de Osuna, is derived not from 'knowing' (*saber*) but from 'tasting' (*sabor*), in particular tasting the delights of the *gustos espirituales*, the spiritual delights. This *gusto espiritual* is 'so excellent that it is almost impossible for a person who has experienced it not to praise it... We should realise that he who tastes spiritual food hungers to taste and enjoy more' (TA:12.6). Here de Osuna gives a quote purportedly from St. Bernard's *De interiori domo*: '*Quanto amplius delectaris...*'. However, as López Santidrián points out (1998:351), this is a misattribution; the passage is from a twelfth-century Cistercian manuscript that transcribes a passage from Richard of St. Victor's *Beniamin Maior*, thus once again relating this tradition of *deleite* and *gusto* to the Parisian school of *theologia mystica* and the 'Affective Dionysianism' we explored in the previous chapter.

De Osuna continues by justifying the use of pleasure as a marker of spiritual progress, dismissing those who object for 'not differentiating among the types of pleasure' and classing them all together. He calls on Gerson to justify his approach, which is, as we saw previously, the emphasis on the importance of experience over understanding. At this point de Osuna employs a quote from Proverbs 8.31 which we shall see later is of fundamental importance to Teresa. The original verse from Proverbs reads:

> The Lord created me at the beginning of his work
> The first of his acts of long ago.
> Ages ago I was established
> At the first, before the beginning of the earth...
> When he established the heavens,
> I was there,
> When he drew a circle on the face of the deep...
> When he marked out the foundations of the earth.
> There I was beside him, like a master worker.
> And I was daily his delight
> Rejoicing before him always.
> Rejoicing in his inhabited world
> And delighting in the human race.
>
> (Proverbs 8:31)

De Osuna transcribes it thus:

> Our souls would delight in an increase of consolation, and, as we delighted in God, he would grant the petitions of our hearts, for it is said that his delights are to dwell in the sons of man so they will cause them to delight in him.
>
> (TA:12.4)[17]

His statements here build on the previous ones made in Chapter Six, developed within the framework of Gerson's writings, especially on the *theologia mystica*:

> Even though the understanding may discover and analyse numerous sublime matters there is good reason for you to believe that

17   As well as Prov 8.31, Osuna also makes reference here to Ps 103:27 and
      Prov 5.19.

complete, fulfilling repose is not to be found through functions of the intellect (*por la operación intelectiva*) and that ultimately the least part of what we do not know exceeds everything we do know.

(TA:12.1)

For de Osuna, 'study steals away everything' and he quotes Ecclesiastes 1:18 '*Cuanto más letrados son, anan más indignados*', 'the more learned one is, the more angry one is':

If having found nothing to satisfy or correspond in magnificence with their knowledge and persumption they go about with sad, flushed faces revealing the anger in their spirit: they are dissatisfied with books, murmur against the authors, yearn for and search out new treatises, thumb through some, then others, grow weary and weighed down with books, pile labour upon labour. Burdened with fetters, burdened with fear. So long as you increase in cleverness and knowledge, you will need more and more books, as they say the cleverer you become, the heavier arms you need. Such people fail to realize that a multitude of books is no more than great spiritual dissolution, excessive work, lack of rest, a burden for the memory, food that will not fill the stomach and cosmetics to cover up deficient knowledge so as to deceive the stupid into believing that since they posssess the books, they must surely understand them.

(TA:12.1; cf. GMT:1.34)

De Osuna's diatribe against book learning here is in contrast to the more nuanced approach to the 'unknowing' of the high medieval tradition described as we have seen in the writings of Gallus, Gerson and Hugh of Balma.[18] In Gerson's writings, for example, the

18 We shall see shortly that Bernardino de Laredo relies more on Balma, whereas de Osuna relies on Gerson. Like Gallus, Balma's view of the relation between *intellectus* and *affectus* is more balanced.

'anti-intellectual element' was sufficiently tempered for his texts to be employed on both sides of the Tegernsee debate regarding Nicholas of Cusa in the fifteenth century. De Osuna goes further than Gerson (who equally preferences the *affectus* to the *intellectus*) to present a more radical championing of the *affectus* which will shape the later Spanish writers such as Teresa: 'The good religious must first seek kindness and devout discipline, then knowledge and insure that his knowledge, like weeds growing among the wheat, does not choke devotion' (TA:12.2). Quoting Bernard and Richard of St. Victor, de Osuna finds this 'way of love' through the 'tasting of the divine goodness':

> No-one is to think that he loves God if he does not wish to taste him, for the fruit of love is the enjoyment of what is loved, and the more it is loved, the more it is enjoyed (*porque el fruto del amor es el gusto de lo que es amado, y mientras más se ama, mejor se gusta*). Accordingly, Richard says about joyful love: 'Love is a sweetness of intimate flavour, and the more ardently one loves, the more sweetly it tastes; and love is the enjoyment of hope' ('*el amor es una dulcedumbre de sabor íntimo, y cuanto con más ardor ama, tanto más suavemente gusta, y el amor es gozo de la esperanza*').
>
> (TA:12.2)

Once again, de Osuna employs the mystical strategy of the *theologia mystica* going beyond Gerson's 'moral purification' into an altogether more sensual and libidinized sense of *eros*, an approach we shall see mirrored in Teresa of Avila. Throughout the medieval *theologia mystica* there is an oscillation from the purity of a 'purged moral *affectus*' to an altogether more libidinal and embodied *eros*. We must 'taste what we understand'/'*gustando lo que entiendes*' to attain the wisdom we are looking for – the '*theología mística*' or, as de Osuna also calls it, the *recogimiento*. In this affective version of the *theologia mystica*, the influence of Bernard is very apparent, and de Osuna quotes his comments with approval:

I wanted a vital juice (*un zumo vital*) to be infused through every vein and into the very marrow of my soul so that it might be freed from every other desire and know that One alone... If the spur of intimate love does not penetrate your soul with divine desire as deeply as before and if the new desire aroused in you is less ardent than other affections it awakened, then you must doubt if the supreme Lover yet possesses the intimate breast of your desire.

(TA:12.5)

As de Osuna comments: 'the absence of pleasure once enjoyed is evidence of your failing', themes we shall return to when we consider Teresa's use of the 'strategy of affectivity' in Chapter Six.

Concluding his chapter, de Osuna once again (as he has so many times in this chapter) quotes Gerson directly from the *Theologia Mystica* in seeing that this 'spiritual savour' is not confined to the intelligentsia (indeed, following from his comments in Section One it would seem that they are the least equipped to receive it) but referencing Gerson again, this knowledge is open to (and perhaps preferenced to?) the 'little woman and the fool'/'*aunque sea mujercilla e idiota*' (TA:12.7; cf. GMT:1.30:5).[19]

The effects of de Osuna's affective-unknowing strategy using the spiritual *gustos* are described in Chapter 21 of the *Tercer Abecedario*: *Intimamente asoseiga y acalla tu entendimiento*/'Intimately calm and quiet your understanding'. Again, at the beginning of this chapter there is a passage that mirrors a similar passage in Gerson and points forward to the writings of Teresa. Here it concerns a theme that has already been mentioned but is further clarified here: *reposo*, or the rest or repose of the soul:

Ultimately security and repose in the heart will not be attained perfectly through speculative meditation (*por meditación escudriñando*) but through recollection, which quiets the heart... we shall find that all natural movements are directed to quietude

19   See also footnote 22, Chapter Four.

and that all things work to that end. Nothing moves except for the purpose of finding that repose which all things seek as their ultimate end.

(TA:21.1; cf. GMT:1.40–42)[20]

This sense of 'quietude, repose or rest', developed by Gerson and adopted by de Osuna, will be used later by Teresa and most memorably by John of the Cross in the final stanza of the *Cántico Espiritual* (see Tyler 2010a). For both Gerson and de Osuna, the sweetness of the spiritual element (de Osuna's *gustos*) brings spiritual relief and repose. Needless to say, by now, this repose is found through love and *affectus* rather than through understanding:

> The silence of love is marvellous and most admirable and praise-worthy, that silence wherein the understanding is profoundly quieted, receiving the sublimely contenting knowledge of experience. We clearly realize that when lovers are present to each other they fall silent and the love that unites them supplies the want of words.

(TA:21.3)

When Teresa comes to this point in the *Vida* and Mansion Four of the *Moradas*, she concerns herself a great deal with the nature of this 'quietening' of the mind. De Osuna deals with this in 21.5. Here he specifies that the '*docta ignorancia*' is not about 'not thinking' but placing thinking in the service of the 'mystical theology' of the affect.

To conclude this passage and 'in support of the entire Third Alphabet' (TA 21:6), de Osuna assembles a series of quotations from 'several authentic doctors' to support his arguments. There are

---

20 'It is necessary that our spirit, when it is united and joined to the highest perfection through perfect love, thereby reaches a state of quietude, fulfilment and stability (*quietetur, satietur and stabilitatur*). Thus matter is fashioned in form as a rock is placed in a centred position, and as anything reaches a state of rest when it obtains its end' (GMT:1.42.2).

no surprises by now among the authors quoted: Gerson, Richard and Hugh of St. Victor, Gregory Nazianzan, Dionysius, Isaac of Stella, Hugh of Balma (attributed to Bonaventure), Augustine and Bernard. In the end the text, despite all his attributions and descriptions, leaves us with the exhortation to engage in *recogimiento* (as he reinvents the *theologia mystica*) without really telling us what it *is*. The practice, as he reiterates many times, can only be comprehended by the practitioner: it remains a 'hidden art' (*ars escondida*). In view of what we have argued as to the *performative* nature of the *theologia mystica* this is perhaps unsurprising.

Thus by combining his exposition of the ancient Jewish texts with the medieval tradition of *theologia mystica* inherited through Gerson and the Victorines, de Osuna provides the materials that Teresa will later incorporate into her mature mystical writing (see also TA:4.3). 'If you enjoy God' (*Si gustas en Dios*) he says, 'you have in your soul the greatest possible sign of God's supreme love and so you should not let anyone frighten you by saying it is self-love'. 'There is nothing', he says, 'which is more delightful than spiritual consolation'. In passages such as this we can see why the young, confused Teresa of Avila took such comfort from the work and found the confirmation of the spiritual journey she was seeking from her confessors and only finding in de Osuna's book: 'her master'. *Los gustos* are for Osuna 'a foretaste of heaven on earth' (TA:5.3): 'God gives the soul spiritual pleasure as a promise of future glory'; 'When you receive it do not be curious about where it comes from but open your hearts to the Lord's gift and accept it.'

We shall see in the following chapter how *embodied* the work of Teresa is. This, I will suggest, is in no small part thanks to her incorporation of de Osuna's approach to the whole spiritual life relying on the mystical strategies he has inherited from the late medieval tradition of *theologia mystica*.

LAREDO AND THE *ASCENT OF MOUNT SION*

Before turning to Teresa and the mystical strategies she would employ
in her writing I will conclude this survey of the Spanish school from
which she emerged by turning to the other Spanish Franciscan writer to
whom she gives specific reference: Fray Bernardino de Laredo.[21] Like de
Osuna, Laredo belonged to that early sixteenth-century reform within
the Iberian Franciscan order that had been encouraged and supported
by Cardinal Cisneros. As with de Osuna we know very few biographical
details about the friar; however, we do know that he was born in Seville
in 1482 and before entering the order had undertaken medical studies at
Seville University. He joined the order in 1510 in which he remained as
a lay brother until he died in 1540, living most of his life in the Friary of
San Francisco del Monte near Villaverde del Río in Andalusia.[22] Working
within the same context as de Osuna there is much in Laredo that is
similar; however, Laredo does not develop the *theologia mystica* of Gerson
in the systematic fashion that de Osuna does as has been related above.
Rather, the emphasis in Laredo is on the work of Balma whom he usually
refers to as Henry of Balma.[23] Although Laredo employs the mystical
strategy of the affective like Osuna, by not relying on Gerson as much as
his Franciscan confrere he can claim a direct inheritance from the tradition
of affective Dionysianism/*theologia mystica* of Balma, the Victorines and
Dionysius. Significantly for Laredo the tradition represented by Jerome,
Augustine and Ambrose is of little importance and Thomas Aquinas,
Bernard and Bonaventure are not cited at all. This is the theological world
that will later have such an impact on the thought of St. Teresa. In fact

21   Teresa of Avila V:23.
22   In this biographical sketch I am drawing upon Allison Peers (1930, 1952),
     Ros (1948) and Gomis (1948).
23   Drawing upon the *Sol de Contemplativos* published in 1514. 'This book',
     writes Andrés Martin, 'is for Spanish mysticism in the 16th and 17th
     centuries what the *Sentences* of Peter Lombard or the *Summa Theologicae*
     of the Angelic Doctor are for dogmatic theology'(Andrés Martín 1975:58).
     Ros (1948:144, 152) gives Balma as the most important influence on
     Laredo. Allison Peers (1952:45) prefers Herp.

Laredo goes so far in Chapter 27 of the *Ascent* to give a 'mystical lineage' of his writing that stretches from St. Paul to Dionysius, the Victorines and Hugh of Balma, Bruno and Gregory to Gerson and Herp.

Allison Peers (1952) feels that Teresa draws from Laredo the ability to map 'the various stages of the contemplative's progress' (1952:49) which would have appealed, he suggests, to 'her orderly mind'. Strangely, however, a few pages later he bemoans Laredo's obscure style and the fact that he 'has no claim whatever to a place in pure literature... his singular lack of literary sense often obscures his meaning and repels would-be readers' (1952:54). However, in view of the argument of this book and our exposition of the *theologia mystica*, could we not turn Allison Peers's criticism on its head and suggest that these verbal jumblings may indeed be part of the 'mystical strategy' of Laredo (as they are of Osuna) and hence of Teresa? Allison Peers, the devout translator, bemoans Laredo's free-and-easy use of personal pronouns and tenses such that meaning and emphasis shift within one sentence alone. He cites Book 3, Chapter 21 of *The Ascent of Mount Sion*:

> Moses here represents any soul that has fed freely upon contemplation, and his people, who were committing idolatry, stand for our sensual nature, the immoderateness of this flesh and of its inclinations, its lack of shame, my utter wretchedness and the poor returns of your harvesting.[24]

Allison Peers duly tidies this up into:

> Moses here represents any soul that has fed freely upon contemplation, and his people, who were committing idolatry, stand for our sensual nature, the immoderateness of the flesh and of its

---

24 *Moisés tiene aquí figura de cualquier anima cebada en contemplación; y el pueblo suyo, que idolatraba, tiene figura de nuestra sensualidad, de esta carne sin mesura, y de sus inclinaciones, y de su poca vergüenza, y de toda mi miseria, y de cuanta poquedad tenéis de vuestra cosecha.* (Gomis 1948:2:356).

inclinations, its lack of shame, its utter wretchedness and the poor returns of our harvesting.

(Allison Peers 1952:148)

Yet could it be, as I will argue in the following chapter with reference to Teresa, that Laredo is *deliberately* destabilizing the narrative here to allow the breakdown of the *intellectus* in preparation for the manifestation of the *affectus*? For, as this study has shown, the text of the *theologia mystica* is forever a performative text that will surprise and challenge its reader as it deconstructs the intellect and softens the affect. Laredo in this passage brings the emphasis around to *you, the reader* – it is *your* warped inclinations that he wants to draw attention to – not some generic 'us'. Similarly, we shall see in Teresa that as she struggles to speak of the spiritual world through the overlap of affect and intellect (as we saw with Dionysius, Gallus, Balma, Gerson and Osuna) she too will craft her own mystical strategies to bring us into the active interaction of 'what is said and what is shown'. The shape of Wittgenstein's own 'mystical thinking' is never far below the surface in passages such as these.

So perhaps then this was the great lesson that Teresa learnt from Laredo, not the ability to 'think straight', but rather to 'think crooked', to realize that the stuttering of 'I know not what' is the beginning of the mystical discourse and not its end (see AM 15).

Another lesson of the *theologia mystica* that Teresa learns from Laredo is his emphasis on the *capacity (capacidad)* of the soul.[25] 'The divine visitation', writes Laredo, 'gives even greater capacity' (ch. 10). A phrase that we shall see in the next chapter begins Teresa's greatest writing, *The Interior Castle*. As with de Osuna there is the emphasis that the 'secret science' of the mystical theology 'cannot be attained by temporal learning, nor can it be understood by the senses of those that are given to temporal things' (AM:10). Showing the influence of Balma, Laredo writes: 'in the sudden uprising of the affective nature, in this secret wisdom or celestial theology, which can bear souls away and

---

25   A term also explored with reference to Dionysius by Golitzin (2003).

unite them in an instant with God... we become suddenly recollected and the wonderings of our incautious thoughts are dispersed.'

As with de Osuna, and later with Teresa, Laredo does not *describe* the divine life but points towards it through implication and the preparation of the *capacity* of the self. The divine life will, as with Wittgenstein, 'make itself manifest', for it cannot be described within the mystical theology. For Laredo it is not an intellectual knowing but 'a knowledge and understanding from experience' (AM:15):

So sublime is this science (mystical theology) that though this or that servant of His can speak of it, as it were stammeringly, only His boundless Majesty can cause it to be understood inwardly, make it to be felt within the soul and implant it into the heart.

(AM:15)

In common with the tradition there is the emphasis on the 'divine unknowing' that began life with Dionysius:

In the secrecy of this wisdom, the soul knows that it is united with the Divine fellowship, through Divine condescension through a bond of love; yet, notwithstanding, its knowledge is such that it understands not how it understands that which it understands. It knows it without knowing how it knows it; it knows that it has a knowledge of God but, because He Whom it knows is incomprehensible, it knows not how to know through understanding.

(AM:11)

As we have seen so many times already, this 'divine unknowing' is linked to the affect which for Laredo is the 'upsurging power' that brings us to God. The surge of love that leads us to God is described in the same direct fashion as Balma so that, unlike de Osuna who relies more heavily on the subtle distinctions of Gerson, we have in Laredo something closer to the strong upsurge described by the early Victorines. The 'mystical theology' is thus for Laredo the *vía de aspiración* or the 'way of aspiration' (AM:11). Where Laredo differs from Osuna is in the emphasis on the strength of this passion. At every point in the *Ascent of Mount Sion* (as with Balma's *Viae Lugent Sion*) the 'upsurge of the affect' threatens to overwhelm the self. Laredo memorably describes it thus:

> The heart, by which is here to be understood the fire of love, must be alive in every contemplative's soul, must of a sudden pour itself wholly forth into infinite love, like a jug full of water when it is turned to face downwards.
>
> (AM:27)

Laredo calls this element of the mystical strategy the 'amative power' or 'loving ability' (*amativa virtud*) which he defines as 'the eager will that attains quiet in love': *'la muy pronta voluntad, que está quietada en amor'* (AM:29). Thus, he says, his writings will 'excite our affective nature' so that we too may experience the 'gentle sweetness' of the divine, 'melting those that have no warmth'.

The *Ascent* concludes in a somewhat scrappy fashion. No doubt Professor Allison Peers would not approve. Yet in line with the view that what Laredo is presenting is *mystical theology* rather than *speculative theology* this seems appropriate. Chapter 39 sets down a 'prayer in preparation for Holy Communion', 'more abundant in meaning than in words' which then leads in Chapter 40 to an extended poem and exposition on the nature of the 'tasty love' that has been expounded throughout the book. As later with St. John of the Cross, Laredo seems to sense the point at which discursive reason must give way to the poetic (see Tyler 2010a). The penultimate chapter is given over to two actual encounters – one with a 'skilled theologian' who is unable to comprehend the mystical theology and the other with a 'poor woman' (the same that we have met in Gallus, Gerson and de Osuna and whom we shall meet in Teresa) for whom the language of the mystical theology makes sense. An encounter with a holy man 'whereupon I learned certain things that I had never thought to learn and cannot set down here on paper' (AM:41) effectively finishes the book. We are back, it seems, in the world of Dionysius and Hierotheus – teaching by encounter and affect rather than through speculative reasoning – a teaching not lost on the young Teresa of Avila, to whom we turn in the next chapter.

PART THREE

Wittgenstein and Teresa of Avila

6

Teresa of Avila's Mystical Strategies

When a number of books in Spanish were taken away from us and we were not allowed to read them, I felt it very much because the reading of some of them had given me great recreation, and I could no longer do so since they were only available in Latin. Then the Lord said to me: 'Don't be upset, for I will give you a living book'.

(Teresa of Avila V:26.6) [1]

In this key passage in her *Libro de la Vida* ('Book of the Life', hereafter V) Teresa hints at some of the external and internal circumstances that led to her own writing career. In this passage we come across some of the key events that were influencing her: the prohibition of spiritual books in the vernacular following the Valdés decree of 1559, her own

---

1 *Cuando se quitaron muchos libros de romance, que no se leyesen, yo sentí mucho, porque algunos me dava recreación leerlos, y yo no podia ya, por dejarlos en latín; me dijo el Señor: 'No tengas pena, que yo te dare libro vivo'*. My translation from the Spanish of the *Obras Completas de Santa Teresa de Jésus* ed. Efrén de la Madre de Dios and Otger Steggink, 9th edn. Madrid: Biblioteca de Autores Cristianos, 1997 and *Santa Teresa Obras Completas*, ed. T. Alvarez, 10th edn. Burgos: Editorial Monte Carmelo, 1998. The English translations of Teresa's works will be either my own or, unless stated, Kavanaugh and Rodriguez (1987). V = *El Libro de la Vida* (Book of Her Life), M = *Las Moradas* (The Interior Castle), CE = *Camino de Perfección* (Way of Perfection), Escorial Codex, CV =*Camino*, Valladolid Codex, CT = *Camino*, Toledo Codex, C = *Meditaciones del amor de Dios*, Exc = *Exclamaciones*. For a biographical sketch of Teresa see the author's *Way of Ecstasy: Praying with St. Teresa of Avila* (Tyler 1997).

reliance on just such vernacular books of spirituality in her early life, and finally the inspiration for her own writing found in the words she received: 'I will give you a living book.' Central to her own vision of her 'mission' is the next sentence:

> I wasn't able to understand why this was said to me for as yet I had received no visions. Afterwards, after only a few days, I understood very clearly. For what I saw presented to me gave me much to think about and recollect (*recogerme*), and the Lord showed me so much love and taught me in so many ways that I had little or hardly any need for books afterwards.
>
> (V:26.6)[2]

Applying the Wittgensteinian *Blick* developed during this book and observing Teresa's communication as it stands, we see that she, like Wittgenstein, is making a move from 'saying' to 'showing', or, in this case, a move from the intellectual book learning of the *letrados*[3] to the 'vision' of 'what the Lord presents' 'in His love'. The key word here is *recogerme* – 'to recollect myself' – a crucial term that links Teresa with the main spiritual currents of her time and especially the writings of the 'vernacular master' she refers to in the previous sentence and had already mentioned in Chapter 4 of the *Vida*:

> When I was on my way, that uncle of mine I mentioned who lived along the road gave me a book. It is called *The Third Spiritual Alphabet* and endeavours to teach the prayer of recollection... And so I was very happy with this book and resolved to follow that path with all my strength... For during the twenty years after this

---

2   *Yo no podia entender por qué se me había dicho esto, porque aún no tenía visions; después, desde a bien pocos días, lo entendí muy bien, porque he tenido tanto en qué pensar y recogerme en lo que vía presente y ha tenido tanto amor el Señor conmigo para enseñarme de muchas maneras, que muy poca u casi ninguna necesidad he tenido de libros.* My translation.

3   Literally 'learned ones', a term used for theologians as opposed to hermits or more 'spiritual' friars and monks.

period of which I am speaking, I did not find a master, I mean a confessor, who understood me, even though I looked for one.

(V:4.7)[4]

As we analyse Teresa's sense of her own vocation as a writer we have a number of circumstances to 'place before us' in Wittgensteinian fashion to help us make sense of her writings. First, there are the circumstances of 1559 which produced the Valdés Index and Teresa's reaction to it. Second, the influence of 'her masters', Francisco de Osuna and Bernardino de Laredo, and what she learnt from them about writing on 'mystical topics'. Finally, the nature of her own approach to 'saying and showing' through 'that presented to her through recollection'.

In the previous chapter we discussed what Teresa would have drawn from the writers of 'recollection' such as de Osuna and Laredo. Therefore before we now look at Teresa's own use of the *theologia mystica* it is necessary to give a brief word on the crisis of *alumbradismo* alluded to in the previous chapter (and the prevenient cause of the Valdés Index) and how Teresa's work reacted to it.

ALUMBRADISMO AND THE VALDÉS INDEX

Writing on Teresa and *alumbradismo*, the North American Teresian scholar Gillian Ahlgren states:

Though Teresa never used the term *alumbrados*, the effects of the movement were probably the most important influence on her literary objectives. The suspicions of prophecy and of women's religious experience which the movement had inflamed affected Teresa's credibility.

(Ahlgren 1996:29)

---

4   *No sabía cómo poceder en oración ni cómo recogerme y así holgué mucho con él y determinéme a seguir aquel camino con todas mis fuerzas.*

Contemporary scholarship differs as to the role, nature and scope of the *alumbrados* (see for example Márquez 1980). The term *alumbrado* (literally: 'enlightened', 'illumined') seems to have originally been one of mockery and abuse used to denote 'excessive piety and to suggest hysteria and hypocrisy and fraudulence' (Hamilton 1992:28). At the beginning of the sixteenth century it began to be associated in Spain with a loose-knit group who were condemned at various times by the Church and state. The propositions for which they were condemned were first collected together in the Edict of Faith issued by the Inquisitor General, Alonso Manrique (Archbishop of Seville) on 23 September 1525. The edict contained forty-eight propositions directed against *'alumbrados, dexados e perfectos'* (literally: 'the enlightened, abandoned and perfect', see Bataillon 1982:166[5]) which comprised a collection of questionable and heretical statements held by and attributed to the group. As well as certain apocalyptic statements they included propositions such as 'prayer must be mental and not vocal'; the denial of the necessity of any sacramental intermediary between God and humans – thus rejecting the efficacy of external works as well as the authority of the Church to interpret scripture and contempt for the cult of the saints, the worship of images, bulls, indulgences, fasting and abstinence. Although the Edict condemned what appeared to be a homogenous and coherent group, scholars such as Bataillon and Márquez have concluded that the 'group' was a fragmentary grouping of various collections of people with differing motives, ideas and spiritualities. It was this emphasis on the importance of personal prayer that caused the most problems for Teresa, as one of the thrusts of her own life and work was the restitution of personal prayer as central to the life of the average Christian.

A key phrase used in the condemnations of the *alumbrados* was *dejamiento* (literally: 'abandonment') which was used to describe the type of prayer advocated by the *alumbrados*. It is unclear what exactly

5   From this time *dejamiento*, as opposed to *recogimiento*, was considered suspect as a form of prayer by official authorities in Spain. Although very fond of using the term *recogimiento* it is notable that Teresa uses the term *dejamiento* only once in her works.

was meant by the term; however, it seems to have arisen as a variant of the prayer of *recogimiento* discussed in the previous chapter. The teaching of *recogimiento,* as Andrés Martín points out, placed an emphasis on the importance of withdrawing from activity once or twice a day, usually to a dark room, for quiet contemplation with lowered or closed eyes. The teaching of *dejamiento*, often ascribed to Isabel de la Cruz, suggested that such a withdrawal was unnecessary and the contemplation could continue in all states and places – even allowing evil thoughts and temptations to arise.

After the Edict of 1525 an inquisitorial process was initiated against Pedro Ruiz de Alcaraz and Isabel de la Cruz of Toledo (See Márquez 1980:244–257) who were found guilty of the practices condemned. In 1529 Alcaraz was flogged, his property confiscated and both parties were condemned to 'perpetual reclusion and habit'. From this time any groups of laypeople, women and those associated with the Franciscan *recogitorios* were suspect of the heresy.[6] Thus, over the next thirty years, effectively culminating with the Valdés Index of 1559, four separate movements within Spanish society began to be conflated by the Inquisition:

- The 'alumbrados'
- The 'Erasmians'
- 'Lutherans' and 'Protestants'
- Remaining non-Christian elements, especially influences from Judaism through so-called *conversos*.[7]

It is notable that a number of the *alumbrado* groups were connected with *converso* or 'New Christian' groups, a group to which Teresa herself belonged. Contemporary commentators have been divided over whether the group was a 'movement' of interior Christianity akin to Erasmianism (Bataillon 1982) or a native, heretical protestant sect with justification by faith as their basic doctrine (Márquez 1980).

6 For a full list of the condemned propositions see Marquez 1980:250.
7 Literally: 'converted Jews and Muslims'.

Hamilton, following Márquez, suggests that their emphasis on the working of the Spirit in the individual, their pessimism about human nature, their interest in St. Paul and their quest for greater simplicity in religion ally them to the movement of Catholic reform at the time of the Northern European Reformation, known as *evangelism*. It is clear, as Bataillon points out (1982:166), that in the minds of the Inquisition, *alumbradismo* had to have somewhere a connection with the wider religious reforms of Northern Europe, even if, as appears likely, little such connection existed in reality.

The condemnation of the *alumbrados* by the Edict of Seville in 1525 marked in many ways the beginning of the end of the wave of openness and 'renaissance' within the mystical tradition in Spain initiated by Cardinal Cisneros and discussed in the previous chapter (See Bataillon 1982:699–737). As a young woman born in 1515, Teresa of Avila was able to have access to many mystical works from the tradition of *theologia mystica* before the close of this 'mystical Renaissance'. We have seen that in the period of unrest and unhappiness that she experienced after her profession at the convent of the *Encarnación* in 1537 (including a period of physical collapse), she relates in the *Libro de La Vida* how, during a stay at the house of her uncle, Don Pedro de Cepeda, she first came across de Osuna's *Tercer Abecedario Espiritual*. The book remained 'her guide' for many years to come as she found no spiritual director who could guide her as well as the book. 'During all those years, except after communion, I never dared begin to pray without a book' (V:4.9).

As well as de Osuna she read Bernardino de Laredo and the classical 'mystical' writers such as Augustine, Gregory and Bernard. However, as her own spiritual life grew and developed, the political climate in Spain began to change again.[8] Following years of tension between the 'Erasmians' and the Inquisition, events in Spain came to a head in 1559 when many works of the 'Cisnerosian Spring' of the early sixteenth century (including Erasmus and Luther) were condemned in the Valdés

---

8   There are many good analyses of the reasons for these changes. In English, see Ahlgren (1996) and Hamilton (1992), and in Spanish, Andrés (1975) and Márquez (1980).

Index. Valid only for Spain, it contained many of the writings of the people who had already fallen foul of Valdés and the Inquisition: Cardinal Carranza, Luis de Granada, Juan de Avila and the works of Erasmus in Castillian and Latin. As has been said, it also incorporated many of the writers and works who had contributed to the Cisnerosian revolution at the beginning of the century: as well as Francisco de Osuna's *Tercer Abecedario* (but not the other *Abecedarios*), it included Herp's *Theologia mystica* and de Balma's *Via Spiritus* (de Bujanda 1984:303–592).

As Hamilton puts it:

> By forbidding so many books published with the approval of Cisneros, the Index could also be regarded as the first official statement condemning his spirituality, the coronation of the trials which had started in the 1520s and of which the *alumbrados* had been the first victims.
>
> (Hamilton 1992:111)

Some works remained uncensored such as those of Alonso de Madrid and Bernardino de Laredo. In total it listed some 253 titles including fourteen editions of the Bible. In addition to the mentioned titles it also created a wider sense of alarm and caution on a whole range of areas.[9] In Ahlgren's words:

> In summary, the Valdés Index of Prohibited Books was not merely a list of books prohibited to the public; it was an edict intended to limit the scope of religious speculation and to define religious faith and practice very narrowly as the province of an educated elite whose task was not speculation but transmission of dogma.
>
> (Ahlgren 1996:17)

---

9   Other entries included books by known heretics, partial or whole translations of the Bible, books in Arabic or Hebrew or that tell of Muslim or Jewish practices, books regarding witchcraft and superstition, and manuscripts that mention biblical tradition or the sacraments of the church. See Ahlgren 1996:17.

For Andrés, the Valdés Index 'tried to banish affective spirituality in its various manifestations, encouraging the traditional spirituality of the practice of virtues and the destruction of vices over other ways of spirituality considered mystical' (Andrés 1976:1:362).

Commentators such as Ahlgren have noted the paradox that the period after 1559, while being one of repression, also encouraged a great flowering of 'mystical literature' (Ahlgren 1996:30). She suggests that Teresa of Avila employed four strategies to survive in the post-Valdés climate:

- She was careful about the literary and theological sources she cited.
- She employed a series of rhetorical devices to justify her right to write as an 'unlettered woman'.
- She practised a form of self censorship in the spirit of Valdés: 'her allusions to controversial subjects, such as her *converso* origins, permitted contemporary readers (especially those who knew her) to understand the subtext, but she never spoke openly enough to attract attention'.
- Finally, in exact language she explained 'mystical phenomena as thoroughly and accurately as possible'. Her overall aim was to show how 'charismatic experience did not have to be viewed as a potential danger to the institutional church but could instead be an important source of Roman Catholic identity'.

As she notes:

As the new mystical pathways opened in the first half of the century narrowed to a dogmatic and disciplined orthodoxy, so did the range of subjects appropriate for theological debate... If the works were to survive intact, certain topics had to be handled with extreme care, and authors used language to hide rather than reveal their intent.

(Ahlgren 1996:19)

As Ahlgren points out, this particularly applied to laypeople and especially women.[10] As most women did not read Latin, the Valdés prohibition of spiritual books in the vernacular posed a particular problem. As these ideological concerns impacted upon Teresa I suggest here that she was able to respond largely because of the 'training' and 'education' she had received from 'her masters' Frays Francisco de Osuna and Bernardino de Laredo and their exposition of the *theologia mystica*. In this respect, I would argue, her schooling in the mystical strategies of the *theologia mystica* was ideal preparation for the challenges of the environment within which her mature work was developed.

TERESA AND THE *THEOLOGIA MYSTICA*

Although, as argued, Teresa relies heavily on the tradition of *theologia mystica* throughout her works she makes only three explicit references to it; these occur in chapters 10–12 of her *Vida*. It is worth while spending some time on these references and their place in the text of the *Vida*.

The decision to write the text of the *Vida* coincided with Teresa's 're-formation' of the Carmelite houses in Spain. In 1561 the Inquisitor of Toledo, Francisco de Soto y Salazar, suggested that Teresa present a description of her experiences and methods of prayer. The first draft was completed in 1562 and the final draft in 1565, which was then to be read by several learned *letrados*: Juan de Avila, her Dominican mentors and probably Balthasar Alvarez, one of her Jesuit mentors. In 1574 the work came under inquisitorial suspicion – due, among other things, to the vindictive malice of the Princess of Eboli, and the manuscript disappeared into the Inquisition's hands until after Teresa's death in 1582. It was later recovered by Ana de Jésus and edited by Luis de Léon.

The context of chapters 10–12 of the *Vida* is that they are preceeded by Teresa's descriptions of how her life of prayer had gone astray once

10   She notes that between 1550 and 1600 no books by female authors were printed from Alcalá.

she had joined the convent of the *Encarnación*. As she describes the sins into which her soul had fallen she makes a telling comment:

> And helping this was that as my sins grew, I began to lose the pleasure and gift in the things of virtue.
>
> (V:7.1)[11]

For Teresa, one of the most distressing things at this time in her life was the loss of the pleasure *(gusto)* of the life of prayer. Deprived of this *gusto* she became 'afraid to pray', instead resorting to 'vocal prayer'. She clearly practised the outward virtues 'So that the nuns had a good opinion of me' while retaining this 'inner dryness'. She contrasts her outer shows of piety and holiness at this time (including instructing others on prayer) with her own interior sense of alienation from the source of her being – God. This period of unrest and unhappiness with her spiritual life dated from her profession at the convent of the *Encarnación* in 1537. Significantly, from the point of view of our study, this period of physical collapse had coincided with a stay at the house of her uncle, Don Pedro de Cepeda, when, as we have seen, she first came across de Osuna's *Tercer Abecedario Espiritual*. The experience of this time is one of *recollection* and dryness punctuated by another state of which she finds it difficult to speak (V:4.8). This period ('of some twenty years': V:8.2) she tells us was a time of neither 'pleasure in God' nor 'contentment with the world' *(yo gozaba de Dios ni traía contento en el mundo)* (V:8.2), for she is adamant that prayer is the source of 'delights/pleasures' *(gustos V:8.9)* from the Lord, it is the place where 'the Lord takes delight in a soul and gives the soul delight/*entrar a regalarse con un alma y regalarla*' (V:8.9) – a theme we shall see reiterated at the beginning of the *Moradas* below and one we have already encountered in Osuna in the previous chapter.

In this place of deconstruction without intellectual concourse (V:4.7, 9.4, 9.5, 9.9) Teresa enters a place to which she gives the name *mística teología*:

11   *Y ayudóme a esto que, como crecieron los pecados, comenzóme a faltar el gusto y regalo en las cosas virtud.*

It used to happen, when I represented Christ within me in order to place myself in His presence, or even while reading, that a feeling of the presence of God would come upon me unexpectedly so that I could in no way doubt He was within me or I totally immersed in Him... I believe they call this 'mystical theology.'

(V:10.1)[12]

Teresa equates this 'mystical theology' with an indubitable sense of the presence of God:

The will loves; the memory appears to me almost lost; the under-standing does not discourse, so it appears to me – it is not lost, but, as I say, it does not work – however it is amazed at how much it can understand, because God wants it to understand how little it can understand of what God represents to it.

(V:10.1)[13]

Using the classical scholastic/Augustinian typology of the memory-will-understanding, Teresa presents here our deconstructive-affective strategy in clear terms. The pull of the text is as though she wants to declare that the reason *(entendimiento)* ceases to work – the most extreme position of unsaying, although her uncertainty allows her to interject the milder *no discurre* – 'does not discourse'. Only the affective/libidinal can function at this point, as stressed in her short statement *ama la voluntad* ('the will loves'): the mystical strategies of the *theologia mystica* are clearly being employed here (See also V:12.5).

---

12 *Acaecíame en esta representación que hacía de ponerme cabe Cristo, que he dicho, y aun algunas veces leyendo, venirme a deshora un sentimiento de la presencia de Dios que en ninguna manera podia dudar que estaba dentro de mí o yo toda engolfada en El... creo lo llaman mística teología.*

13 *Ama la voluntad, la memoria me parece está casi perdida, el entendimiento no discurre, a mi parecer, mas o se pierde; mas, como digo, no obra, sine está como espantado de lo mucho que entiende, porque quiere Dios entienda que de aquello que Su Majestad le representa ninguna cosa entiende.*

As she states in 12.5 this 'stopping of the intellect' is not something that is done by voluntary action, but something received from God, 'for otherwise we would be left like cold simpletons'. The intellectual should 'delight in God' (13.11) rather than 'wearing themselves out in composing syllogisms'.

Her next mention of the 'mystical theology' in V:11.5 is to distinguish it from the beginning stages of prayer (or as she calls it 'mental prayer') which will form a small discourse from chapters 11–22 – the famous analogy of the 'four waters' (see Kavanaugh and Rodriguez CW I:470). In Chapter 23 she returns to her 'mystical theology'; this, she says, is distinguished by being the stage where we 'enjoy' God's presence: *'lo más es gozar'* ('the more to enjoy it') (V:11.5). The beginning 'mansions', as she will later call them in the *Moradas*, are places lacking in *gustos y ternera*[14] – these are the special attributes of the *teología mística* (see V:8.5, 9.9. 10.2 and 25.11). At this earlier stage the 'understanding' continues to 'work' and for this she recommends books such as Alonso de Madrid's *Arte de servir de Dios* (V:12.2). The great delight in the Lord's presence in the soul (V:14.2, 14.9) reflects the opening of the *Moradas*:

> This quietude and recollection is something that is clearly felt through the satisfaction and peace bestowed on the soul, along with great contentment and calm and a very gentle delight in the faculties.
>
> (V:15.1)[15]

STRATEGIES OF UNKNOWING IN TERESA

The climate, then, in which the mature Teresa was writing books of affective spirituality for her sisters was clearly one of *odium theologicum*

---

14   See discussion of these terms below.
15   *Esta quietud y recogimiento del alma es cosa que se siente mucho en la satisfacción y paz que en ella se pone, con grandísimo contento y sosiego de las potencies y muy suave deleite.*

towards an intelligent woman presuming to teach men, a daughter of *converso* stock and someone whose teachings came perilously close to that of *alumbradismo* (See Llamas-Martínez 1972; Rivers 1984). We remember the famous quote from the Inquisitor Fray Alonso de la Fuente, made in 1589, some seven years after her death:

> The author of the said book passes it off and recommends it as a doctrine revealed by God and inspired by the Holy Spirit; but if in fact the author was that nun whose name is on the title page, it is a matter *praeter naturam* for her to have written something taught by an angel, because it exceeds a woman's capacity. In any case it could not have been a good angel, but a bad one, the same one that deceived Mohammed and Luther and the other leaders of heretics. This being the case, the so-called miracle of the nun Teresa of Jesus, that her body is today intact and uncorrupted, is a fabulous business, either the work of Satan or the invention of heretics.
>
> (Llamas-Martínez 1972:396)

Within this climate it appears to us now that Teresa deliberately used her own 'vulgar style of substandard written Spanish' (Rivers 1984:120) to survive. Indeed, within the context of the *theologia mystica* her 'anti-rational' style makes complete sense. Her style, as Rivers points out, deliberately avoids the syntax and style of the newly developing Romance Spanish then popular with Renaissance Spanish humanists such as Luis de Granada and Juan de Valdés:

> Teresa's written Spanish is in fact hard for us to read and under-stand in a wholly rational way; it is comparable, within an American context, to something composed by a writer of Black English, who deliberately tries to avoid the academic sound of white bourgeois correctness.
>
> (Rivers 1984:121)

Just how important style was for Teresa may be seen by observing the differences between the various versions of the *Camino/Way of Perfection* (see Weber 1990:78–80).[16] As Ahlgren points out, Teresa criticizes the Valdés Index in no less than four places in the *Camino*, albeit indirectly (Ahlgren 1996:89). She famously remarks, for example, that 'even they [The Inquisition] cannot take the *Our Father* and the *Hail Mary* away from [the sisters]' (CE:21.8). To which García remarks: 'she seems to be reproving the Inquisitors for prohibiting books on prayer'.[17]

'In sum', as Weber puts it, 'Teresa repeatedly denies possessing any literary skill, much less theological certainty or authority. Disorder, digression and imprecision – these are the tactics that disguise a charismatic text as women's chatter' (Weber 1990:108). Like Wittgenstein, dressed as his 'old woman', it seems that Teresa too would deceive us that the mess and disorder in her writing is just confusion and chaos. As we saw with Wittgenstein, so with Teresa; once we start to examine her style we realize that there is 'method in the madness'.

The argument in this book is that taking her cue from de Osuna and Laredo and the tradition of *theologia mystica*, Teresa is engaging in her own form of 'unknowing' all the better to teach the truths of the contemplative life. We turn now to her ways of doing this.

16   The original text, begun between 1562 and 1566, her next literary venture after the *Vida,* is conserved in an autograph manuscript in the Escorial (Herafter CE) which was then amended by García of Toledo. Between 1566 and 1569 Teresa recopied this manuscript incorporating García's corrections as well as reorganizing chapters and headings; this is known to us as the Valladolid codex (Hereafter CVA). As copies of the *Camino* proliferated Teresa planned a version for publication using CVA as its basis. This third version is named the Toledo codex (Hereafter CT); clearly, as Efrén de la Madre de Dios and Otger Steggink put it, the intention in writing this text was 'to reach the general public' (1962:181). One instance that we have where Teresa intended her writings to circulate beyond the sisters of the reform to have a wider reading public. As Weber remarks: 'The revisions of the *Way of Perfection* allow us to observe, with particular clarity, not only the degree to which Teresa's stylistic decisions were deliberate but also the extent to which style was, for Teresa, a pragmatic issue' (Weber 1990:80).

17   *Haced bien, hijas, que no os quitarán el Pater nóster y el Avemaría... Parece que reprehende a los Inquisidores que prohiben libros de oración.*

The direction of locution

After Teresa's death in 1582 the Discalced Carmelites, on the recommendation of St. John of the Cross, approached the Augustinian friar and professor of Hebrew at Salamanca University, Fray Luis de León, to edit her texts for publication. Luis, a theologian with a humanistic bent and from *converso* origins himself and who had spent five years in the prisons of the Inquisition, knew something of the dangerous climate within which such mystical texts would be received and engaged in his task with perception and insight (See Rivers 1984:122). The first edition of her works was published with remarkable speed in 1588 with a dedicatory letter to Ana de Jésus, Prioress of the Discalced in Madrid and close friend of John. Luis begins his letter by stating:

> I never knew, or saw, Mother Teresa of Jesus while she lived on earth; but now that she lives in Heaven I do know her, and I see her almost continuously in two living images of herself which she left us – her daughters and her books.
>
> (Peers CW III:368)

From the beginning Luis recognized how 'alive' Teresa's texts were and how dependent they were on the 'oral community' of Carmelites that she had created:

> I believe that your reverences are important witnesses, for you are quite similar models of excellence: I never remember reading her works without imagining that I am listening to Your Reverence's voices, nor, conversely, do I ever hear you talk without feeling that I am reading the words of the Mother. Those who have experience of this will know that it is the truth.
>
> (Peers CW III:372)

For Luis, Teresa's writings *must* be understood within the context of the oral community. Like Wittgenstein's, they benefit from being read aloud and strive to repeat the patterns, rests and pauses of speech with which she was familiar. The texts are peppered with '*errs*', '*umms*' and '*puess*' as she seeks at headlong pace to transcribe the oral to the written. Take, for example, this breathless interruption to the exposition of the 'Prayer of Quiet' in Mansion Four of the *Moradas*:

> God help the mess I've gotten into! I've already forgotten what I'm writing about as business and poor health have forced me to put this work on one side until things were better, and as I have a bad memory everything will come out confused as I can't return to read it all over again. Perhaps everything I say is confused – that's what it feels like anyway.[18]

> (M:4.2.1)

Commenting on Teresa's style, and possibly having in mind passages such as the above, the Spanish critic Menéndez Pidal wrote:

> St. Teresa does not really write, but speaks through writing; thus the excitement of her emotional syntax constantly overflows the restrictions of ordinary grammar.
>
> (Menéndez Pidal 1942:135)

Like Wittgenstein she is not adverse to giving snatches of reported dialogue and will often introduce more than one narrative voice into the text:

> O Lord, Lord! Are You our Model and Master? Yes, indeed! Well then, what did Your honour consist of, You who honoured us? Didn't you indeed lose it in being humiliated unto death? No, Lord, but You won it for all.
>
> (CVA:36:5)

---

18   *¡Válame Dios en lo que me he metido! Ya tenía olvidado lo que tratava, porque los negocios y salud me hacen dejarlo al major tiempo; y como tengo poca memoria irá todo desconcertado,por no poder tornarlo a leer, y an quizás se es todo desconcierto cuanto digo. Al menos es lo que siento.*

She presents us her readers with open questions:

> And supposing my Lord that there are others who are like myself, but have not realized this?... Oh God help me sisters! If we only knew what honour really is and what is meant by losing it!
>
> (CVA:36:3)

> Why do we serve the Lord in so doubtful a way...? Who is plunging you into those perils?
>
> (CVA:18.9)

Like Wittgenstein, too, she puts questions in her interlocutors' mouths so that she can answer them:

> But why, you will say, does the Prioress excuse us? Perhaps she would not if she knew what was going on inside us.
>
> (CVA:10.7)

> What do you think His will is, daughters? That we should be altogether perfect, so as to be one with Him and with the Father, as in His Majesty's prayer. See how far we are from attaining this!
>
> (M:5:3)

As de Certeau suggests, when we read passages such as these later ones from the *Moradas* where she has perfected her craft it is almost as though we can see the sisters round us, pressing nearer to hear what she has to tell us (see also M:6.4, 3.1, 4.1, 4.2). Her discourse, then, presupposes and arranges a community of discourse – a Wittgensteinian *Sprachspiel* in a *Lebensform*.

Contradiction

In his dedicatory letter Luis de León also defended Teresa's habit of 'failing to carry her argument to its conclusion, but introducing other arguments which often break the thread of her sense' (Peers CW III:373). Throughout her writings Teresa is not concerned to reproduce the classical Latin style of the new Renaissance humanism. Hers is a 'rough-and-ready' style whose directness is its appeal.

As befits the *stulta sapientia* of the *theologia mystica* Teresa, like de Osuna, frequently employs paradox to shift meaning to the point where it begins to break down. The soul in the third degree of prayer in the *Vida* is:

> Rejoicing in this agony with ineffable joy... the state is glorious folly... a heavenly madness... delectable disquiet... So delectable is this distress that life holds no delight which can give greater satisfaction.
>
> (V:24)

In this respect Menéndez Pidal describes her style in a similar vein to Luis de León when he writes:

> Her incessant ellipses; confused grammatical arguments; enormous parentheses, which cause the reader to lose the train of thought; lines of reasoning that are never completed because of interruptions, verbless sentences.
>
> (Menéndez Pidal 1942:135)

I suggest here that Teresa *deliberately* writes in this confusing way as a true daughter of the *theologia mystica* of de Osuna, Laredo and *Los Recogidos*. The understanding, as for de Osuna, must be thwarted to allow the soul's direct access to God through *recogimiento*. The tumbling morass of sentences, adverbs, meandering constructions and exclamations only helps to serve that purpose. Rivers again:

> She refuses to accept the analytical or linear sequentiality of linguistic discourse, and she strives for simultaneity, for saying everything all at once, as it actually happens, 'writing with many hands'.
>
> (Rivers 1984:127, see e.g. CV:20:6)

Avoiding conclusions: humility

The whole groundwork of prayer is based on humility and that the more a soul lowers itself in prayer the more God raises it up.

(V:22.11)

In an important essay on Teresa's *Moradas* published in 1983 (Flasche 1983) Hans Flasche points out the importance of the verb *parecer* – 'it seems, it appears' in *Las Moradas*. *Parecer,* he writes, 'is one of the most important words in Saint Teresa's lexicon' (Flasche 1983:447). She uses the verb repeatedly in all her texts, creating a deliberate atmosphere of incertitude and provisionality which can only assist in the 'disguising' of Teresa's intentions with regard to her exposition of the 'mystical theology'. Pictures and suggestions are 'offered' to the reader as possible solutions and answers she has found: once again we have the familiar 'stammering, broken voice' of Teresa.[19] In the *Moradas,* for example, it appears frequently: '*Paréceme que aun no os veo satisfechas* /It seems to me that you're still not satisfied' (M:5:1). '*Paréceme que estáis con deseo de ver qué se hace esta palomica*/It seems to me you have a desire to see what this little dove is doing' (M:5.4). '*Paréceme que os estoy mirando cómo decís*/It seems to me that I can see you asking' (M:6.6). Once again the rhetorical strategies we identified above are coming into play. Accompanying this studied incertitude is Teresa's continual insistence that as an unlettered '*mujercilla*' she is not qualified to talk on such lofty matters:

For the love of God, let me work at my spinning wheel and go to choir and perform the duties of religious life, like the other sisters. I am not meant to write: I have neither the health nor intelligence for it.

(Peers CW:1.xxxix)

19   See, for example, the opening passage of *Las Moradas* that was considered in the Introduction and to which we will return shortly.

She frequently repeats the claim that she is unqualified and useless to the task (see M:4.2.1 quoted on p.148 above). It is notable that these linguistic devices become more evident when Teresa talks of the more 'inexpressible' elements of prayer such as in the Fourth Mansions of the *Moradas* quoted above. The phrase 'little woman' or 'stupid woman' was a typical theological attack on women's inadequacy when it came to questions of doctrine or theology. Bartolomé de Medina had denounced her as '*mujercilla*', saying that her nuns would be better off 'staying in their convents and praying and spinning' (Weber 1990:36).

As Weber shows in her classic exposition of this tactic, Teresa's defence was to 'embrace stereotypes of female ignorance, timidity, or physical weakness but disassociate herself from the double-edged myth of woman as seducible/seductive' (1990:36). For example, in *Vida* 11:14:

> As for a poor woman (*mujercita*) like myself, a weak and irresolute creature, it seems right that the Lord should lead me on with favours (*regalos*), as He now does, in order that I may bear certain afflictions with which He has been pleased to burden me. But when I hear servants of God, men of weight, learning and understanding (*de tomas, de letrados, de entendimiento*) worrying so much because He is not giving them devotion, it makes me sick to listen to them... They should realise that since the Lord does not give it to them they do not need it.

As Weber remarks: 'With disarming modesty she concedes to women's intellectual inferiority in a way that frees her to explore a new theological vocabulary' (1990:38):

> I shall have to make use of some comparison, for which I should like to apologise, since I am a woman and write simply what I am ordered to write. But this spiritual language is so difficult to use for anyone who like myself has not gone through studies, that I shall have to find some way of explaining myself, and it may be

that most of the time I won't get the comparison right. Seeing so much stupidity will provide some amusement for your Reverence.

(V:11.6)

To which Weber comments:

> In these passages, and in many others, Teresa concedes to women's weakness, timidity, powerlessness and intellectual inferiority but uses the concessions ironically to defend, respectively, the legitimacy of her own spiritual favors, her disobedience of *letrados*, her administrative initiative, her right to 'teach' in the Pauline sense and her unmediated access to scripture.
>
> (Weber 1990:39/40)

For both reader and writer, then, humility is required. The opening sections of the *Moradas* stress the need for 'humility', not just morally but intellectually. Only by this *stulta* can the means be prepared for God to impart *sapientia*. Teresa's 'little woman' is thus the first cousin of the 'unlettered woman' presented by Gallus, Gerson, Laredo, de Osuna and the other masters of the *theologia mystica*.

Disorientation

In Luis de León's letter to Ana de Jésus mentioned above he points out that he does not feel it is necessary to amend the style with which Teresa presents her writing:

> I have neither amended them verbally nor adopted the considerable changes which copies now in circulation have made in the text of them either through the copyists' own carelessness or out of presumption or error... If her critics had a real understanding of Castilian, they would see that that of the Mother is elegance itself. For even though, in certain passages of what she writes, before she completes the sentence that she has begun, she contaminates it with other sentences and breaks the train of thought, often beginning anew with interpolations, nevertheless she inserts her digressions so

skilfully and introduces her fresh thoughts with such grace that the
defect itself is a source of beauty, like a mole on a lovely face.

(Peers CW:III.373)

As we have seen, Luis, her first editor, recognized at the outset that,
as with Wittgenstein, the meaning of Teresa's message was inextricably bound up with the medium of the message: that rag-tag bag of
flooding prose full of errors, inconsistencies, *puess*, *buts* and *errs*, the
very same style that makes the whole work come alive for the reader.
Exclamations litter Teresa's text, as do lengthy repetitions and interpo-
lations in the text. In the *Vida* in particular the sentences tumble out,
making it difficult for the reader, and the translator, to keep up:

At first these things did me harm – so it appeared (*me parece*) – and
it shouldn't have been her fault, but mine; for afterwards my own
wickedness was bad enough, together with the servants we had,
whom for every wrong they were able to assist; that if one had given
me good counsel, to benefit me; rather self-interest blinded them as
did desire me. And because I was never inclined to much wrong
– because I naturally abhorred bad things –, but to the pastime of
pleasant conversation; yet, placed in the situation, I was in the hand
of danger, and would be placing my father and brothers in it as well.

(V 2.5)[20]

20   My translation. This is a very difficult passage to translate and should really
be left as it stands: *Al principio dañáronme las cosas dichas – a lo que me
parece –, y no devía ser suya la culpa, sino mía; porque después mi malicia
para el mal bastava, junto con tener criadas, que para todo mal hallava en
ellas buen aparejo; que si alguna fuera en aconsejarme bien, por ventura me
aprovechara; mas el interese las cegava, coma a mí la afeción. Y pues nunca
era inclinada a mucho mal – porque cosas deshonestas naturalamente las
aborrecía –, sino a pasatiempos de Buena conversación; mas puesta en la
occasion, estava en la mano el peligro, y ponía en él a mi padre y hermanos.*
    Kavanaugh/Rodriguez and Allison Peers both give two varying transla-
tions which at times verge on the ungrammatical like my crude translation
above. I give both in full to illustrate the problems and pitfalls of translating Teresa:

Teresa seems to recognize that in order to convey the vitality of the spiritual world she is trying to communicate to her reader she must also retain the rough-edged inconsistency of speech in real time. Like Wittgenstein's texts, her texts 'show' as much through what they do not say as through what they do. Accordingly, Teresa will often use pictures, metaphors and images to 'disorientate' the discursive intellect and take it to places it would rather not go. We shall see this shortly when we discuss her later work the *Moradas*.

As we have seen above, Teresa frequently uses the 'rhetoric of incompetence'. Thus in *Moradas* 1.2.7 we find the following passage:

> These interior matters are so obscure for our minds *(tan oscuras de entender)* that anyone who knows as little as I will be forced to say many superfluous and even foolish things in order to say something that's right. Whoever reads this must have patience, for I have to have it in order to write about what I don't know. Indeed

> 'These things did me harm, I think, at the beginning, and it wasn't her fault but mine. For afterward my malice was sufficient, together with having the maids around, for in them I found a helping hand for every kind of wrong. If there had been one of them to give me good counsel, I perhaps would have benefited by it; but self-interest blinded them as my vanity did me. I was never inclined to great evil – for I naturally abhorred indecent things – but to the pastime of pleasant conversation; yet, placed, in the occasion, the danger was at hand, and my father's and brothers' reputation was in jeopardy as well' (Kavanaugh and Rodriguez CW I:59).

> 'At first, I believe, these things did me harm. The fault, I think, was not my friend's but my own. For subsequently my own wickedness sufficed to lead me into sin, together with the servants we had, whom I found quite ready to encourage me in all kinds of wrongdoing. Perhaps, if any of them had given me good advice, I might have profited by it; but they were as much blinded by their own interests as I was by desire. And yet I never felt the inclination to do much that was wrong, for I had a natural detestation of everything immodest and preferred passing the time in good company. But, if an occasion of sin presented itself, the danger would be at hand and I should be exposing my father and brothers to it' (Allison Peers CW I:15).

sometimes I take up the paper like a fool (*'una cosa boba'*),[21] for I
don't know what to say or how to begin.

(M:1.2.7)

Following Gerson and de Osuna, the 'fool' or 'little woman' is the one who
is wise in the *'theologia mystica'*.[22] Again, Teresa refers to these things *'tan
oscuras de entender'* – is this another reference to the dark and obscure
knowledge of Dionysius's *theologia mystica* which we have already
analysed? Perhaps, she implies, all of us, writer and reader alike, must
become fools before we can enter the strategy of the 'mystical theology'.

Humour

The soul sometimes laughs to itself when it sees seriously religious
and prayerful persons make a big issue out of some rules of
etiquette which it has already trampled under foot.

(V:21.9)

As is attested by many of her contemporaries and is clear from her
writing, humour was always an important part of Teresa's armoury in
her struggles to establish the Discalced reform. Although examples of
this abound throughout her work perhaps the clearest examples are in
the *Libro de Las Fundaciones* ('Book of the Foundations', hereafter F)
describing in open fashion the recent events around the founding of her
convents in Spain. As Weber points out (Weber 1990:126), the topics
dealt with had to be done so with tact and care, as many of the protago-
nists were still alive and the tension between the Discalced reform and
the Carmelites of the Mitigated Rule remained high (see Tyler 2010a).
She describes her style in the Prologue to the book as *tan pesado* ('too
heavy') and suffering from too much *grosería* ('coarseness'). Weber
describes the history as 'picaresque':

21   Cf. De Osuna and Gerson on the 'fools and women'.
22   Cf. Wittgenstein doing philosophy 'disguised as an old woman': see above.

She slyly reveals that in her determination to do God's work she must rely on her charm, ingenuity, and, at times, deception in order to outwit unenlightened souls, be they landlords, town councilmen, or archbishops.

(Weber 1990:128)

A few examples will suffice:

Chapter 31 describes the difficult foundation at Burgos. Here the Archbishop, Don Cristóbal Vela, was initially enthusiastic, encouraging the sisters to come prior to his granting a licence for the foundation.[23] Teresa describes the struggles to get to Burgos, the rivers in full spate and her own illness. Having finally arrived, Teresa describes how the Archbishop does not want them there and tells them that if they do not have an income and a house of their own they should leave, to which Teresa comments: 'The roads of course were charming and it was such nice weather!' (F:31.21).

Chapter 19 describes the foundation of Salamanca with the full vigour of the picaresque. The house they had chosen (which still stands on the Plaza de Santa Teresa) had previously been occupied by students, and Teresa's description of the first night of herself and an elderly sister, terrified of the evicted students returning on Hallowe'en, is a masterpiece:

When my companion found herself shut up in the room, she seemed to be a little calmer about the students, though she did nothing all the time but look about her fearfully, first in one direction then in another... 'What are you looking for?' I asked her. 'Nobody can possibly get in here.' 'Mother', she replied, 'I am wondering what you would do all alone if I were to die here.'... So I said to her: 'Well, sister, I shall consider what is to be done if the occasion arises: now let me go to sleep'.

(F:19.5)

---

23   His uncle was Teresa's godfather; see Peers CW III:184 fn 2.

One of the most interesting depictions of humour occurs in Chapter 6 which begins with Teresa back with her favourite topic of the *Vida* and the *Moradas* – namely the spiritual life and how progress can be made in prayer. Almost immediately she reaches the 'point of unknowing': 'I wish I knew how to explain myself here, but it is so difficult that I do not know if I shall be able to do so' (F:6.2). However, in this chapter she touches on the controversial subject of raptures and ecstasies, so easily associated with the *alumbrados*. The chapter also deals with the controversial topic of the relationship between spirituality and sexuality and the proximity of sensual with spiritual delights. She gives clear guidelines that prioresses should beware these prolonged 'swoons' or 'raptures' and not encourage them in their sisters. To make her point with humour she refers to an incident that took place at Medina del Campo with a choir nun, Alberta Bautista, and lay sister Inés de la Concepción (See Peers CW III:30 fn 1). In their desire to experience ecstasy they asked for frequent communion from their confessor: 'the result was such an increase in distress that unless they communicated daily they thought they were about to die' (F:6.10). Teresa realizes how unhealthy this attachment has become but has to deal with an obdurate confessor who refuses to believe this can cause anything but good for the sisters. Let Teresa complete the story herself:

> I started to talk to the nuns and to give them many reasons, sufficient, in my opinion, to prove to them that the idea that they would die without this particular help was pure imagination. But the notion was so deeply rooted in their minds that no argument could eradicate it and it was useless to reason with them further. So, seeing that it was in vain, I told them that I had those very desires myself and yet I should stay away from Communion, so that they might realize that they ought not to communicate except when all the nuns did so together: we would all three die together, I said.
>
> (F:6.11)

Potential heretics, timid and difficult nuns, wavering clerics: Teresa encounters each with humanity and warmth, allowing her humour to pepper the narrative and convince us, her readers, of the correctness of her remedies and solutions.

Perhaps the key to her use of humour in the *Fundaciones* lies at the beginning of the Prologue where she stresses the need for humility (*humilidad*) in the enterprise (see 'Humility', above). Humility, humour and grounded or ordinary language: all three rotate around each other to produce the necessary effect on the reader. As we read the accounts we realize that she is gently laughing at us the readers – with all our pomposities, obsessions with prayers, worldly concerns and judgemental attitudes. Yes, we can laugh at the targets of her humour in the *Fundaciones,* but we must always remember that her comments are directed equally at us, her readers.

Ordinary speech

As we have seen, Teresa is conscious of her style; she calls it 'my rough style rather than that of those more elegant/*mi grosero estilo que por otros elegantes*' (CVA:16.9) full of 'imperfection' and 'poverty' (CVA:Prologue). As Allison Peers points out in his 1953 essay *Saint Teresa's Style: A Tentative Appraisal* (Allison Peers 1953), the key note in her style is down-to-earthiness and naturalness. Here again she appears to be a disciple of de Osuna and the *Recogidos* and the simple direct style of the *theologia mystica* of the *Tercer Abecedario*. She states that the manner of writing (like talking) adopted by nuns should be:

> Simple, frank and devout, rather like that of hermits and people who live in retirement. They must use none of the newfangled words – affectations, as I think people call them – which are current in a world always eager for new-fangled things. In all circumstances let them give preference to common expressions rather than to unusual ones.
>
> ('Method for the visitation of convents of the Discalced
> Carmelite nuns' in Allison Peers CW:3.251)

As Allison Peers comments, she avoids learned words (Allison Peers 1953:84) and her text is notable for the lack of precise theological terms especially concerning 'mystical theology'. Indeed, as we have seen, the word 'mystical theology' is only used a handful of times in the *Vida* before it is dropped, not to be used again in her work. The humility of ordinary language is close to the humility of humour and central to the effect she wants to produce in her readers.

In his study *The Vernacular Mind of St. Teresa* (Rivers 1984), Elias Rivers points out how Teresa's 'vernacularism' was a part of the sixteenth-century Spanish humanist movement which deliberately sought to communicate to 'ordinary people' through Castilian rather than Classical Latin. Rivers suggests that in this the simple Latin of Augustine's *Confessions*, as we have already seen an important influence on the young Teresa, was clearly formative for the young woman:

> Teresa of Jesus knew very little Latin, and she deliberately refused to imitate the new style of classical Spanish prose; in a true patristic spirit, she invented her own vulgar style of substandard written Spanish, a style that is clearly anti-academic and even anti-rational.
>
> (Rivers 1984:120)

Thus, in her prose we find that 'classical' Castilian spellings are twisted and subverted, often using more phonetic spelling than grammatical. Thus she uses *ylesia* and *yglesia* for *iglesia* ('church'), *naide* for *nadie* ('no one'), *relisión* for *religion* ('religion') as well as a host of diminutives and familiarizations of words: *mariposita* (little butterfly), *pastorcito* (little shepherd boy), *avecita* (little bird). Allison Peers suggests that she creates words of her own invention, 'charging them with emotional content which another language can only approximately express' (Allison Peers 1953:85): *un disgustillo* (V:12), 'a little annoyance/a little feeling of frustration'; *estos temorcillos* (V:31), 'these little fears'; *centellica pequeñita* (V:15), 'the tiniest of tiny sparks' – this latter being her appropriation of the classical phrase *scintilla* from the *theologia mystica* to describe the point at which the soul meets the divine.

Her conversational and immediate style, Rivers suggests, is deliberate and intentional:

She learned to read Spanish fluently as a young girl and knew that she had an advantage there that she could never have in the official Scholastic language of the Western Church, with its exclusively male priesthood. Her Spanish was not structured, as Louis of Granada's and John de Valdés's was, by a familiarity with written Latin, whether ecclesiastical or neo-classical. When she wrote, she neglected, or perhaps deliberately avoided, the normal spelling and syntax of the Spanish texts that she had voraciously read.

> (Rivers 1984:121)

If this is the case, Teresa in her 'rough speech' is deliberately positioning herself in her writings with her beloved *espirituales* of the *recogimiento* movement such as Pedro de Alcantara rather than the sophisticated *letrados* with their more polished and scholastic Latin rhetoric. Teresa's *Sprachspiel*, then, may be considered coarse, vulgar or stupid, but she is happy with this as it serves the purpose she wants, namely to 'change the aspect' of her reader:

Your behaviour and language must be like this: let any who wish to talk to you learn your language; and, if they will not, be careful never to learn theirs: it might lead you to hell. It matters little if you are considered coarse (*groseras*) and still less if you are taken for hypocrites: indeed, you will gain by this, because only those who understand your language will come to see you.

> (CVA:20:4–5)

As with Wittgenstein her texts 'show' as much as they 'say', and they 'show' through her (un-)grammatical and linguistic devices in the text. Just as Wittgenstein uses his aporias, strange stories and constructions to create the necessary *Überblick*, so too Teresa uses similar devices to convey the nature of spiritual transformation through *recogimiento*. She is using her text, as does Wittgenstein, as a 'guide to the perplexed' – a way of prodding and prompting us, through hints, sarcasm, humour and ordinary language so that we may eventually see all that lay before us from a new perspective. Like Wittgenstein, she helps remove the scales from our eyes so that we may have a clearer vision of 'all that is the case' (T.1).

TERESA'S STRATEGIES OF AFFECTIVITY

> I would like to know how to explain myself here and it is so difficult that I do not know if I shall be able to do so... I am quite sure, however that souls who are deceived in this way will under-stand if only they will believe me. I know some, souls of great virtue, who have been in such a state for seven or eight hours and everything appeared to them to be rapture (*arrobamiento*), and every virtuous exercise affected them in such a way that they immediately relinquished control of themselves, because they thought that it was not right to resist the Lord; and little by little they might die or become fools if a remedy is not procured. What I understand to be the case here is that when the Lord begins to caress (*regalar*) the soul, our nature, being so fond of pleasure/ delight (*deleite*), abandons itself completely to this pleasure (*gusto*) such that it would not move, or lose what it has gained, for anything in the world. For, in truth, it is much more pleasurable than anything of the world.
>
> (F:6.2)

So far in this chapter I have argued how Teresa uses six strategies of deconstruction or unknowing to soften the rational defences of the reader. To conclude the chapter I will now turn to the other side of the unknowing-affective strategy: the affective element. I will turn first to Teresa's very special and deliberate vocabulary.[24]

---

24 A version of the following passage has already been printed in *Sources of Transformation: Revitalising Christian Spirituality*, ed. E. Howells and P.M. Tyler (Continuum, 2010). There I enlarge the discussion of this chapter to include Teresa's *Meditations on the Song of Songs* which space does not permit me to enlarge upon here.

Gustos, gozos, regalos, deleites and *sabors* pepper Teresa's works. On the one hand, as Allison Peers argues (Allison Peers 1944:xxi), they may be seen as manifestations of her 'rough hewn style', the homely style of ascetics and hermits that I analysed above; a desire to avoid the hifalutin' terms of a spiritual elite (the *letrados)* for more simple, homely words to which her audience will respond. However, on the other hand, the words themselves are ambiguous and Teresa's use of them opens up a whole new 'epistemology of delight' for her exploration of the supernatural and mystical. In her use of the erotic and spiritual, the blending of *eros* and *agape*, the human and divine, the key style and tone, as we may have become accustomed to by now, is *ambiguity*. Before we analyse her use of the terms it is useful to review them.

Gusto is a favourite of Teresa's. Despite attempts to 'tidy up' her prose, both Allison Peers (1944) and Kavanaugh and Rodriguez (1987) convey something of the ambiguity in their translations. In all, the word appears 185 times in her works, 52 in the *Vida,* 20 in the *Fundaciones,* 19 and 22 in the *Camino* Valladolid and Escorial codex respectively, 32 in the *Moradas* and 33 in the *Meditaciones*. As her writing and style evolve so does her subtlety and use of the word.

The term first appears in Chapter 3 of the *Vida* where Teresa contrasts her new (enforced) life in the Augustinian convent of *Santa María de Gracia* with her previous life of sensuality: '*Mirava más el gusto de mi sensualidad y vanidad quo lo bien que me estava a mi alma/*I looked more to the pleasure of sensuality and vanity than to what was good for my soul' (V:3.2). Thus at its earliest appearance *gusto* is associated with the dubious sensual pleasures she had described in the previous two chapters:

I began to dress in finery and to desire to please and look pretty, taking great care of my hands and hair and about perfumes and all empty things in which one can indulge, and which were many, for I was very vain.

(V:2.2)

This process led eventually to some sort of sensual dalliance with one of her cousins. This struggle between the 'things of God' and the *'contentos y gustos y pasatiempos sensuales'* (V:7.17) continues throughout the early stages of the young girl's journey to discover herself. Teresa herself was clearly a lady of some sensuality and she found in prayer a difficulty to reconcile the two 'so inimical to each other'. At this stage in the *Vida*, and in her writing about these experiences, Teresa contrasts the *gustos* and *contentos* with the *mercedes*, the greater 'favours' that the Lord will give her in prayer (V:7.17). Yet already by Chapter 8 she talks of the *gustos* 'bestowed by God'; one of her first uses of the term as a description of that which occurs in prayer rather than that which is connected purely with the sensual appetites. Of these *gustos* ('delights' [Kavanaugh and Rodriguez CW:8.9], 'consolations' [Allison Peers 1944:8]), as she now begins to call them, she will tell us more later. But she makes clear, and this will be a constant theme throughout her writing, that one of the purposes of prayer is *gusto* – delight, sensuality, sensuousness – and 'The Lord' will indeed 'take delight' *(regalarla)* by entering the soul. This new description of prayer in terms of sensuality and delight climaxes towards the end of *La Vida* in passages such as the famous description of the soul caressed by the Golden Cherub in the *Vida* 29:13 (and so memorably immortalized by Bernini's great statue of 'Teresa in Ecstasy' at Santa Maria della Vittoria in Rome). However, before this point we find this memorable passage from V:27:

> In this other case, nothing: even that little bit of just listening, which it did in the past, is all gone. One finds everything already cooked and eaten, there's nothing to do but enjoy, *(gozar)*, like someone who without learning or working to know how to read, or even studying at all, would suddenly find all knowledge already known in itself, without knowing how or where, for he hadn't even ever worked even to learn the ABC's.
>
> (V:27:8)

As we have seen above, Teresa's ambiguous use of *gusto* is often accompanied by *regalo*. Of the two terms it is perhaps the more ambiguous.

Although Allison Peers translates it as 'comfort of the soul' in the passage from the *Fundaciones* with which we began this section he adds the following note:

> The real meaning of this ubiquitous word here is 'show signs of affection for'; and 'pet', 'caress', 'fondle' though hardly seemly in the context, would not, as far as the actual sense is concerned, be too strong.
>
> (Peers CW:iii.27)

What we see in the passage from the *Fundaciones* with which we began this section is some of Teresa's most mature reflection and use of the terms. Allison Peers is not the only one to feel unease with her sensual and ambiguous language here, a strategy that she will employ in those other two mature works, the *Moradas* and the *Meditaciones*.[25] Further on in this passage Teresa describes how love will cause the novice 'sense pleasure' *(gusto en el sentido)*. Jerónimo Gracián, one of the first of her reader-editors, substituted this with *sensible en el sentido* which is perhaps less ambiguously sensual than *gusto en el sentido*. However, her later editor Báñez restored the original. Such problems arise throughout the manuscript and suggest the problems her first readers had with her sensual language (see Allison Peers 1944:27; De la Madre de Dios and Steggink 1997:693–695). Despite, or perhaps because of this ambiguity *regalo* remains one of her favourite words for describing things of God and occurs frequently in her works, especially her later works.

Like *regalos* and *gustos*, *deleites*, *gozos* and *sabor* again occur with abundance throughout her works. *Deleites* appears 108 times, almost as many as *gustos*, and *gozos* 82 times. Together with *sabor* Teresa frequently uses them to convey the right mixture of the sensual and spiritual that she hopes to achieve. By these means, I am suggesting here, she is able to initiate the necessary *transformation of affect* so central to her 'mystical strategy'.

25 See Tyler 2010c.

STRATEGIES OF AFFECTIVITY IN *LAS MORADAS*

An examination of Teresa's last great work, *Las Moradas* (literally, 'The Mansions' or '*El Castillo Interior*/The Interior Castle', hereafter M), shows how she has finally honed her use of the strategies of the *theologia mystica* to present her own *Summa* of affective spirituality, the teaching and propagation of which had been her lifelong task.

Following conversations reported with Jerónimo Gracián (see Allison Peers CW:ii.188) and others, Teresa tells us that she began work on the *Moradas* on Trinity Sunday (2 June 1577) in Toledo. Five years before her death, she was 62 years old, and her reform of the order was going badly.[26] As well as conflict between the Discalced and Carmelites of the Mitigated Observance, Teresa's health was poor at this point (she writes of headaches, nausea and a 'great noise in her ears' in M:4). The most high-profile casualty of this conflict was St. John of the Cross who was imprisoned in Toledo (see Tyler 2010a). From this time we also have the famous description of her by the new papal nuncio in Spain, Felipe Sega, who took up his post in June 1577:

> A troublesome, restless, disobedient and stubborn female, who under the guise of devotion invented bad doctrines, running around outside the cloister against the order of the Tridentine Council and prelates, instructing like a teacher in defiance of what St. Paul taught, who ordered women not to teach.[27]

---

26 For more detail see Efrén de la Madre de Dios y Otger Steggink, *Tiempo y vida de Santa Teresa*, Madrid: Católica, 1977:701–805.

27 *Fémina inquieta, andariega, desobediente y contumaz, que a título de devoción inventaba malas doctrinas, andando fuera de la clausura contra el órden del concilio tridentino y prelados, enseñando como maestra contra lo que San Pablo enseñó, mandando que las mujeres no enseñasen* in Francisco de Santa María *Reforma de los descalzos de Nuestra Senora del Carmen de la primitiva observancia, hecha por Santa Teresa de Jesús* (Madrid 1644–1655 1:556).

In July, seemingly as a result of Sega's appointment, she left Toledo and completed the work at San José, Avila on 29th November the same year – a remarkably short six months required for completion. Due to crises within the order both at Toledo and Avila, commentators suggest that she spent a mere three months in actual writing. This included being re-elected Prioress of the *Encarnación* in October, an election which was later reversed by Tostado (Commissary General of the Spanish Carmelites appointed in 1576), and the appearance of a scurrilous pamphlet denouncing both Teresa and Gracián (See Kavanaugh and Rodriguez CW:ii.265).[28]

Gracián described her decision to write the *Moradas* in a conversation recorded after the event:

Being her confessor and speaking with her once in Toledo about many things concerning her spirit, she said to me: 'Oh, how well that point is written in the book of my life, which the Inquisition has!' And I said to her, 'Well, since we can't recover it, write down what you remember, and other things, and write another book, and explain the basic doctrine without identifying the person who has experienced what you say there.'[29]

Which suggests that, like the *Vida*, the dialectic of concealment with the Inquisition was present in the work from its inception. Weber notes, referring to the oftentimes ramshackle rhetoric of the *Moradas*: 'A bride is hidden in Teresa's castle: the dangerous language of erotic

28 As well as the original autograph held in the convent of the Discalced sisters in Seville there are several copies. The Toledo copy bears the date 1577 which seems to have been the copy made as Teresa wrote. The Discalced sisters of Córdoba hold a copy in Gracián's hand while the University of Salamanca possesses P. Ribera's copy (1588).

29 Quoted in Ahlgren (1996:61) from Gracián, *Anotaciones al P Ribera* in Antonio de San Joaquín *Año Teresiano, diario histórico, panegyrico moral, en que se descruben las virtudes, succesos y maravillas de la seráphica y mystica Doctora de la Iglesia Santa Teresa de Jésus* (Madrid 1733–1769, 7:149).

spirituality is concealed by a proliferation of competing images. Her avowed incompetence constitutes in reality a rhetoric of obfuscation' (Weber 1990:99). For Weber, the 'bride' of the Interior Castle, both 'concealed and protected' by Teresa's rhetoric, is erotic spirituality itself, so dangerous in open expression in Spain of the 1570s (Weber 1990:118–122).

Whereas I would agree that Weber is right to see a sensual or erotic side in the *Moradas,* the argument of this book is that Teresa, true heir of the masters of the *theologia mystica,* sees the need to engage with the *affectus* if contemplative transformation is to be effected in the listener. However, it would be a mistake to see Teresa as understanding this process as an end in itself. For Teresa the end of the sensual self-examination of the *affectus* is to return us to the world, our responsibilities to our fellow human beings and the possibilities that arise from our human relationships with each other. In Weber's interpretation the erotic is an end in itself for Teresa, and although, as she says, 'Teresa, who found herself on the frontiers of contemporary orthodoxy, nevertheless felt the idea of spiritual marriage so crucial that she was willing to continue to take risks' (Weber 1990:121), it is not so clear from her description just *why* Teresa should go to these great lengths and what she was hoping to achieve by them. One of the attractions of interpreting Teresa's writings from the perspective of the Wittgensteinian 'strategy of affectivity' presented here is that, unlike Weber's notion of 'concealed erotic spirituality' this question is answered. As we have seen, Teresa, using her heritage and understanding of the *theologia mystica* inherited from de Osuna and Laredo, is able to couple a strategy of unknowing with a strategy of affectivity which will lead to deeper prayer, 'good works' (*Obras*) and responsible action in the world for others.

Weber has argued that Teresa deliberately obscures the erotic spirituality of the *Moradas* – 'like a bride in the castle' – all the better to protect it from the Inquisition. She suggests that in the 1560s when Teresa wrote the *Meditaciones* it was possible to be more explicit about the 'erotico-maternal' matrix that she describes there in her commentary on the Song of Songs. By 1577 the situation had become more difficult, exemplified by Gracián's order for Teresa to burn the text of the *Meditaciones* in 1580 (See Weber 1990:117; Tyler 2010c). None other than Luis de León had been imprisoned between 1572 and 1575 for publishing his vernacular version of the Song of Songs. Weber also mentions the *beatas* of Llerena, burned at the stake in 1579 for reporting, among other things, erotic visions of Christ's humanity and his union with his followers (See Llorca 1980:103–121; Weber 1990:120).

While accepting that Weber's thesis reveals something of the tension that went into the writing of the *Moradas* I would argue here that the work may have been more than an attempt to 'conceal or hide erotic spirituality'. As we have seen throughout this book, from Dionysius through the Victorines, Balma, Gerson, Laredo and de Osuna a mystical strategy runs throughout the medieval Western Christian tradition. As we have argued, this tradition possesses several strategies, that of affectivity being one of them.[30] Starting with Dionysius, *eros* has a vital role to perform in the 'mystical dance' and Teresa's *gusto*-led affectivity is but the latest manifestation of the thread that has been traced throughout this book.

Therefore, I suggest here that the *Moradas* is better interpreted, from the Wittgensteinian perspective of this book, as using linguistic strategies of unknowing and affectivity to lead the reader to personal affective transformation for engagement in *Obras* in the world. There is insufficient space here to give a full exposition of the *Moradas*, but I will draw out some of the main passages that support this interpretation.

---

30 Using a Wittgensteinian approach this book has examined two strategies of the *theologia mystica*: that of unknowing and affectivity. However, I do not wish to suggest that these are the only strategies of the tradition of *theologia mystica*. The argument here is that these two are clearly visible and their influence from one set of writers to another can be clearly traced, as has been done here. It seems from the authors surveyed here that this 'thread' forms an essential component of the tradition of *theologia mystica*. However, I also acknowledge that there may be other, equally important threads that future studies will reveal. Weber's concentration on the strategy of concealment is a good candidate and needs further investigation.

THE FIRST MANSIONS

If we see the *Moradas* along the lines that are being suggested here,
then in the very first paragraph of the 'first mansion' we see laid out the
strategy we have presented in this chapter: [31]

> While I was beseeching our Lord today to speak for/through
> me (*por mí*), as I was unable to find a thing to say (*no atinaba a
> cosa que decir*), or how to begin to comply with this obedience,
> what I will say now presented itself (*ofreció*) to begin with this
> starting point: that we consider our soul to be like a castle, totally
> of diamond or very clear crystal, where there are many abodes
> (*aposentos*), as in heaven there are many mansions. Now if we
> consider it carefully, sisters, the soul of a just person (*el alma del
> justo*) is nothing else but a paradise where He says he takes his
> delights (*El tiene sus deleites*). Well then, what do you think such
> an abode would be like where a King so powerful, so wise, so pure,
> so full of good things, takes his delight? I cannot find anything with
> which to compare the great beauty and capacity (*capacidad*)[32] of
> the soul; and truly our intellects will no more be able to grasp this
> than they can comprehend God, no matter how keen they are, for
> He Himself said that He created us in his own image and likeness.
>
> (M:1.1.1)

Our intellects (*nuestros entendimientos*) cannot grasp that which we
seek – whether it be the nature of God or the nature of the soul (Teresa
boldly implies that epistemologically they present the same situation to
the intellect). Rather than presenting an intellectual or conceptual notion
of the soul, something 'presents itself' to her.[33] Teresa seems quite precise

---

31 See footnotes to this text presented in the Introduction.
32 Cf. Laredo; see previous chapter.
33 *ofreció*, literally 'offers itself'; it is not 'thought' as Kavanaugh and
    Rodriguez and Allison Peers translate it, nor is it an 'idea' as other trans-
    lators present it (e.g. Benedictines of Stanbrook translation 1906).

in her language that the image or trope of the Castle offers itself or presents itself rather than is thought, since, as she says, our intellects and understanding cannot grasp what is being presented. Rather, it is talked about in terms of being 'enjoyed' (*se deleita*) by 'the King'. The dialectic of affectivity lies at the heart of this epistemology. The true nature of ourselves, our relation to God, and God in God's self are described in terms of affectivity and delight. Just as de Osuna quoted Proverbs 8:31 in his chapter on the *sabrosa saber*, so again Teresa makes allusion to the same passage when she describes the soul as the place 'wherein our Lord takes delight'. As with de Osuna, so with Teresa, knowledge is obtained from 'tasting' the delights of the *gustos espirituales*, and this will become apparent as the reader moves through the 'castle'.

Within the context of the linguistic strategies of unknowing presented earlier, this passage is revealing. Teresa presents a series of metaphors, one after another, for the soul – each one is piled one after the other: a castle; totally of diamond or other clear crystal; of many abodes, like the heavenly mansions; a paradise where He takes His delights; and like God in God's self. The effect certainly leads to spatial and emotional disorientation.[34] This spatial instability continues throughout the chapter, and indeed the whole book. As she states in M:1.1.3, the aim of this disorientating metaphor is to illustrate the 'favours' which the Lord will grant:

> It is necessary that you keep this comparison in mind. Perhaps God will be pleased to let me use it to explain something to you about the favours He is happy to grant souls and the differences between these favours.
>
> (M:1.1.3)

The recipients will be 'delighted and awakened/*se regalarán y despertarán*' (M:1.1.4) by these favours, since the castle itself is not just beautiful but 'full of delight/*deleitoso*' (M:1.1.5) to those who enter it. It defines itself in terms of 'delight'.

---

34 In 1.2.1 more metaphors are introduced: 'this pearl from the Orient, this tree of life'. In 1.2.8 it is a 'palmetto fruit'.

As well as the necessity for delight the first part of the mansion frequently mentions 'self-knowledge/*el propio conocimiento*' (M:1.1.8, 1.2.8,[35] 1.2.9, 1.2.13[36]) this is not the 'head knowledge' of ideas and thought, but more an 'experiential knowledge' closely connected to the libidinal springs of delight, the *affectus* of the Victorines. 'Without experience/*Si no hay experiencia*' (M:1.1.9), she says, it is difficult to understand what she is talking about. Experiential reflection is a necessary component of her presentation – her 'offering'.

Self-knowledge, humility and delight: all the components of our strategy of unknowing/affectivity are presented in these dense first pages of the *Moradas*. The final element of Teresa's strategy – the 'mystical strategy as transformational' – is brought out towards the end of the first mansions. Here she notes that the soul 'will not be able to enjoy' (M:1.2.14) the pleasures of the Lord if there are impediments in our outer life such as 'possessions, honour or business affairs'. To proceed further, 'to enter the second dwelling place', the seeker 'must give up unnecessary things and business affairs' (M:1.2.14). Only by transforming our 'outer' attachments can 'inner' attachments be altered. In Wittgenstein's terms, only by a new 'Form of Life' can we be liberated from the 'fly-bottle' in which we find ourselves. As with Wittgenstein (and Augustine), a *confessio* is necessary to prompt a 'change of life'. In M:1.2.16 she describes the necessity of each individual sister making 'a good beginning', observing faults and that which leads us from the interior transformation to the exterior. This leads inevitably to her final paragraphs:

> Let us understand, my daughters, that true perfection consists in love of God *and neighbour* (my emphasis); the more perfectly we keep these two commandments the more perfect we will be.
>
> (M:1.2.18)

35 'Oh but if it is in the room of self-knowledge! How necessary this room is – see that you understand me – even for those whom the Lord has brought into the very dwelling place where He abides.' M:1.2.8.
36 'Self-knowledge is the most important thing for us.'

She concludes her impressive opening chapter by giving an example to illustrate the embodied, practical, ethical action she is recommending. In this case, sisters, especially superiors, must be careful about admonishing one another and how they upbraid others for not keeping convent rules, since 'much discretion is necessary'.

The first mansion of the *Moradas* is a *tour de force* of mystical strategy, combining as it does all the elements of unknowing and affectivity which I have presented in this book. The movement in the chapter from the opening passages saturated in metaphor and scriptural allusion, the subtle use of strategies of unknowing and affectivity, and the final presentation of a practical 'case study' will be typical of how she proceeds throughout the book. Each chapter will contain all three elements and, seemingly to emphasize the point, each chapter will end with a very practical example to illustrate the points that have been made. Mansion Four, for example, having discussed the 'prayer of quiet' and 'raptures', gives some guidelines at the end on how to deal with nuns who appear to be suffering from such raptures but are simply physically ill. This is done with humour (see above), discretion and discernment:

> Since [these sisters] feel some consolation interiorly and a languishing and weakness exteriorly, they think they are experiencing a spiritual sleep (which is a prayer a little more intense that the prayer of quiet) and they let themselves become absorbed. The more they allow this the more absorbed they become because their nature is further weakened, and they fancy they are being carried away with rapture [*arrobamiento*]. I call it being carried away in foolishness [*abobamiento*] because it amounts to nothing more than wasting time and wearing down one's health... By sleeping and eating and avoiding so much penance the person got rid of the stupor.
>
> (M:4.3.11)

This recurring structure is typical of the *Moradas* and marks it out, I suggest, as her most mature expression of all the elements of the *theologia mystica* that she has inherited from the tradition.

THE REMAINING MANSIONS

As already stated, space does not permit a line-by-line account of the *Moradas*. Indeed, it could be argued that the main themes are sketched out in the first mansions and then developed throughout the book: the strategies are constantly present throughout the work and numerous more examples than are enumerated here may be cited to support the interpretation. As is clear, each chapter takes the same general form of the first chapter and encourages the reader to move, through unknowing, self-awareness and affectivity, towards that transformed place which will allow the necessary *Obras* as we return to embodied existence in the world around us.

In overview, the *Moradas* takes the basic form of three mansions which prepare the self in the way described for transformation. True to her roots in the *theologia mystica* she does not describe this transformation, but through the sort of verbal strategies we have explored suggests how this may come about for the person. Thus, after the preparations of the first three mansions, the fourth is essentially the 'mansion of transformation' where the change may occur. Thereafter the final three mansions discuss the consequences of the transformation with particular emphasis on the move from 'rapture' to 'works'/*obras*. We recall the passage:

When I see people very diligently observing the sort of prayer that they have and very wrapped up in it when they have it (for it seems that they will not let the thought move or stir in case they lose a small morsel of the *gusto* or devotion that they have had), I realise how little they understand of the road to the attainment of union. They think that the whole business lies in such things. No, sisters, no! The Lord desires works and that if you see a sick woman to whom you can give some help, never be affected by the fear that your devotion will suffer, but take pity on her: if she is in pain you should feel pain too; if necessary, fast so that she may have your food, not so much for her sake as because you know that the Lord desires it.

(M:5.3)

Thus, in the second and third mansions she emphasizes (M:2.1.7; cf. Vida:4.2, 11.10–15) that the *gustos* should not be strived for: 'souls shouldn't be thinking about consolations *(regalos)* at this beginning stage'. Our non-thinking extends towards not desiring the *regalos*. Once again she emphasizes that this is an *experiential* process and we, the readers, 'cannot begin to recollect yourselves by force but only by gentleness/*y cómo no ha de ir a fuerza de brazos el comenzarse a recoger, sin con suavidad*' (M:2.1.10). As always with this experiential learning, 'it is very important to consult persons with experience' (cf. Dionysius and the initiation of Hierotheus). In these second mansions Teresa talks of the disturbance of the intellect: 'Here the intellect *(entendimiento)* is more alive and the faculties *(potencias)* more skilled. The blows from the artillery strike in such a way that the soul cannot fail to hear' (M:2.1.3). The devils 'represent the esteem one has in the world, one's friends and relatives, one's health and a thousand other obstacles'. The power of intellectual representation is clearly a block to *recogimiento*, and in Teresa's language is used by the devil for that purpose. The dangers of the intellect are clearly delineated here. Insofar as the intellect is to be used, it is to remind the person of the importance of persevering with *recogimiento* (M:2.1.4); it must not be used as a critical tool in itself.

Even in these early mansions, the intellect is there to serve the function of helping the soul find *gustos, mercedes* and *regalos* within *recogimiento*, rather than striving after intellectual comprehensions. We are being prepared '*para gozar su gloria*' – 'to enjoy his glory' (M:2.1.11).

Regarding the third mansions, she characterizes the people at this stage of the journey as being:

Fond of doing penance and setting aside periods for recollection [*horas de recogimiento*]; they spend their time well, practising works of charity towards their neighbours; and are very balanced in their use of speech and dress and in the governing of their households.

(M:3.1.5)

Clearly the *entendimiento* is well-developed! To pass this level, which she compares with the rich young man of Matthew 19:16–22, we must pass into the place of unknowing and delight/*gusto*:

> Let us prove ourselves, my Sisters, or let the Lord prove us, for He knows well how to do this even though we often don't want to understand it.
>
>   (M:3.1.7)

The action required 'must not be fabricated in our imaginations but proved by deeds' (M:3.1.7): the person must move from interior reflection to embodied action. As she says in M:3.1.9, a certain humility of intellect is required for this process to work: 'The Lord will give you understanding of them so that out of dryness you may draw humility – and not disquiet, which is what the devil aims after.' The possession of the *entendimiento* is also connected with worldly success:

> After these years, when it seems they have become Lords of the world or at least clearly disillusioned in this regard. His Majesty will try them in some minor matters, and they will go about disturbed and afflicted that it puzzles me and makes me fearful.
>
>   (M:3.2.1)

She helps these people by 'compassion/*sentimiento*' and not 'contradicting their reason' (M:3.2.2). The process of unknowing is not initiated through the intellect but the affect. For these people, 'their reason is still very much in control. Love has not yet reached the point of overwhelming reason' (M:3.2.7).[37] She exhorts us to 'let us abandon our reason (*dejemos nuestra razón*) and our fears into His hands' (M:3.2.8).

This 'letting go of the reason' and the move to the affect will occur in the all-important fourth mansions of transformation. At the beginning of this mansion (M:4.1.1) she once again returns to the dilemma that

---

37   *Porque su razá muy en sí; no está aún el amor para sacar de razón.*

she had encountered in the *Vida*: how can the *theologia mystica be explained*? What literary mechanisms, or indeed *strategies*, can be employed to do this?[38]

Her solution is to take Wittgenstein's path: from saying to showing to acting. She cannot *explain* the process:

> As these mansions are much closer to where the King lives, they have great beauty and there are things so delicate to see and understand there, which the understanding does not have the capacity to grasp them, although something might turn out to be well put and not at all obscure to the inexperienced; those who have experience, especially a lot of it, will understand very well.
>
> (M:4.1.2)[39]

As we saw with Wittgenstein, she appeals to those 'who may have had these thoughts already' (cf. T:3) and she will demonstrate by *showing* rather than *saying*. The unknowing of the *theologia mystica* will be maintained, although the *gustos* will be an important part of that transformative process when eventually they too will fall away as the importance of embodied existence in the *Obras* takes hold.

Consequently, as well as delineating the nature of the 'mystical strategy' as an unknowing-affective strategy, Teresa goes into greater depth here than she has ever done before to map this affective territory. Following Weber's suggestions, Teresa must know of the dangers here (The *Meditaciones* had not long been burnt), so she treads very carefully in defining her 'pleasures of the Lord' ('*gustos*') in such a way

---

38   'Although I think I now have a little more light about these favours the Lord grants to some souls, knowing how to explain them is a different matter' (M:4.1.1).

39   *Como ya estas moradas se llegan más adonde está el Rey, es grande su hermosura y hay cosas tan delicadas que ver y que entender, que el entendimiento no es capaz para poder dar traza cómo se diga siquiera algo que venga tan al justo que no quede bien oscuro para los que no tienen experiencia; que quien la tiene muy bien lo entenderá, en especial si es mucha.*

as to retain their affective power but to protect her from unwelcome attention (and suppression) from the Inquisition.

She distinguishes these *gustos* from the '*contentos*':

> The *contentos* appear to me that what we can call we have acquired from our meditation and petitions to our Lord, which proceed from our natural nature, although in the end God helps this.
>
> (M:4.1.4)[40]

The '*contentos*' are, for Teresa, associated with the *entendimiento* (intellect) and their reception is linked with the work of the intellect described in the first three mansions. During this fourth mansion, the move to the unknowing-embodied strategy is emphasized, and with it the move from the '*contentos*' to the '*gustos*' (delights):

> For we obtain them [the *contentos*] through thoughts [*con los pensamientos*], assisting ourselves, using creatures to help our meditation, and tiring the intellect [*cansado el entendimiento*].
>
> (M:4.2.3)

For Howells (2002:94), the process is defined by a 'developed knowledge or familiarity with the field of prayer', as opposed to 'learning that comes from books'. She describes this as a distinction between 'having experience *of* something' and 'having experience *in* something':

---

40 *Los contentos me parece a mí se pueden llamar los que nosotros adquirimos con nuestra meditación y peticiones a nuestro Señor, que procede de nuestro natural, aunque en fin ayuda para ello Dios.*' Kavanaugh and Rodriguez translate this passage as: 'the term consolations, I think, can be given to those experiences we ourselves acquire through our own meditation and petitions to the Lord'. Teresa, significantly, does not use this language of 'naming experiences'. Here as in many other passages Kavanaugh and Rodriguez show that they are tending towards an epistemological bias based on 'modern mystical' experientialism (see Chapter 1, this volume).

Experience is the skill brought by one who knows not just something *about* the object under view but how to orient and position oneself in *relation* to this object in order to grasp it accurately.

(Howells 2002:94)

As Howells makes clear in his footnote here, he understands the problem with a 'modern mystic', 'experiential' (or indeed Jamesian) interpretation of Teresa:

In modern English, feelings suggest a merely *emotional* sense, whereas Teresa's emphasis is on the *sensory*, epistemological value of these feelings, which the translators judge is better rendered as "experience". The problem is that Teresa's distinction between feelings and experience is then lost.

(Howells 2002:182)

I would go further, in accord with the general thrust of this book, by arguing that on such interpretation hangs Teresa's use of the language of *theologia mystica* to describe the *affective changes* she is asking her reader to respond with. This, as with Wittgenstein, is done through *showing* rather than *saying*, a movement that seems akin to Wittgenstein's increasing familiarity with the 'Field of Language' which ultimately comes from *Lebensformen*. Only precisely *this* sort of knowledge can effect transformation, not 'head knowledge' or 'book knowledge'.

In this vein Teresa now makes very clear (M:4.1.5) that the unique locus of the mystical knowledge is not the 'understanding' but the 'heart' (*el corazón*). At this point she again dissembles claiming: 'I don't know much about these passions of the soul [*estas pasiones del alma*] for I am very stupid [*muy torpe*]'. Again we hear the 'stuttering, broken voice' of the strategy of unknowing using the strategies of contradiction and humility (that voice with which we are now so familiar from Dionysius to Gerson to de Osuna/Laredo). To proceed on the spiritual journey, she says, we must 'not think much but love much/*no está la cosa en pensar mucho, sino en amar mucho*' (M:4.1.7; cf. F:5.2: 'and so do that which best stirs you to love'). This love, this '*amar*' is seen in *deeds* rather than in thoughts.

In M:4.3 she returns to her earlier thoughts in the *Vida* by relating what she is presenting to the prayer of *recogimiento*. As with Osuna, there is a clear statement that the *recogimiento* is connected with 'unknowing': 'Don't think this *recogimiento* is acquired by the intellect (*entendimiento*) striving to think about God within itself, or by the imagination (*imaginación*) imaging Him within itself' (M:4.3.3).[41] However, such 'unknowing' is accompanied by the increase of the affect and cannot exist on its own: 'love must already be awakened' (M:4.3.4). The *entendimiento* cannot be stopped without this:

> When His Majesty desires the intellect to stop, He occupies it in another way and gives it a light so far above what we can attain that it remains absorbed. Then without knowing how the intellect is much better instructed than it was through all the soul's efforts not to make use of it.
>
> (M:4.3.6)

Thus the intellect moves into unknowing as the affect is quickened by the encounter with God. 'Without any effort or noise the soul should strive to cut down the rambling of the intellect [*el dicurrir del entendimiento*] but suspending either it or the *pensamiento*' (M:4.3.7). Teresa seems here to be treading the fine path between ending the discursive intellect and recognizing the danger of an *alumbradismo* like quietism. Her compromise – 'cutting down the rambling' without suspending it – seems to suggest a way out. She has moved from de Osuna's total reliance on the affect at the expense of the intellect. However, although this is what she states in M:4.3 there are enough contradictory statements, as we have seen above, to suggest an alternative reading and that her position is not so far from de Osuna's (and

41   Two explicit references to Osuna in this chapter in 4.3.2 and 4.3.3 show that she is clearly thinking of de Osuna at this point.

possibly the *alumbrados*) as she would have us believe. The soul must 'enjoy' the new place without trying to understand it (M:4.3.7).[42]

As we have seen, Teresa ends the fourth mansions with spiritual advice warning sisters who experience a sort of 'spiritual stupor' which she calls being carried away with 'foolishness' – *abobamiento*. Although there is an element of tongue-in-cheek, Teresa is of course strengthening her anti-*alumbrado* credentials by these sorts of remarks while using the strategy of humour we described earlier. Unlike the *Vida* which contained lengthy accounts of these practices, visions, levitations, locutions and so on, the *Moradas* presents the considered views of a spiritual master on how such phenomena should be treated.

The final three mansions of the *Moradas* are thus concerned with showing how the living out of the transformation she has described is effected through action in the world. What she is proposing is *union with God through action in the world*.

Again, she emphasizes that 'the intellect is not capable of understanding' the 'riches treasures and delights' (*la riqueza y tesoros y deleites*: M:5.1.1) of the fifth mansions. As we would expect by now, although they cannot be grasped by the intellect they can be 'enjoyed' (*gocen*). Yet from this point on she emphasizes 'service of the Lord' (*el servicio de nuestro Señor*) as much as 'self-knowledge' (M:5.3.1). Through a virtuous life one affects others and so ultimately does God's work. She returns once again to her earlier theme, namely the importance of love of neighbour as much as love of God:

> The Lord asks of us only two things: love of His Majesty and love of our neighbour. These are what we must work for...The most certain sign, in my opinion, as to whether or not we are observing these two laws is whether we observe well the love of neighbour... The more advanced you see you are in love for your neighbour the more advanced you will be in the love of God.
>
> (M:5.3.7–8)

---

42 *Goza sin ninguna industria.*

From this she concludes her fifth mansion with the customary practical example of holy living and the exhortation to 'good works' we have already quoted above. This, for her, 'is the true union with His will' (M:5.3.11).

These final mansions enshrine a movement we can also see in Wittgenstein's writings to which we will return to in the following chapter. That is:

- An inextricable link between the theological and the ethical.
- The need for self-knowledge, as the true source of contemplation.
- A strategy that returns the reader to the 'relationships of everyday life'.
- A strategy with transformative power to make a difference in those relationships.

All this takes place within the threefold Wittgensteinian path of saying-showing-acting. For Teresa, this is based on an epistemology of affect, coupled with the path of unknowing. Thus by the time of the sixth mansions Teresa talks of the *vista* of the soul with God[43] – not 'seen in a way that can be called seeing, even by the imagination', but the encounter is determined and defined by desire and 'enjoyment' *'que todo su deseo es tornarla a gozar/*(the soul's) whole desire is to enjoy it once again' (M:6.1.1). Knowledge and vision are gone; only desire remains.

The first chapter of the sixth mansions looks back on the 'trials' of the previous mansions (and the previous forty years of Teresa's life; see M:6.1.7) again couched in familiar terms of the incomprehension of the intellect when faced with the stirrings of the affect (and, also, often the body): *'porque no estaba el entendimiento capaz/*for the understanding had no capacity to comprehend' (M:6.1.9).[44] Looking back on her

---

43 Allison Peers translates as 'sight', Kavanaugh and Rodriguez as 'meeting': from the sense of the first passage of 6.1 'sight' would seem to be a more appropriate translation.

44 *Capaz/Capacidad*. Again, the favourite word of Laredo we explored in the previous chapter and a regular component of *Las Moradas*.

experiences she sees that intellectual comprehension was of little help in dealing with it:

> In sum, there is no remedy in this tempest but to wait for the mercy of God. For at an unexpected time, with one word alone or a chance happening He so quickly calms the storm that it seems there had not been even as much as a cloud in that soul, and it remains filled with sunlight and much more consolation [*consuelo*].
>
> (M:6.1.10)

The process was one of suffering and difficulty, 'having seen itself totally incapacitated' to 'make it understand its nothingness' (*nuestra nonada* M:6.1.11). At such times, for Teresa, 'the best remedy is to engage in external works of charity' (6.1.13). The *gustos* that led us to this place our now transcended, as we have seen, to allow the fullness of the life of 'action in union'.

Having clearly moved from the intellectual discernment of the earlier mansions much of the rest of these mansions are given over to the question of discernment within the realm of unknowing and the affect. Thus in M:6.3 she talks of locutions received, often 'when in darkness of intellect' (M:6.3.5: *oscuridad del entendimiento*) and how they are to be discerned from God, the devil or 'melancholy'.[45]

As Teresa points out in M:6.7.13, the *gustos* of the 'prayer of quiet' are not an end in themselves and although she uses the mystical strategies we have delineated they are for her a 'means to an end', in this case 'the prayer of union' or '*vista*' that she mentions at the beginning of the sixth mansions. These moments of union involve the theological entrance into deep relationship with Christ, the Trinity and the Mother of God. Throughout it all, however, the faculty of the intellect has to be circumvented and the Strategy of Unknowing remains:

---

45 Teresa's term for what we would now refer to as 'mental illness'. See Tyler 2010a.

> You will ask how if nothing is seen one knows that it is Christ, or
> a saint, or His most glorious Mother. This, the soul will not know
> how to explain, nor can it understand how it knows, but it does
> know with the greatest certitude.
>
> (M:6.8.6)

Teresa stipulates throughout a 'divine unknowing' – the Dionysian *stulta sapientia* we described in Chapter Three – and this, for Teresa, is the 'realm of the supernatural' (see M:6.9.18). She concludes these extraordinary sixth mansions by suggesting two aspects that remain from the states she has mentioned here: the one is pain, the other is 'overwhelming joy and delight/*muy excesivo gozo y deleite*' (M:6.11.11). Even through it all, and the discussions of the supernatural unknowing of these states, she returns to the epistemology of delight. Although mixed with pain, as we shall see in the seventh mansions, that delight remains to the end, long after the pain has dropped away. The pain of this union is that which achieves the 'true union' rather than the 'delightful union'. As Howells makes clear (Howells 2002:106–107) this 'true union' – the union with God in the world – is achieved by transcending the *gustos* and so reaching true embodied service in the world. For Teresa, unlike Wittgenstein, this can only be achieved through identification with Christ. At this point we have one of the clearest contrasts between Teresa's approach and Wittgenstein's. Wittgenstein can allow for the possibility of this *Lebensform*, but his job is to provide a vision of it through a *Weltbild*. Teresa, on the other hand, is able to choose the Christian *Weltanschauung* which enables the self to be 'grabbed and turned round' by the passion of union with Christ.

Therefore the final seventh mansions present both the strategy of affect combined with the newer 'true union' of action in the world. This, of course, all happens through her theological eyes in union with Christ in Trinitarian perspective.

At the beginning of the seventh mansions, Teresa repeats her phrase from the first page of the first mansions (alluding to the Book of Proverbs), when she states that the soul is the place where 'The Lord finds his delight/*almas con que tanto se deleita el Señor*' (M:7.1.1). However, in contrast to the earlier mansions she seems to imply that in this 'spiritual marriage/*el matrimonio espiritual*', as was the case implied with the raptures and the prayer of union in the previous mansions, there is here a passing over of the strategies of affect and unknowing, 'for all the faculties are lost'. There is a vision of the Trinity and a 'certain representation of the truth'. At this point Teresa has moved completely into the theological realm – a realm of 'theological' not 'intellectual' knowing. (e.g. M :7.3.8, what Howells refers to as the 'mystical knowing' of Teresa; see Howells 2002). It is a time of quiet 'like the building of Solomon's temple when no sound was heard' (M:7.3.11). 'There is no reason for the intellect to stir or seek anything… the faculties are not lost here, but they do not work, remaining as though in amazement.' The theological content is at its strongest here which fits with Teresa's theological strategy of returning us to Christ through the processes of the *theologia mystica*. Yet, as commentators such as Howells point out (Howells 2002:117), Teresa must 'work hard' to bridge philosophico–psychological divides in her picture of the self with theological imagery and thought, centred around the resemblance of the self to Christ's own union of two natures – the divine and the human. Needless to say, Wittgenstein's anthropology never moves in this direction and does not have such tensions to deal with.

Although Teresa insists that the soul has now 'gone beyond delight' she persists in using the language of delight to describe this place: 'Here one delights [*se deleita*] in God's tabernacle' (M:7.3.13). To the end she seems happy to use paradox as a linguistic strategy to *show* rather than *say* what she is trying to express in these last mansions. Yet, as has been stressed repeatedly, for Teresa, the end-point of her *theologia mystica* is the 'good works, good works/*Obras, Obras*' which will enable action in the world:

This is the reason for prayer, my daughters, the purpose of this spiritual marriage: the birth always of good works, good works… I repeat it is necessary that your foundation consist of more than prayer and contemplation. If you do not strive for virtues and practice them, you will always be dwarfs.

(M:7.4.6)

Weber was right to state that at the heart of the *Moradas* lies an 'erotic spirituality'; however, as Teresa makes clear in this final chapter such erotic spirituality, and by implication the strategy of unknowing, has ultimately, for her, to be directed towards 'good works' and the 'practice of virtues'. This is her means for discerning the authenticity of the spiritual path that has been followed: 'Let us desire and be occupied in prayer not for the sake of enjoyment but so as to have this strength to serve' (7.4.12).

Yet, despite it all, and though the end of the journey is clearly the creation of good works, twice in the epilogue Teresa exhorts her sisters to 'delight in the castle' (M:Ep.1–2).[46] Even though ultimately the strategy of affect must fade away, Teresa clearly intends it as a key strategy to help bring her daughters (allied with the strategy of unknowing) to the place of theological union with the Trinity that she herself underwent. She concludes with the reflection of those verses from Genesis and Proverbs with which she began and which we have seen re-echo throughout the lines of the *Moradas*, forming as it were a counterpoint to the strategy of desire throughout the castle:

> Although no more than seven dwelling places were discussed, in each of these there are many others, below and above and to the sides, with lovely gardens and fountains and labyrinths, such delightful things [*cosas tan deleitosas*] that you would want to be dissolved in praises of the great God who created the soul in His own image and likeness.
>
> (M:Ep.1)

Teresa's remarkable achievement in the *Moradas* is to blend the linguistic strategies of the *theologia mystica*, to which she was heir, with theological imagery to present a radical proposal of how the Christian should act in the world through 'embodied unknowing' in selfless action. The final result is a sophisticated text which reflects the Wittgensteinian tripos of saying-showing-acting, giving the text an

---

46 *A gozar de esta Castillo.*

unprecedented experiential force in the literature of Western Christian spirituality. In this respect it is a supreme example of *mystical* writing carefully using 'mystical strategies' developed, I have argued, over the previous 300 years.

7

Wittgenstein and the Return to the Mystical

One of the things Christianity says amongst others, I believe, is that all sound doctrines are useless. You have to change your *life* (Or the *direction* of your life). It says that all wisdom is cold; and that you can no more use it for sorting out your life than you can forge iron when it is *cold*.

The point is that good teaching need not necessarily *grab* you; you can follow it as you would a doctor's prescription. – But here you need something to grab you and turn you round. – (i.e. this is how I understand it.) Once you have been turned round, you must *stay* turned round.

Wisdom is passionless. But faith by contrast is what Kierkegaard calls a *passion*.

(VB:1946)

Throughout this book we have taken some themes from the writing of Wittgenstein to help an exploration of what I understand to be the Christian mystical tradition of *theologia mystica*. I have argued that this tradition arises in the High Medieval interpretations of Dionysius and, as I have demonstrated, reaches its apotheosis in the sixteenth-century writings of the Spanish school, exemplified in the work of Teresa of Avila. By doing this I hope to have demonstrated how a Wittgensteinian

Blick can be useful for understanding the aims of the *theologia mystica* as a particular and unique 'strategy of performance'.[1]

To conclude our time together I would like to return to the writings of Wittgenstein and see, first, how the ideas developed in this book can be applied to his own writings (perhaps discovering his own 'mystical strategies'), and finally to elucidate that elusive Wittgensteinian 'religious point of view' with which we began the book.

FAITH AS PASSION

As we saw at the beginning of this book, Wittgenstein was always buffeted by the *passion* of faith. His *Nachlass* shows that Wittgenstein was constantly searching for religious certainty and essentially saw religious faith as a *passion (Leidenschaft)* – a phrase he borrowed from Kierkegaard – a search which was to preoccupy most of his adult life. One of the key texts for throwing light on Wittgenstein's attitude to religion is the recollections of his pupil Maurice Drury (in Rhees 1987).[2] The most important period of his recollections of Wittgenstein dates from the period after the Second World War when Wittgenstein was living in Ireland and Drury was working in St. Patrick's Hospital in Dublin.[3] After Drury's death in 1976 his recollections were collected and published by Rhees. Commenting on the reason for publishing the remarks Drury stated:

1   The discussion of this book may be extended to the works of St. John of the Cross. I have undertaken this task in my *St. John of the Cross: Outstanding Christian Thinker* (Tyler 2010a).
2   Drury had originally gone up to Cambridge to study for the Anglican priesthood at Westcott House. However, after he had come under the influence of Wittgenstein he abandoned his ordination training and spent two years working with unemployed people in Newcastle and Merthyr Tydfil. With Wittgenstein's encouragement he began to study medicine in 1934 and qualified in 1939.
3   The hotel Wittgenstein lived in during this period, 'The Ross Hotel', sadly has now been modernized and refurbished. On a visit in 2010 no trace remained of his stay.

The number of introductions to and commentaries on Wittgenstein's philosophy is steadily increasing. Yet to one of his former pupils something that was central in his thinking is not being said.

Kierkegaard told a bitter parable about the effects of his writings. He said he felt like the theatre manager who runs on the stage to warn the audience of a fire. But they take his appearance as all part of the farce they are enjoying, and the louder he shouts the more they applaud.

Forty years ago Wittgenstein's teaching came to me as a warning against certain intellectual and spiritual dangers by which I was strongly tempted. These dangers still surround us. It would be a tragedy if well-meaning commentators should make it appear that his writings were now easily assimilable into the very intellectual milieu they were largely warning against.

(Rhees 1987:xi)

Many of the key themes of Wittgenstein's writing which have been explored in this book are contained in this quote: the difficulty and oddness of Wittgenstein's writing and how it stubbornly resists easy (or sloppy) academic assimilation; the notion of certain 'intellectual and spiritual temptations' that his philosophy helps us to overcome; the existential relevance of the *passion* of his philosophy and the challenges it presents. His philosophy, so Drury suggests, should not leave us cold:

Christianity says that wisdom is all cold; and that you can no more use it for setting your life to rights than you can forge iron when it is *cold*.

(CV:53e)

One of the key influences on Wittgenstein's notion of religious belief was his encounter with Tolstoy's *Gospel in Brief* (Tolstoy 1895) which he had first come across while he was a soldier in the First World War. McGuinness and Monk tell the strange story of how, shortly after arriving in Galicia during his war service in 1914, he walked into a bookshop which contained only one book – Tolstoy's *Gospels*. At this time he was feeling particularly low and, in Monk's words, he was quite literally 'saved by the word' (Monk 1990:115). He carried it with him wherever he went for the rest of his service and became known to his fellow troops as 'the man with the gospels' (See Monk 1990:115; McGuinness 1988:220): 'He read it and re-read it, and thenceforth had it always with him, under fire and at all times' (letter from Russell to Lady Ottoline Morrell, LR:20.12.19). As he later wrote to von Ficker: 'If you are not acquainted with it, then you cannot imagine what an effect it can have upon a person' (letter from Wittgenstein to Ludwig Ficker, LF:24.7.15).

In later life Wittgenstein would tell Drury (Rhees 1987:86) that there were only two European writers of recent times who had anything important to say about religion: Tolstoy and Dostoyevsky. In the book Tolstoy calls Christianity 'a very strict, pure, and complete metaphysical and aesthetic teaching above which human reason has not risen' (Tolstoy 1895:384). Churches, as well as universities, for Tolstoy, do not expound it and it is found through following the 'passion of conscience' very much in the way advocated by Kierkegaard. 'Simple language', 'the language of millions of simple, unwise men' (Tolstoy 1895:4), for Tolstoy, is better than any fine or fancy language for getting this truth across: a common ground, as we have seen, between Wittgenstein's and Teresa of Avila's style.

The zeal and passion of the Tolstovian Gospel stayed with Wittgenstein throughout his life, tempered as we have seen with the passion of Kierkegaard which he read avidly during his 'break from philosophy' in the 1920s. This slightly idiosyncratic faith, mixed with a dash of Tagore, perhaps explains his later remark to Drury with which we began this book and was to so influence Malcolm and many other Wittgensteinian commentators: 'I am not a religious man but I cannot help seeing every problem from a religious point of view' (Rhees 1987:94).

Thus it is possible to interpret the later remarks found, for example, in Drury, as a commentary on Wittgenstein's belief in the importance of faith as *passion* while remaining sceptical as to religious institutions and behaviour *tout court*. Thus if we are to make sense of Wittgenstein's contribution to the philosophical problems arising from religious faith we would do well to look at his conviction of the *passion* of religious faith as much as the 'logical structure' of any supposed religious 'language games'. This is an approach that has been favoured by several recent commentators,[4] and is the favoured perspective adopted here.

WITTGENSTEIN AND *THE MYSTICAL*

The final passages of the *Tractatus Logico-Philosophicus* completed while Wittgenstein was on active service in the First World War and a prisoner in Monte Cassino, Italy, contain his most consistent, and some would say notorious, comments on *das Mystische*:

6.44   *Nicht wie die Welt ist, ist das Mystische, sondern dass sie ist/*
        What is mystical, is not how the world is but that it is.

6.45   *Die Anschauung der Welt sub specie aeterni ist ihre*
        Anschauung als – begrenztes – Ganzes.
        Das Gefühl der Welt als begrenztes Ganzes ist das mystische/
        The view of the world *sub specie aeterni* is the view of it
        as a limited whole.
        The feeling of the world as a limited whole is the mystical.

6.52   We feel that even when all possible scientific questions have
        been answered, the problems of life remain completely
        untouched. Of course there are then no questions left, and
        this itself is the answer.

6.521   The solution of the problem of life is seen in the vanishing
        of the problem.

6.522   *Es gibt allerdings Unaussprechliches. Dies zeigt sich, es ist*
        das Mystische.

4   As well as those referred to: see also Kallenberg 2001, McCutcheon 2001
     and Tanesini 2004.

> There are indeed, things that are inexpressible. They *show*
> *themselves*. That is the mystical.

7   What we cannot speak about we must pass over in silence.

On first reading, like the writings of Teresa which we examined in
the previous chapter, Wittgenstein's remarks can evoke puzzlement,
confusion and contradiction. When Frank Ramsey went to Austria in
1923 to help with the English translation of the *Tractatus* he wrote back
to his mother:

> Some of his sentences are intentionally ambiguous having an
> ordinary meaning and a more difficult meaning which he also
> believes.
>
> (LO:78)

Thus it is perhaps unsurprising that this somewhat gnomic style,
especially in these remarks on *das Mystische* coming at the end of
what purported to be a thesis on logical form, should perplex his
earliest commentators, not least Bertrand Russell. Although his former
mentor and friend paid fulsome praise to the work in his Preface ('a
book no serious philosopher can afford to neglect'), he did not accept
the conclusions, especially the references to 'the mystical'. Consequent
commentary has often sided with Russell (and most members of the
Vienna Circle) in finding the 'mystical remarks' a sideshow or hindrance
to the main action of the *Tractatus* which is seen as concerned primarily
with logical form or the nature of meaning. Another approach has been
to co-opt Wittgenstein's remarks into a wider search for the 'mystical'
as an ontological, cross-credal category along the lines of 'modern
mysticism' discussed in Chapter One – something, again, which does
not seem to be Wittgenstein's purpose.

Of commentators in recent years, perhaps Cyril Barrett (see Barrett
1991 and Harris and Insole 2005:61–75) has come closest to recognizing the full import of the final paragraphs of the *Tractatus* for a
wider understanding of Wittgenstein's approach to faith, belief and

what he himself called 'the problem of life'. The contemplation of which problem, Barrett claimed, lay closest to Wittgenstein's heart. For Barrett:

> Wittgenstein's lasting message is first, the inexpressibility of religious belief, ethical principles and aesthetic judgements in empirical terms and hence, second, the absurdity of attempting to give an empirical account of them.
>
> (Harris and Insole 2005:63)

Barrett wants to stress the importance of silence to Wittgenstein and allies his approach to the strategy of pure apophasis that we discussed in Chapter Three with reference to Dionysius. In Barrett's opinion, Wittgenstein does not take the Kantian road to the transcendental, but rather 'returns to Hume and turns him on his head' (Harris and Insole 2005:64). That is to say, he agrees that expressions of value and metaphysics cannot be empirically meaningful, but 'their nonsensicality was their very essence: they are an attempt to say the unsayable in order to make sense of the sayable.'

Of the other (sparse) writing on Wittgenstein and 'the mystical', mention must be made of Sontag's (2000) study, *Wittgenstein and the Mystical*. Of the writing on this subject his is the most intriguing; however, the book assumes an understanding of what the author means by 'the mystical' or 'the mystic'. Insofar as Sontag does define his terms, he seems, like so many commentators, to be preoccupied with the mystical as an ontological cross-credal entity in the 'modern mysticism' model, something explicitly rejected throughout this book. This is perhaps where most of the philosophers of religion who tackle the question of Wittgenstein and 'the mystical' become unstuck.[5]

McGuinness, on the other hand, in his instructive essay on 'Mysticism' (McGuinness 2002), relies upon the characterization of 'the mystical' from Russell's 1914 essay 'Mysticism and Logic' which was probably not read

---

5   In this respect, a similar strategy is adopted by Weeks's (1993) work *German Mysticism from Hildegard of Bingen to Ludwig Wittgenstein*.

by Wittgenstein at the time he wrote the *Tractatus*. Russell's account, like McGuinness's, relies on a Jamesian notion of the mystical which we have already critiqued. Being imbued with the Jamesian spirit, McGuinness concerns himself with the somewhat tangential question of whether 'Wittgenstein is entitled to have a single doctrine of mysticism' (2002:187), a question whose legitimacy has already been questioned. In this respect it is noticeable that McGuinness concerns himself with whether or not 'Wittgenstein had a mystical experience during the war', or as he later puts it, 'a genuine mystical experience', a category itself that we have already challenged. Using Zaehner and James in an essentialist way McGuinness concludes by stating that 'we cannot know whether Wittgenstein had mystical experiences'. As we have seen, such a conclusion is unsurprising due to the nature of the category itself. As opposed to Barrett, who grasps the full metaphysical implications of the final remarks of the *Tractatus*, McGuinness remains rooted with the question of whether Wittgenstein's so-called 'mystical experiences' can be verified or not, a question, it seems, that Wittgenstein's own approach rules out as illegitimate. It is precisely to challenge such unhelpful classifications of Wittgenstein's so-called 'mysticism' that this book arises. Accordingly, I will conclude this book by presenting what I believe are Wittgenstein's own 'mystical strategies', again adopting the unknowing-affective schema that we observed in the *theologia mystica* and applying it to Wittgenstein's own method of 'showing' his readers what must remain 'unsaid'.

WITTGENSTEINIAN STRATEGIES OF UNKNOWING AND DECONSTRUCTION

Anything your reader can do for himself leave to him.

(Wittgenstein VB:1948)

I should not like my writing to spare other people the trouble of thinking. But, if possible… to stimulate someone to thoughts of his own.

(Wittgenstein PI:Preface vi)

As has been stated throughout this book, it is not possible to make a direct comparison between the Christian mystical writers we have been discussing and Wittgenstein. Even if this were possible it would probably not be desirable. However, what we can say, and what is being argued for here, is that all these writers in coming across the blocks to their expression; in the case of Wittgenstein the limits to meaning in logical form of language, and in the case of a writer like Teresa of Avila, the limits to expression of the 'spiritual' nature of the self, adopt similar 'strategies of elucidation' or 'performative discourse'. What we may call 'strategies of elucidation' or 'performative discourse'. In all such 'strategies of elucidation' style is as important as content, none more so than in the use of a subversive or deconstructive strategy. Wittgenstein clearly states that he does not want to spare his readers the trouble of 'thinking for themselves' (PI:viii). As he says of his later philosophy:

> I do philosophy now like an old woman who is always mislaying something and having to look for it again: now her spectacles, now her key.
>
> (OC:532)

As we have seen, this 'new way of doing philosophy' no longer produces the systematic treatise but rather a sequence of numbered remarks designed to beguile and interact with the reader so that the discourse would have the desired performative effect on the person who engaged with it:

> They point or gesture towards ends that are somewhat alien to our current preoccupations. In fact they are written in the form of 'striking similes' and 'arresting moments' – they have a 'poetic quality', their function is to change our 'way of looking at things' (PI:144).
>
> (Shotter 1997:1)

If we look at Wittgenstein we can see certain 'strategies of unknowing' which resemble those of a writer such as Teresa of Avila, both having the aim to subvert and elude their readers' expectations – in both cases, the goal is 'pure performance'. For Wittgenstein our words become tools, instruments to challenge and wake us up; he refers to them as 'the levers in the cabin of a locomotive' or 'tools in a toolbox'. Throughout his writings he uses them carefully and develops and traces his strategic elucidations with care and caution. Teresa, on the other hand, is using her performative discourse to urge her readers – primarily but not solely her sisters – to *act* through prayer to reach closer union with God in their lives. As we saw in Chapter Two, Shotter (1997:14) isolates four 'linguistic strategies' adopted by Wittgenstein:

1. To arrest or interrupt ('to deconstruct') the spontaneous, unself-conscious flow of our ongoing 'mental' activity. These strategies provoke us into examining whether there is 'more to it' than we expected. We are shocked into 'standing back'.
2. To use certain 'instructive forms of language' that provoke us to give 'prominence to distinctions which our ordinary forms of language easily made us overlook' (PI:132). They are 'instructive gestures' which point and show.
3. To suggest new ways of thinking by the use of carefully selected images, similes and metaphors which can help the process giving 'first form to such sensed but otherwise unnoticed distinctions, thus to make reflective contemplation of their nature possible' (Shotter 1997:15).
4. To use the comparison of different 'language games' to present 'an order in our knowledge of the use of language: an order with a particular end in view; one of many possible orders; not the order' (PI:132).

We also saw that as part of this subversive linguistic toolkit, Genova (1995:130) isolates four 'subversive stategies' used by Wittgenstein:

1. Talking to himself
2. Contradicting himself
3. Avoiding arguments and conclusions
4. Refusing orientating structures.

To these four what we call 'performative strategies of unknowing' we added two more – use of humour and ordinary language – to suggest the six strategies of unknowing within Wittgenstein's texts that we also found in Teresa:

1. The Direction of Locution
2. Contradiction
3. Avoiding Conclusions: Humility
4. Disorientation
5. Humour
6. Use of Ordinary Speech.

All six, I have argued, are knowingly used by both Wittgenstein and Teresa to 'change the aspect' of the reader. This, I have argued, is part of the 'mystical strategy' common to both. As with Teresa, let us look now at Wittgenstein's use of each in turn.

The direction of locution

> Nearly all my writings are private conversations with myself.
>
> (VB:1948)

Throughout his *corpus* Wittgenstein talks to himself. As Genova points out, the boundaries between self and others breaks down: 'most times he talks to a host of imagined interlocutors who are fragments of himself and others' (1995:130). Several positions are stated and explored, sometimes all at once. The alternating narrative voice is both disconcerting and liberating; it is almost at times as though he had written the script of a play or film rather than a philosophical treatise.[6]

He conducts dialogue with imaginary others and with himself, including 'the author of the *Tractatus*' who takes on the third person:

6   In reference to this see Derek Jarman's comments on this aspect of Wittgenstein's work used in the making of his own film *Wittgenstein* in Jarman (1993).

PI:113 'But this is how it is-------' I say to myself over and over again. I feel as though, if only I could fix my gaze absolutely sharply on this fact, get it in focus, I must grasp the essence of the matter.

PI:114 (*Tractatus Logico-Philosophicus*, 4.5): 'The general form of propositions is: This is how things are.' -------- That is the kind of proposition that one repeats to oneself countless times. One thinks that one is tracing the outline of a thing's nature over and over again, and one is merely tracing round the frame through which we look at it.

Central to Wittgenstein's approach is his relationship with the reader, us, and how we are going to react to his remarks. Even the punctuation and arrangement of the script are important, as he states: 'I really want my copious punctuation marks to slow down the speed of reading. Because I should like to be read slowly (as I myself read)' (VB:1948). As we have also seen with Teresa we are invited into an imaginary conversation with the narrator. He constantly asks us questions, challenges us, asks us to undergo thought experiments, a technique also found in Teresa. Fundamental to both is *our own experience*: how we write interpretation depends upon the pages of our own experience; in both cases we are understanding something that is already there. In the case of Wittgenstein, 'all that is the case' (T:1), in the case of Teresa, the *Moradas* that present themselves when we begin to look at and consider ourselves in a prayerful fashion.

Wittgenstein's 'technique', then, as a philosopher, may be said to be one of constructing a series of 'reminders' to us. We have the answers all along; his task is to nudge us in the right direction so 'the fly can escape the fly bottle'. His written style therefore consists of series of these nudges and winks:

If it is asked: 'How do sentences manage to represent?' – the answer might be: 'Don't you know? You certainly see it, when you use them?' For nothing is concealed.

How do sentences do it? – Don't you know then? For nothing is hidden.

But given the answer: 'But you know how sentences do it, for nothing is concealed' one would like to retort 'Yes, but it all goes by so quick, and I should like to see it as it were laid open to view'.

(PI:435)

The direction of locution, then, helps Wittgenstein in his task of letting his work be a 'series of reminders'. His work, like Teresa's, is essentially dialogic (Incandela 1985:463) – 'it needs someone else and invites response'. We have to struggle to understand what Wittgenstein is trying to put across; the answers will not come easily or lightly.

Contradiction

Wittgenstein enters into the deconstructive game with his own contradictions and cross-examples (see e.g. OC:400–405, PI:352 or his debates with 'the author of the Tractatus', e.g. PI:113–115). As we saw in Chapter Two, in contrast to the proponent of the *Weltanschauung*, the proponent of the *Weltbild* can only suggest and cajole. She cannot declaim. As with the writers of mystical and psychotherapeutic discourse, Wittgenstein can never present a complete and watertight system. It flows with the stream of life, sometimes hardening into the channel, sometimes fluid with the stream – 'now losing her spectacles, now her key' (OC). The method of elucidation acts through games, strategies and reminders, some of which will contradict each other. Its special function requires a special form. This is the form of Wittgensteinian analysis or, for that matter, mystical discourse.

Avoiding conclusions: humility

There is accordingly no fixed end-point for the discourse: world, language and discourse are endless. His writings contain no final conclusion, rather:

The real discovery is the one that makes me capable of stopping doing philosophy when I want to. – The one that gives philosophy peace, so that it is no longer tormented by questions which bring *itself* in question.

(PI:133)

We do not need to *win* an argument; rather our aim is to *bring peace* to ourselves and to our interlocutors.

As Anthony Kenny points out (Kenny 1959:235) the *Philosophical Investigations* contains 784 questions, only 110 of which are answered and seventy of these are meant to be wrong! The arraigning of questions is clearly a positive strategy by Wittgenstein to elicit the change of *Weltblick* that he seeks. In *Zettel*:457, for example, he quotes Augustine with approval: '*quia plus loquitur inquisition quam invention*/because the search says more than the discovery', and perhaps Augustine is the 'missing link' for both Teresa and Wittgenstein. Both were profoundly influenced by reading the *Confessions*, and both Teresa's *Vida* and Wittgenstein's *Philosophical Investigations* reveal more than a passing desire to *confess*. As we saw earlier, for Cavell (1976:71) the style of the *Investigations* is that of Augustine's *Confessions*; the problems of the *Investigations* contain:

> What serious confession must: the full acknowledgement of temptation(s) ('I want to say...'; 'I feel like saying...'; 'Here the urge is strong...') and a willingness to correct them and give them up ('In the everyday use...'; 'I impose a requirement that does not meet my real need...').
>
> (Cavell 1976:71)

As we know from Monk, Wittgenstein at many times in his life made a 'full confession' and the confessional mode was familiar and attractive to him (See Monk 1990:367–371). The 'voices of temptation and correctness' (Thompson 2000:14) are familiar from above – they hover before us and may either lead us in the right direction or against where we want to be.

Hauerwas, in his comments on Wittgenstein in 'Aquinas, Preller, Wittgenstein and Hopkins' (Hauerwas 2004:98), suggests that the

Philosophical Investigations is 'a form of training in humility'. He quotes Wittgenstein's remarks with approval: 'The edifice of your pride has to be dismantled. And that is terribly hard work' (VB:1937). For Hauerwas, pride is clearly an aspect of the self that stops us 'seeing how things really are'. It obstructs the *Übersichtliche Darstellung*.

Wittgenstein's aim, as Incandela points out (Incandela 1985:460), was 'not explaining or setting out a position as much as he was confessing temptations – not for others to believe, but for them to test by their own lights, to engage in self-scrutiny, and only then to accept or reject them'. This can only happen if the author has the humility to step to one side; the ladder, as it were, 'is pulled up' once it has been used:

> My propositions serve as elucidations in the following way: anyone who understands me eventually recognises them as nonsensical, when he has used them – as steps – to climb up beyond them. (He must, so to speak, throw away the ladder after he has climbed up it.)
>
> He must transcend these propositions, and then he will see the world aright (*dann sieht er die Welt richtig*).
>
> (T:6.54)

As Kallenberg comments:

> The use of the adverb 'rightly' (*richtig*) here to modify the verb 'to see' (*sehen*) was deliberate: Wittgenstein's aim was that the reader attain a correct *manner* of viewing rather than secure a correct picture of reality, because, as he would summarize some years later, 'the search says more than the discovery'.
>
> (Kallenberg 2001:22)

As with Teresa, humility within the author can allow this process of self-reflection in the reader to happen. Rather than 'confessions', it may be better to see his later writings more as 'collections of reminders' (See Fann 1969:107):

The work of the philosopher consists in assembling reminders for a particular purpose. If one tried to advance *theses* in philosophy it would never be possible to debate them, because everyone would agree to them.

(PI:127)

The philosophers who seek to construct a *Weltanschauung* or overriding theory will need to produce arguments, proof and reasoning. For the philosopher who seeks the *Weltbild* the 'collection of reminders' will be sufficient. As Wittgenstein reminds Drury, we must avoid trying to become professional philosophers churning out academic research papers when we have nothing new to say to one another.

Disorientation

For a philosopher there is more grass growing down in the valleys of stupidity than up on the barren heights of cleverness.

(VB:1949)

Throughout Wittgenstein's texts we are forced to lose our way. We wander around trying to find a coherent way, but do not achieve it. The text is alive and constantly changing. As we have seen, Wittgenstein himself would worry endlessly about the order of his sentences, experimenting, as with a kaleidoscope, with differing versions of the propositions. In Shotter's words he seeks to arrest or interrupt 'the spontaneous, unreflective flow of our ongoing, routine activities' (2006:4) so that he may give 'prominence to distinctions which our ordinary form of language easily make us overlook' (PI:132). As we have seen, the works are constructed in ways that make them difficult to read as parts of a systematic treatise. They are full of exclamation marks, non-sequiturs, blind alleys. 'Think of...'; 'Imagine...'; 'It is like...'; 'Suppose...' and similar expressions pepper the text, as well as odd or unusual scenes or thought experiments.

Take, for example, the opening paragraphs of the *Philosophical Investigations* where we are confronted with no less than five differing thought experiments describing four different situations of '*Sprachspiele*', namely:

- The description of Augustine's encounter with ostensive definition from his account of his childhood in *The Confessions* (PI:1).
- The person sent shopping with a slip marked 'five red apples' who has the shopkeeper perform strange activities much like a *Monty Python* comedy sketch (who says Wittgenstein has no sense of humour!) (PI:1).
- The activities of two builders who utter the monosyllabic 'slab', 'block', 'pillar' and 'beam' (memories here surely of Wittgenstein's time as a builder-architect constructing his sister's house in Vienna in the 1920s) (PI:2).
- 'Moving objects about on a surface according to certain rules' – descriptions of board games (PI:3).
- An actor interpreting a script 'in which letters are used to stand for sounds, and also as signs of emphasis and punctuation' (PI:4).

For the opening of the last major work by one of the leading thinkers of the twentieth century, it makes for an odd and disconcerting experience. No wonder some people question Wittgenstein's grasp of form, or indeed reality, in these last seemingly confused and confusing jottings. Yet, as has been argued throughout this book, Wittgenstein knows exactly what he is doing and if we return to our proposal of the importance of the *Überblick* in Wittgenstein's writings as argued above, the message becomes very clear. As he says in PI:5:

> We may perhaps get a sense of how much this general notion of the meaning of a word surrounds the working of language with a haze which makes clear vision impossible. – It disperses the fog if we study the appearances of language in primitive kinds of application in which one can have an overview (*übersehen*) of the aim and functioning of words.[7]

---

7   My translation.

The aim of the disconcerting thought experiments is to pull the readers from their habitual way of viewing the world, disconcert and re-orientate them so that they 'see the world aright':

> His acceptance of the new picture consists in his now being inclined to regard a given case differently: that is, to compare it with this rather than that set of pictures. I have changed his way of looking at things [*Anschauungsweise geändert*].
>
> (PI:144)

Humour

> Humour is not a mood but a *Weltanschauung*.
>
> (VB:1948)

Wittgenstein famously once said that he wanted to write a work that consisted entirely of jokes but didn't have the necessary sense of humour to do it! Humour is an essential part of Wittgenstein's strategy of moving us into the *Überblick*, and in this he shares the attribute with Teresa. The examples are numerous:

> PI:250: Why can't a dog simulate pain? Is he too honest?

> PI:268: Why can't my right hand give my left hand money?

The philosophical *Blick* he is trying to achieve in his writings can use humour as much as anything else. As we saw at the beginning of the book, by stating that 'philosophy leaves everything as it is', Wittgenstein was as much trying to change *nothing* as to change *everything*, which is exactly, as he realized in his later writings, how humour works. It is a fundamental *change of aspect*. So with humour, the whole can be changed by a certain comical 'aspect seeing':

> What is incomprehensible is that *nothing*, yet *everything* has changed.
>
> (RPP2:474)

Thus, humour and 'getting the joke' can be just as much part of the process of 'changing aspect' as logical argument or rational discourse. In this respect, humour is a central plank or tool of Wittgenstein's strategies:

> What is it like for people not to have the same sense of humour? They do not react properly to each other. It's as though there were a custom amongst certain people for one person to throw another a ball which he is supposed to catch and throw back; but some people, instead of throwing it back, put it in their pocket.
>
> (VB:1949)

Ordinary speech

> It is wrong to say that in philosophy we consider an ideal language as opposed to our ordinary one. For this makes it appear as though we thought we could improve on ordinary language. But ordinary language is all right.
>
> (BB:28)

One of the key components of the Wittgensteinian *Blick* is to redirect our gaze away from the abstract entities of theoretical speech to the ordinary that lies before us. As we have seen, he is not concerned with developing a new body of systematic theory (PI:109, 126) but 'putting everything before us' so nothing is either explained or deduced. *Ordinary* use and *ordinary* speech is of vital importance to his *Blick*:

> When philosophers use a word ---- 'knowledge', 'being', 'object', 'I', 'proposition', 'name' ---- and try to grasp the *essence* of a thing, we must always ask ourselves: is the word ever actually used in this way in the language which is its original home ---- *We* bring the words back from their metaphysical to their everyday use.
>
> (PI:116)[8]

8   My translation. Anscombe translates *Sprache* with 'language game' rather than 'language' – which seems to me to introduce an unnecessary level of 'Wittgensteinian' terminology (see Chapter Two).

By such means the Wittgensteinian *Blick* brings us back from 'one or another piece of plain nonsense' (PI:119) to a clearer understanding of the way we relate to the world. For philosophy can 'in no way interfere with the actual use of language, it can in the end only describe it' (PI:124).

Again, Wittgenstein *reminds us* how we *use language in ordinary life* (cf. the opening pages of the *Philosophical Investigations*) as a solution to our problems. As we saw in the previous chapter, Teresa is also very clear that her sisters should use 'ordinary language' when they talk to each other and the faithful, especially when talking about things of God. She is, of course, working within the context of the *letrados/ espirituales* debate, yet, like Wittgenstein, she seems to be able to sniff out 'metaphysical claptrap' and is all for plain speaking when talking of 'things of the spirit'. As with Teresa, there is a suspicion that this language may be 'too coarse and material' (PI:120), but as Wittgenstein says 'How can another be constructed?' and 'How strange that we should be able to do anything at all with the one we have!' Therefore his 'clear and simple language games are not preparatory studies for a future regularization of language' (PI:130) but rather a means to enable a person to say 'now I can go on'.

As with Teresa, we have then six performative strategies by which Wittgenstein deliberately disconcerts us and leads us into 'unknowing':

1. The Direction of Locution
2. Contradiction
3. Avoiding Conclusions
4. Disorientation
5. Humour
6. Ordinary Speech.

In both cases the two authors do not want to impose dogma or a certain way of thinking on the reader but leave the reader to 'do what they can themselves'. For Wittgenstein this is the resolving of 'one or other piece of philosophical nonsense', for Teresa it is the individual soul's journey to God occurring in a place of freedom. Both are natural rebels, but they are rebels who respect the importance of the system they find around them and, in Wittgenstein's phraseology, 'use the ladder' they find around themselves to achieve what they want, 'before throwing away the ladder'.

STRATEGIES OF AFFECTIVITY IN LUDWIG WITTGENSTEIN

When we regard the use made of Wittgenstein's *Nachlass* by his later editors, as Baum (1992) and others have argued, there seems to be a fear to engage with the notion of Wittgenstein as an embodied being – both humanly and sexually. In particular, with regard to his view of the 'religious' and 'mystical' there is the need to take seriously his description of religious faith as 'a passion', and as he clearly states in the quotation that heads the next chapter, the need to see religion as essentially tackling *Lebensfrage* (Questions of Life) or else talking rubbish. Out of this, I have argued, flow his views on the religious life as an ethical life, inspired by his reading of, amongst others, Tolstoy in the First World War trenches. In this respect, and in the perspective of the later remarks in the *Tractatus* wherein Wittgenstein deals with *das Mystische*, I would like to suggest here that the key moment in the young Ludwig's development was his experience on the Eastern Front in the latter stages of the First World War.

Accordingly, I will conclude this chapter by analysing his remarks during this period to relate them to the 'strategy of affectivity' which will emerge in his subsequent writing. In this respect, the so-called *Geheime Tagebücher/Secret Diaries* of 1914 to 1916 and the *Koder Tagebuch* from the 1930s both illustrate the points that are being made; that is, that Wittgenstein's approach to life and philosophy can only be understood through the need for embodiment and what he terms the *passion of religious belief*.[9]

---

9 It is notable that both works are not available in English translation and in this chapter I will work from the *Bergen Electronic Edition* (BEE).

The *Tagebücher* first came to light in 1952 in the possession of Wittgenstein's sister, Margarethe Stonborough, shortly after Wittgenstein's death (see GT:162). Wittgenstein, during his last visit to Vienna in 1950, had suggested that they should be destroyed, but fortunately this did not occur. They were subsequently deposited in the Wren Library at Cambridge and classified by von Wright as 'Notebooks 101–103' in the *Nachlass* (See PO:486). The *Tagebücher* were first translated and published in English as *Notebooks 1914–16* by Elizabeth Anscombe in 1961. In her Preface Anscombe suggested that the Notebooks were being published 'as an aid to students of the *Tractatus*' (NB:v) which seemed to justify quite a radical editing of the work that has come in for a lot of later criticism. Although she states that 'very little has been left out' the subsequent publication of the complete Notebooks, both in the *Nachlass* and Baum's edition show, as we shall see, just how much Anscombe had decided to omit. She had once remarked that 'if by pressing a button it could have been secured that people would not concern themselves with his personal life, I should have pressed that button' (LPE:xiv); yet her desire to 'clean up' Wittgenstein's works has inevitably led to a distortion of the impact of his writings, not least in the questions investigated here around affect and desire.

If we read the Preface to the 1977 edition of *Vermischte Bemerkungen* (published in English with the title *Culture and Value* in 1980) von Wright states that the criteria for publishing his collection were as follows:

> In the end I decided on the only principle of selection that seemed to me unconditionally right. I excluded from the collection notes of a purely 'personal' sort – i.e. notes in which Wittgenstein is commenting on the external circumstances of his life, his state of mind and relations with other people – some of whom are still living. Generally speaking these notes were *easy* to separate from the rest and they are on a *different* level of interest from those which are printed here.
>
> (CV:Preface)

Subsequent commentators, some of whom have already been mentioned in Chapter Two, while acknowledging the sterling work of von Wright *et al.* in the publication of Wittgenstein's Notebooks, have also recognized that von Wright's hidden hermeneutic may have distorted a balanced reading of Wittgenstein's work – especially the notion that his 'philosophy' can be extracted from his 'life'. As we saw earlier, the groundbreaking biographies of Monk and McGuinness raised the question of a reintegration of Wittgenstein's life and writings to enable an understanding of his philosophy (see Klagge 2001 for an extended discussion on this). Accordingly, as we approach the question of Wittgenstein's strategy of affectivity here we have no hesitation in reuniting the published version of his Notebooks by Anscombe, von Wright *et al.* with the 'personal' notes, often unpublished and only available through study of the *Nachlass*.

With respect to the First World War diaries considered here it became clear that once the *Nachlass* was in the public domain there was not only a fuller 'notebook' but also an encrypted, so-called 'secret notebook'. This had a simple encryption of replacing a with z, b with y and so on. Thus the first edition of what became known as the 'Secret Notebook' was first published, through the efforts of Baum and Pascual in Spanish, Catalan and German in the Spanish journal *Saber* in 1985. This eventually appeared in a German–Spanish edition published by Alianza in Madrid in 1991. For Baum, the publication of the work showed the importance of understanding Wittgenstein's context and interpretation through 'Christian Form of Life with Religion as one of the chief matrices for understanding his work' (GT:175). To date, as has been pointed out, no English translation has yet appeared.

To illustrate the importance of embodiment and the passion of embodiment to Wittgenstein's philosophy, we will concentrate on the diary entries from 1916. Wittgenstein, serving as an ordinary soldier for the Austrian army on the Russian front, was moved on 21st March of that year from a place of relative security to great danger in the fourth battery of the fifth Field Howitzer Regiment (See McGuinness 1988:238).

The placement was one of the worst experiences of his life and the diaries detail his struggle to make sense of it all. On 21st April he finds himself in battle for the first time; at this time he remained in solitary duty on the observation post. On 4th June the Austrian offensive was followed by an equally severe Russian offensive. Wittgenstein clearly acquitted himself well during this hellish time and was awarded a silver *Tapferkeitsmedaille* Second Class on 6th October. His decoration recommendation stated:

> Ignoring the heavy artillery fire on the casement and the exploding mortar bombs he observed the discharge of the mortars and located them... On the Battery Observation Post, Hill 417, he observed without intermission in the drumfire, although I several times shouted to him to take cover. By this distinctive behaviour he exercised a very calming effect on his comrades.
>
> (McGuinness 1988:242)

Although not at Wittgenstein's battalion, the Russian offensive was ultimately successful north of Wittgenstein's location. The Austrian army was thus plunged into a chaotic retreat in July of which Wittgenstein was part so that his unit had to seek shelter in the Carpathian mountains.

By the time Wittgenstein was withdrawn from the front line in August he had been continuously in the firing line for five months. Of the notes made at this time McGuinness comments: 'they testify to a change in his thinking as great as that which he himself saw in his countenance... It was as if he had bridged – or was about to bridge – some gap between his philosophy and his inner life' (1988:245). From this point onward there is no separation between the remarks on logical form and remarks on religion, ethics and the general *Lebensfrage* which we cited at the beginning of the chapter: 'Yes my work has broadened out from the foundations of logic to the essence of the world' (NB:2.8.16). Both of his biographers, namely Monk and McGuinness, suggest that at this point in his life, having pushed himself hard on the logical boundaries of language both in Cambridge with Russell and on his own in his retreat in Norway before the outbreak of the First World War, it was as though he 'sought embodiment' and needed the experiences of the trenches to bridge gaps between how he experienced his thought and how he experienced his life. In this respect his experiences on the

Eastern Front in 1916 are, I argue, central for understanding the move in his philosophy from the disembodied exploration of logical form to the embodied researches of the later (or perhaps better 'post-1916') Wittgenstein.

Anscombe gives us the first entry for 15th April 1916 as follows:

> We can only foresee what we ourselves construct.
> But then where is the concept of a simple object still to be found?
> This concept does not so far come in here at all.
> We must be able to construct the simple functions because we must be able to give each sign a meaning.
> For the only sign which guarantees its meaning is function and argument.
>
> (NB:71e)

As they stand, these bald statements do bear a resemblance to the *Tractatus*, especially 5.556, but how much richer they become when we add the coded entries from the full notebook:

> In eight days we go into the Firing Line. May I be fortunate enough to wager my life in a challenging position!
>
> (BEE:103)[10]

The 'pure' philosophizing of the *Tractatus* seems to have arisen from a distinctively embodied context, one that includes *Glaubensfragen*, prayers and entreaties to God:

> Now comes inspection. My soul shrivels up. God give me light! God give light to my soul!
>
> (BEE:103:29.3.16)[11]

---

10   '*In 8 Tage gehen wir in Feuerstellung. Möchte es mir vergönnt sein, mein Leben in einer schweren Aufgabe aufs Spiel zu setzen!*' All the quotes that follow are from the Bergen Electronic Edition, my translation.

11   *Jetzt Inspektion. Meine Seele schrumpft zusammen. Gott erleuchte mir! Gott erleuchte meine Seele!*

The following day he adds:

> Do your best. You cannot do more: and be cheerful... Help yourself
> and help others with all your strength. And at the same time be
> cheerful! But how much strength should one need for oneself and
> how much for others? It is hard to live well!! But the good life is
> beautiful. However, not mine, but Thy will be done.
>
> (BEE:103:20.3.16)[12]

The fervent and passionate quality of his entries at this time is
almost certainly a result of the two works which he carried with him
throughout his time in the War: Tolstoy's *Gospel in Brief* (discussed
above) and Dostoyevsky's *Brothers Karamazov.*

We have seen that the *Gospel in Brief* had a galvanizing impact
on Wittgenstein, turning his philosophy from 'an analysis of logical
symbolism' to 'the curiously hybrid work which we know today,
combining as it does logical theory with religious mysticism' (Monk
1990:116). Monk sees this period as one of increasing 'separation
between body and spirit', which would make sense if he understands
'mysticism' in terms of the 'modern mysticism' we defined in Chapter
One. Yet if, as has been argued throughout this book, we dispense with
the illusion of 'modern mysticism' and concentrate, in Wittgensteinian
fashion, on the *Sprachspiel* of the 'mystical performative discourse',
then it is possible to interpret Wittgenstein's remarks in the diaries as a
growing sense of embodiment and, as Monk puts it, 'duty' towards the
world and fellow people. Yes, there is no doubt that Wittgenstein found
the encounter with his fellow soldiers *feuchterlich ('dreadful'),* but the
reading of the diaries presented here suggests a desire to struggle with
this situation, knowing that here, rather than in the logical abstract

---

12 *Tu dein Bestes! Mehr kannst du nicht tun: und sei heiter... Hilf dir selbst
    und hilf anderen mit deiner ganzen Kraft. Und dabei sei heiter! Aber
    wieviel Kraft soll man für sich, und wieviel für die anderen brauchen?
    Schwer ist es, gut zu leben!! Aber das gute Leben ist schön. Aber nicht
    mein, sondern Dein Wille geschehe!*

symbolism of Cambridge, he will find what he is looking for in terms of the embodied life.[13] On 5th September 1914, shortly after reading *The Gospel in Brief*, he writes: 'I am on the path to a great discovery, But will I reach it?!' (5.9.14), followed by 'I feel more sensual than before. Today I masturbated again'.[14] Rather than a separation of mind and body, even Monk recognizes that for Wittgenstein, from this point onward 'sensuality and philosophical thought were inextricably linked – the physical and mental manifestations of passionate arousal' (Monk 1990:117). Despite later getting hold of the Eighth Volume of Nietzsche's collected works, including *The Anti-Christ,* it seems as though his original inspiration from Tolstoy was not shaken; so much so that he could write on 8th December 1914:

> Christianity is indeed the only sure way to happiness but what if someone spurned that happiness?! Might it not be better to perish unhappily in the hopeless struggle against the external world? But such a life is senseless. But why not lead a senseless life? Is it unworthy?
>
> (BEE:103)[15]

In his exposition of Tolstoy, Sontag (2000) notices the similarities between Tolstoy's relation to Christianity and the position Wittgenstein will ultimately adopt to philosophy. Both want to 'leave everything as it is' and allow the scriptures/ordinary language to speak for themselves.

13 Which would surely also explain his immediate desire after the war to dispense with his immense fortune and live in the hardest and demanding conditions of an ordinary primary school teacher in Upper Austria. Indeed, much of the later life of Wittgenstein after 1916 is marked by this need to 'be embodied' and to act ethically.

14 *Ich bin auf dem Wege zu einer grossen Entdeckung. Aber ob ich danhinge-langen werde ?! Bin sinnlicher als früher. Heute wieder onaniert.*

15 *Gewiss, das Christentum ist der einzige sichere Weg zum Glück. Aber wie, wenn einer dies Glück verschmähte?! Könnte es nicht besser sein, unglücklich, im hoffnungslosen Kampf gegen die äussere Welt augrunde zu gehen? Aber ein solches Leben ist sinnlos. Aber warum nicht ein sinnloses Leben führen? Ist es unwürdig?*

Tolstoy, like Kierkegaard, believes that Christianity must be stripped down to its essentials, leaving each person to make their own decision on its truth uninfluenced by the rhetoric and opinions of the Churches. 'Truth,' Sontag notes, 'can be found in simple language, as it was for Wittgenstein too' (Sontag 2000:125). Yet Sontag, like Monk, is still keen to talk about Wittgenstein's 'mysticism' without explaining what this may be, apart from something akin to our 'modern mysticism'. Wittgenstein, he says, 'adds a mysticism that is missing in Tolstoy', a statement which I hope by now the arguments in this book have shown to be questionable, if only because of the incomprehensibility, and sheer un-Wittgensteinian notion, of 'adding' 'mysticism' as a quasi-ontological category to something. Rather, as has been argued throughout, if we want to discover the filiations between Wittgenstein and Tolstoy we would be better off looking at the *Sprachspiele* and *Weltbild* within the two writers, and also how they relate to the *Lebensformen* expressed through our threefold progression of 'thinking-seeing-acting'. If it was not a case of Wittgenstein 'finding mysticism' (whatever that means) in Tolstoy, what then did he find there?

Reading the first lines of Tolstoy's *Gospel* again it is not surprising that it had such an explosive impact on Wittgenstein, after the logical searching of Cambridge, Norway and the pre-war years. The words could have been Wittgenstein's own:

> Reason without faith had already brought me to despair and to a denial of life, but when I once really examined into the life of humanity, I became convinced that despair cannot be the destiny of man, and that people have lived, and are now living by faith...
>
> I tried to arrange my life after the lives of those who believe, tried to become one with them, to fulfill the same rules of life and laws of conduct, imagining that in this way the idea of life would be revealed to me also.
>
> (Tolstoy 1895:xv)

It is perhaps not too fanciful to compare the effect these sentences had on the young Wittgenstein to the effects de Osuna had on the young

Teresa. Both were in turmoil, loneliness and despair at the time – physically, psychologically, emotionally and spiritually. Both found in their 'masters' a person who writes for the need of personal transformation, commitment and, most of all, engagement with the world. In the case of Tolstoy through the adoption of a life of faith, in the case of de Osuna through the 'path of the heart' embodied in the *theologia mystica* rather than the *theologia speculativa*. In this sense we can understand Tolstoy's work as an example of *theologia mystica* (in contrast to *theologia speculativa* – something which he is at pains to dismiss in his book) rather than as an example of 'modern mysticism' which we critiqued at the beginning of the book:

> At first I sought counsel and a solution to my difficulties from priests, monks, bishops and learned theologians (cf. Teresa's *letrados*). But I often noticed in them a want of frankness, and still more frequently flagrant self-contradictions in their explanations and interpretations.
>
> (Tolstoy 1895:xvi)

Having turned his back on the *theologia speculativa* with its hair-splitting, creeds and dogmas, Tolstoy rather finds what he is looking for in 'such people who carried out in the works of their lives the teaching of Christ'. Where Tolstoy (and probably Wittgenstein) would differ from Teresa and de Osuna is in the role of the Church in living out this faith. For Teresa and de Osuna it is absolutely central; for Tolstoy the truth is received directly to the individual without any intermediary.

So, then, the Wittgenstein who approached the Front in spring 1916 was not the young logician who had left Cambridge some two years earlier; his own questing spirit and the encounter with Tolstoy had led him to see the necessity for a form of knowledge that was not just 'head knowledge' (*intellectus*) but rather the embodied knowledge of which Tolstoy talks about. With this in mind the entries from his arrival on the Front begin to fall into place. As he approaches the batteries he writes:

Tomorrow or the day after we will be in the firing line. Therefore, *Courage!* God will help.

(BEE:18.4.16. 103 5v) [16]

God improve me! Then I would be become more joyful. Today will probably be in the Firing Line. God help me.

(BEE:20.4.16. 103 5v) [17]

This did indeed prove to be the beginning of the firing after which he writes:

Have been a few days in the Firing Line. The whole day is taken up with *heavy* physical work, no time to think. God help me; I have a monstrous amount to suffer. I have asked today to be put in the Observation Tower. Half the people here hate me because no-one understands me and because I am no saint! God help me!

(BEE:23.4.16) [18]

Now I am almost always with people who hate me. And this is the one thing that I have never been able to come to terms with. The people here are wicked and heartless. It is virtually impossible to find even a trace of humanity in them. God help me to live… God be with me! Amen.

(BEE:27.4.16) [19]

16   *Morgen oder übermorgen in die Feuerstellung. Also Mut! Gott wird helfen.*
17   *Gott bessere mich! Dann werde ich auch froher werden. Heute wahrscheinlich schon in Feuerstellung. Gott helfe mir.*
18   *Seit ein paar Tagen in neuer Stellung. Den ganzen Tag über schwere körperliche Arbeit; ausserstande zu denken. Gott helfe mir. Ich habe ungeheuer viel zu leiden. Habe heute angesucht, auf den Beobachtungsstand zu kommen. Beim Halbzub hasst mich alles, weil mich keiner versteht. Und weil ich kein Heiliger bin! Gott helfe mir!*
19   *So bin ich jetzt fast immer umgeben von Leuten, die mich hassen. Und dies ist das Einziges, womit ich mich noch nicht abfinden kann. Hier sind aber böse, herzlose Menschen. Es ist mir fast unmöglich, einen Spur von*

Finally, Wittgenstein, from his new position on the watch tower, finds himself in the mortal danger he has long sought:

> Afternoon during reconnaissance I was shot at. Thought of God. *Your* will be done! God be with me!
>
> (BEE:29.4.16)[20]

> Again during the firing today returned to the insight: People *only* need God.
>
> (BEE:30.4.16)[21]

> It is very difficult! God protect me and stand by me. Amen. Would that this bitter cup passed me by.[22] However *Your* will be done.
>
> (BEE:3.5.16)[23]

This climaxes in the entry for 4th May, 1916:

> Tomorrow I will perhaps be sent to the Observation Post, at my own request. Then the War will finally begin for me. And – perhaps – Life too!
>
> Perhaps the nearness of Death will bring me the light of life. May God enlighten me! I am a worm however through God I will become a human being. God stand by me. Amen.[24]

    Menschlichkeit in ihnen zu finden. Gott helfe mir zu leben... Gott sei mit mir! Amen

20 *Nachmittags bei den Aufklären. Wurden beschossen. Dachte an Gott. Dein Wille geschehe! Gott sei mit mir.*

21 *Gehe heute während eines Feuerüberfalls wieder zu den Aufklären: Nur Gott braucht der Mensch.*

22 Cf. Matthew 26:39.

23 *Habe es schwer! Gott beschütze mich und stehe mir bei. Amen. Möchte der schwerste Kelch an mir vorübergehen. Aber Dein Wille geschehe.*

24 *Komme morgen vielleicht auf mein Ansuchen zu den Aufklären hinaus. Dann wird für mich erst der Krieg anfangen. Und kann sein – auch das Leben! Vielleicht bringt mir die Nähe des Todes das Licht des Lebens.*

The 'nearness of death' and his constant prayer seemed to slowly affect his attitude to his fellow soldiers with whom he had tried so hard to get on. On 8th May he writes:

> The people I am with are not so much nasty as *terribly* limited. This makes relations with them almost impossible as they almost always misunderstand me. They are not stupid, but limited. Within their circles they are clever enough. But they lack character and with that a breadth of understanding. 'The right-believing Heart understands everything'.
>
> (BEE:8.5.16. 103 10v)[25]

A study of these diaries reveals two aspects of Wittgenstein's character and philosophy that are central to the exposition presented here. First, there is the need to understand his logical investigations within the context they were written. Out of these terrible experiences on the Eastern Front during the Brusilov Offensive of spring/summer 1916 would not only arise the final sections of the *Tractatus*, including the passages on *das Mystische* with which we began this chapter, but the major shift in Wittgenstein's consciousness that produces the unique fusion which is his later philosophy. If we want to try and understand what Wittgenstein understands by *das Mystische* in *Tractatus* 6 we cannot ignore the context out of which they arose – his experiences on the Front and in particular the 'nearness of Death which will bring some light'. Thus many of the passages that will later form the end of the *Tractatus* arise from these very notebooks:

Möchte Gott mich erleuchten. Ich bin der Wurm, aber durch Gott werde ich zum Menschen. Gott stehe bei mir. Amen.

25 *Die Leute, mit denen ich beisammen bin, sind nicht so sehr gemein, als ungeheuer beschränkt. Das macht den Verkehr mit ihnen fast unmöglich, weil sie einen ewig missverstehen. Die Leute sind nicht dumm, aber beschränkt. Sie sind in ihrem Kreise klug genug. Aber es fehlt ihnen der Charakter und damit die Ausdehnung. 'Alles versteht das rechtgläubige Herz'.*

The solution of the problem of life is to be seen in the disappearance of this problem.

(NB 6.7.16)

Cf. *Tractatus* 6.521:
The solution of the problem of life is seen in the vanishing of the problem.
(Is not this the reason why those who have found after a long period of doubt that the sense of life became clear to them have then been unable to say what constituted that sense?).

Again:

Death is not an event in life. It is not a fact of the world. If by eternity is understood not infinite temporal duration but non temporality, then it can be said that a man lives eternally if he lives in the present.

(NB 8.7.16)

Cf. *Tractatus* 6.4311:
Death is not an event in life: we do not live to experience death.
If we take eternity to mean not infinite temporal duration but timelessness, then eternal life belongs to those who live in the present.
Our life has no end in just the way in which our visual field has not limits.

Second, there is the influence of Tolstoy, in particular the importance of *Menschlichkeit* and the 'return to the ordinary', finding God in the everyday, and especially in the muck, slime and profanity of the Front. Wittgenstein is at this point no longer seeking enlightenment through books or transcendentalism, but rather in the ordinary living out through the everyday in embodiment. He neither repudiates nor denies the sexual either and it is noteworthy that during this period he is sustained by letters from his beloved David Pinsent, who is killed during the war and to whom he will eventually dedicate the *Tractatus,* with the epigram from Kürnberger: 'Whatever a man knows, whatever is not mere rumbling and roaring that he has heard, can be said in three words.'

Finally, there is no doubting the depth and authenticity of Wittgenstein's religious faith at this point in his life. Despite attempts to downplay it, it is clear from reading the passages above that this is a *passionate* faith (he would later appreciate this point in Kierkegaard) which admits of no middle way. Here again the influence of Tolstoy (and Dostoyevsky) is manifest. It is a faith that does not *transcend* the world but a faith that brings us *into* the world, with all its mess, human relationships and tragedy. Ultimately the goal is to live and to '*Lebe Glücklich!* Live Happily!' (NB 8.7.16):

> The happy life seems to be justified, of itself, it seems that it is the only right life.
>
> (NB 30.7.16)

Some commentators have argued that Wittgenstein's faith and attitudes expressed in the War Diaries were a 'flash in the pan' which he did not sustain throughout his life. Yet, the argument in this chapter has been that the events of 1916 mark a watershed in Wittgenstein's life, which ultimately finds expression in the 'mystical' final two sections of the *Tractatus*. In this respect they form the springboard out of which the later 'interactional' philosophy, famously expressed in the *Philosophical Investigations,* arises. This was characterized earlier in this book as the move from 'saying to showing to acting'. The position is clearly stated in two diary entries from *Nachlass* notebooks 125:1942, interestingly enough again written during bombardment in war, but now the Second World War. This time Wittgenstein had asked for a simple job (he became porter at Guy's Hospital, London) in an area of aerial bombardment in London. As in the First World War he showed great courage under continual bombardment and was able to encourage the younger doctors and nurses who were inexperienced in such things.

This notebook entry was written during a brief break with John Ryle's family in Sussex (see Monk 1990:434):

3.1.42
Every word stands in a field of relationships, at a distinctive point of the speech-field (*Sprachfeld*): if then we choose this word rather than another we are choosing *one* place in the field rather than another, one group of relationships rather than another.

(BEE:125 2v)[26]

Our words, our speech, cannot be extracted from our life and our meaning in words comes from the *Sprachfeld* – the series of relationships within which we dwell. Again, from the same notebook:

9.2.42
I am not interested in an unmediated understanding of a Truth, but the phenomenon of unmediated understanding. Not a particular *seelische* understanding but understanding in the affairs of people. Yes, it is as though the idea-picture of experience is led into particular channels so that we can now see one experience laid together with another. (like an optical instrument brings together light from different sources in a particular way to produce a picture).

(BEE:50r)[27]

26 *Jedes Wort steht in einem Feld von Beziehungen, an einem bestimmten Punkt des Sprachfeldes: wer also geneigt ist dies Wort zu wählen und nicht jenes, wählt einen Ort des Feldes statt eines anderen, eine Gruppe von Beziehungen statt einer anderen.*
27 *Mich interessiert nicht das unmittelbare Einsehen einer Wahrheit, sondern das Phänomen des unmittelbaren Einsehens. Nicht (zwar) als einer besondern seelischen Erscheinung sondern als einer Erscheinung im Handeln der Menschen. Ja; es ist, als ob die Begriffsbildung die Erfahrung in bestimmte Kanäle leitete so dass man nun die eine Erfahrung mit der andern auf andere Weise zusammensieht (Wie ein optisches Instrument Licht von verschiedenen Quellen auf bestimmte Art in einem Bild zusammenkommen lässt).*

The complexity of 'ordinary life' in the 'affairs of people' will finally reach its fullest exposition in the *Investigations*. Yet, as these unpublished remarks show, Wittgenstein was keen to make his readers realize the need for *embodiment* in the 'field of relationships' which constitutes the *Sprachfeld*.

'*Bring der Mensch wieder in das richtige Element*/Bring the person into the right element' he writes on 18th May 1942: '*und alles wird sich entfalten und gesund erscheinen*/ and everything will unfold and appear well' (BEE:125 58r).

As with his philosophical life so with his personal life Wittgenstein realized at this later period the need of what he had expressed in the *Koder* diary in 1930:

> I often feel as though there is something in me like a lump which, if it melted, I would then be able to cry or find the right word (or perhaps a melody). But this 'something' (Is it the Heart?) feels like leather and cannot melt. Or am I perhaps too cowardly to allow the temperature to rise enough for this to happen? There are people who are too weak to break. I belong to this type. The only thing in me which might break sometime, and this I am anxious about, is my reason.
>
> (BEE:183:3/26.4.30)[28]

Parallel to the openness to the possibilities of embodiment held in these entries we find that the heartfelt declamations of faith presented in the War Diaries are still there, and again, the influence of Tolstoy and his *Gospel in Brief* remain apparent. Thus on 15th February 1937 we find him writing:

28 *Oft fühle ich dass etwas in mir ist wie ein Klumpen der wenn er schmelzen würde mich weinen liesse oder ich fände dann die richtige Worte (oder vielleicht sogar eine Melodie). Aber diese Etwas (ist es das Herz?) fühlt sich bei mir an wie Leder und kann nicht schmelzen. Oder ist es dass ich nur zu feig bin die Temperatur genügend steigen zu lassen? Es gibt Menschen die zu schwach zum Brechen sind. Zu denen gehöre auch ich. Das Einzige was vielleicht ein Mal an mir brechen wird und davor fürchte ich mich manchmal ist mein Verstand.*

As the insect buzzes to the light, so I return to the New Testament.

(BEE:183:168)[29]

As Monk points out (1990:364), the turn of 1936/1937 was again a key moment in Wittgenstein's life as he tried the first formulation of his later thoughts in the *Brown Book* which he had taken with him to Norway. As would finally be the case with the beginning of the *Investigations*, his thoughts returned to Augustine (who, as we have seen, was such an important influence on Teresa) whose *Confessions* he was rereading and wanted to emulate. Monk writes that for Wittgenstein '*All* philosophy, in so far as it is pursued honestly and decently, begins with a confession' (Monk 1990:366). As we saw earlier, the true path of philosophy must pass through humility and unknowing:

The edifice of your pride is broken down. And that is terrible work.

(VB:1937)

The remarks he wrote at this time, which would basically form untouched the first 188 paragraphs of the *Investigations* (about a quarter of the book), were written, as Monk points out, 'at a time when he was most ruthlessly honest about himself – when he made the most intense efforts to "descend into himself" and admit to those occasions on which his pride had forced him to be deceitful' (Monk 1990:367); both in his personal life and in his public life, such as the time he struck schoolchildren when he worked as a schoolteacher in Upper Austria after the First World War. His desire for confession and humility led him to return to the village he had taught in and ask forgiveness from his former pupils (movingly described in Monk 1990:370–371).

This period of confession was still linked with his entreaties to God, and in the Private Diaries we see the clearest expression of these thoughts:

---

29 *Wie das Insekt das Licht unschwirrt so ich ums Neue Testament.*

God! Help me come into a relationship with you in which I can
be happy with my work. Believe that in every moment God can
demand *everything* from you! Is really conscious of you! Then ask
that he gives you the gift of life!

(BEE:16.2.37, 183:202)[30]

It is clear that even in 1937, twenty years after the incidents on the
Eastern Front, Wittgenstein still somehow felt the need to engage with
the theistic; however, and perhaps more importantly from the point of
view of our investigation here, that engagement took the form of seeing:

1. The inextricable link between the ethical and the philosophical
2. The need for confession, as the true source of philosophy
3. The proposal of a linguistic strategy that returned the reader to the
    'relationships of everyday life'
4. A linguistic strategy with transformative power.

As he makes clear in one of his later attempts to codify his philosophy,
the so-called *Big Typescript* of 1932 (BT), for the 'later' (post-1916)
Wittgenstein, the aim of philosophy is to produce transformative
change through working on *affect* as much as *intellect*: 'a resig-
nation, but one of feeling and not of intellect' is required for 'work on
philosophy is – as work in architecture frequently is – actually more
of a kind of work on oneself. On one's own conception. On the way
one sees things' (PO:161/2). Again, as has been argued throughout this
book, it is precisely *this* process of affective change that we have already
observed in the tradition of *theologia mystica* and it is by understanding
Wittgenstein's remarks on 'the mystical' through this interpretative tool
that we can, I believe, come closest to what he hoped to present to us,
his readers, in these challenging and often misunderstood remarks.

---

30 *Gott! Lass mich zu dir in ein Verhältnis kommen, in dem ich fröhlich sein
    kann in meiner Arbeit! Glaube daran dass Gott von Dir in jedem Moment
    alles fordern kann! Sei Dir dessen wirklich bewusst! Dann bitte dass er Dir
    das Geschenk des Lebens gibt!*

A Concluding Unscientific Postscript: A 'Life Question' or 'Empty Chatter'?

'There is indeed that which is unutterable. This makes itself *manifest*, it is the mystical' (T 6.522) (but not a 'bluish haze surrounding things' and giving them an interesting appearance [as Wittgenstein once said in conversation]).

(Paul Engelmann in LPE:98)

If you and I are to live religious lives, it mustn't be that we talk a lot about religion, but that our manner of life is different.

(Wittgenstein to Drury quoted in Rhees 1987:114)

It is now time to draw together the main arguments of this book and to highlight its conclusions. We began with a quote from Wittgenstein's conversations with Drury and we begin these conclusions with another, together with some recollections of Wittgenstein's friend and fellow architect, Paul Engelmann. Together the two quotes encapsulate some of the key arguments of this book; namely:

1. That we find in Wittgenstein's writings a method of looking at 'the mystical' by means of employing his essential division between

227

'saying and showing'. The 'mystical' for Wittgenstein is unutterable, but, it can however *be manifest through showing*.

2. The 'perspicuous view' suggested by Wittgenstein enables us to 'see connections' in discourse as we relate them to a 'form of life'. We shall, in his words, 'see a new aspect'.

3. Consequently, if we look at religious texts and life we are as much concerned with *acting* as with *thinking*. For Wittgenstein, 'a religious form of life' *must* be embedded in action.

At the beginning of this book we explored the dilemma of how the words *mysticism, mystical* and *the mystic* were to be meaningfully employed in academic discourse, especially in relation to the Christian tradition. To this end we reviewed the *use* to which the words had been put, primarily in the twentieth century, and argued that an essentialist view of 'the mystical' had arisen that suggested 'the mystical' was an ontological, cross-credal, experientialist category which was termed 'modern mysticism'. Applying a Wittgensteinian *Blick* I argued that such a 'perspicuous view' frees us from the 'bluish haze' of 'modern mysticism' and allows us to concentrate on *mystical discourse* rather than the 'occult entity' of mysticism. In the analysis of James, Vaughan, Inge and Underhill in Chapter One I demonstrated how such an 'occult entity' can pervade our talk of the mystical. Central to the notion of 'mystical strategy' in this book has been the sense of holding the balance between saying *and* showing. As we have seen, Wittgenstein was concerned throughout his life with not only the boundary of what may be said and what may be shown but also how he could express this in his writing. As his writing developed he realized increasingly that for philosophy to lead to action, or as Cavell has called it, 'therapy', it cannot use the traditional methods of theoretical treatises and discourse. Rather, as his later writings show (although as we argued in the previous chapter it is also apparent at the end of the *Tractatus*), the *style* of writing must change to reflect the new purpose or *way of doing philosophy*.

Similarly, when we turn to a 'mystical' writer such as Teresa of Avila we should not expect a theoretical *Denkweise* but an equally unsystematic and arresting *style* that forces us to reappraise our relation to ourselves, the transcendent and the world around us. This arresting style, I have suggested here, is the 'mystical strategy' of the *theologia mystica*. In this respect, we may conclude that Teresa can best be interpreted as a master of 'practical theology' whose primary concern is not theoretical speculation on, for example, the nature of the Trinity, but rather provoking *practical transformation* in the lives of her readers. In this, I have argued, she is a true heir to the great medieval tradition of *theologia mystica*.

Shotter (1996) sees the revolutionary nature of Wittgenstein in the following three aspects:

1.   He orientates us to a new task
2.   He introduces us to a new set of methods relevant to its pursuit
3.   He 'opens up a strange new creative space, a relational space in which we can originate new forms of life, new living connections and relations between aspects of our lives not before noticed' (Shotter 1996:404).

The argument of this book has been that both Wittgenstein and the medieval mystical writers covered, by similar means, challenge conventional ways of seeing to open up a new 'creative, relational space' where new 'connections and relations between aspects of our lives' may be opened up. Wittgenstein uses the tools of linguistic philosophy to subvert that very genre into a 'new way of seeing', whereas the Christian medieval writers use the tools of the venerable tradition of *theologia mystica* (ultimately derived from their interpretation of Dionysius) to present an equally subversive 'way of looking' that changes our way of viewing, our way of being and ultimately our way of acting in the world. All of them were unconcerned with generating 'grand theories'. In the case of Wittgenstein his work often explicitly challenges this notion which he sees as being all-pervading in the modern Western world:

It was true to say that our considerations could not be scientific ones. It was not of any possible interest to us to find out empirically "that contrary to our preconceived ideas, it is possible to think such-and-such" ---- whatever that may mean. (The conception of thought as a gaseous medium.) And we may not advance any kind of theory. There must not be anything hypothetical in our considerations. We must do away with all *explanation* and description alone must take its place.

(PI:109)

On the other hand, Teresa of Avila, for example, is not concerned with the theorizing of the *letrados* and the *theologia speculativa* but rather with the 'change of life' that can occur through the *theologia mystica*.

FAMILY RESEMBLANCES

The real discovery is the one that makes me capable of stopping doing philosophy when I want to.

The one that gives philosophy peace, so that it is no longer being tormented by questions which bring itself into question.

Instead we now demonstrate a method by examples; and one can break off the series of examples.

But more correctly, one should say: Problems are solved (uneasiness//difficulties//eliminated), not a single problem...

But then we'll never get finished with our work!

Of course// certainly // not, because it doesn't have an end.

(PO:195)

Once you have been shown how to enjoy this castle, you will find rest in everything – even those which give you the most trouble –, with hope you will return to it, which no one can take from you.

Although no more than seven dwelling places were discussed, in each of these there are many others, below and above and to the sides, with lovely gardens and fountains and labyrinths, such delightful things that you would want to be dissolved in praises of the great God who created the soul in His own image and likeness.

(M:Ep. 2.1)

For Wittgenstein, as we have seen, philosophical problems arise from a certain sense of unease or discomfort about particular propositions, phrases, twists in the fabric of our language:

The philosopher strives to find the liberating word, that is, the word that finally permits us to grasp what up until now has intangibly weighed down our awareness.

(It is as if one had a hair on one's tongue; one feels it, but cannot grab it, and therefore cannot get rid of it).

(PO:165)

It was the contention at the beginning of this book that the terms *the mystical, the mystic* and *mysticism* present such an intangible discomfort. They cause problems in use and we tie ourselves up in knots using them. Throughout this book I have made a Wittgensteinian case against the following uses of the words:

1. Seeing 'mysticism' as a cross-credal ontological *category* that is somehow *possessed* by a religion such as Christianity. I have given numerous examples of this, arising, as argued, with people such as James, Underhill, Inge and Vaughan and continuing to be used in this way by many academics.[1] I have argued that the 'myth' of 'mysticism' as an 'occult entity' arises from an error of our speech. We want to talk about 'it' as an entity and so want to suppose it is a distinctive category. It is, however, more a manner of speaking and writing than an entity. It is as much a verb as a noun.

1   See, for example, the following phrase from *Mystics of the Christian Tradition* (Fanning 2002:5): 'among the seemingly myriad differences of Christian denominations and the competing claims of the world's faiths, it is in mysticism that they meet on a common ground'.

2. To talk about the 'mystical experience'. Taking the cue from writers such as Lash it has been argued that the notion of a discreet 'mystical experience' is equally meaningless. To ascribe an experiential existence to such an entity is likewise an error of the use of our language.

3. To refer to individuals as 'mystics'. Just as we must be cautious of how we use the terms 'mysticism' and 'mystical experience' I have argued that it is equally meaningless to talk about so-and-so as 'being a mystic'. If the first two categories are empty then this third one is equally so.

Having warned, in Wittgensteinian fashion, against the use of these terms in quasi-ontological style I have also wanted to argue against a pure constructivism that reduces 'mystical language' to pure form lacking any psychological content. To make this point I have suggested that the 'mystical language game' may best be compared to a Wittgensteinian choreography between 'saying and showing'. From this choreography arises the third necessary aspect of the 'mystical language game' – ethical action in the world.

Applying this approach to Teresa of Avila I aim to have shown how we can acquire an innovative and original sense of her works which involves seeing them as a language game which is part of the wider language game of the tradition of what I have termed *theologia mystica*. In focusing on this language game I have not wanted to concentrate on 'destroying the idol' of mysticism by 'creating a new idol' of 'no idols' (cf. PO:171). Rather, in the Wittgensteinian approach to the medieval mystical writers adopted here I have argued for a play of light and shadow as the agent of 'mystic speech' works on the edge of language and meaning.

By necessity this 'mystic speech' will be broken, stammering, untheoretical and contingent: there is an incompleteness to the 'mystic speech act' which is a necessary part of its existence. Throughout this study, in the case of Wittgenstein, Dionysius, de Osuna, Laredo and Teresa, there have been numerous examples of well-meaning translators and executors trying to 'tidy up' the rough-and-tumble of 'mystic speech'.

On the contrary, I have suggested that this 'broken-down nature' is intrinsic to the very nature of mystic speech. In examining Christian mystical writings in this way I hope to have demonstrated that we should not look for perfection and smoothness in those writings. The very coarseness and inconsistency is what makes them alive and gives them the 'passionate intensity' as they grapple with the transcendent.

The other main theme of this book has been how the investigation of the Christian tradition of *theologia mystica* throws light on Wittgenstein's own religious search. Rather than bracketing him as a 'modern mystic' (*pace* Sontag) I have argued that his religious faith, or as he put it, his 'religious point of view', may best be understood as belonging to the tradition of *theologia mystica* as 'mystical speech act'. In his use of aporia, unknowing, embodiment and humility he is about the same 'game' as writers such as Teresa to 'turn his reader around' to see the world aright. For Wittgenstein, as has been demonstrated, 'seeing the world aright' is about seeing beyond the dominant Western *Weltanschauung* of positivistic scientism to a *Weltblick* that 'sees connections' within ourselves, those around us and the world we inhabit, eventually leading to ethical action in the world and for wider society. Although I do not want to conclude that Wittgenstein is 'a mystic' I want to suggest that Wittgenstein is engaging in the same linguistic strategies – what I have termed here 'mystical strategies' – as writers such as Teresa of Avila. In this respect, one of the key arguments of this book has been that one of the central 'family resemblances' between Wittgenstein and Teresa is their shared preoccupation with 'making pictures' to stimulate a 'change of aspect' in our way of seeing and acting in the world. Accordingly I conclude that their writing is fundamentally *transformational* in character. As Wittgenstein put it:

I wanted to put this picture before your eyes, and your *acceptance* of this picture consists in your being inclined to regard a given case differently; that is, to compare it with *this* series of pictures. I have changed your *Anschauungsweise* (way of viewing).

(Z:461)

In his survey of various approaches to Wittgensteinian interpretation, Kallenberg concludes:

> I suspect that each 'discovery' of a supposed central feature of Wittgenstein's thought has the grip it does on each author not because he or she has an objective grasp on Wittgensteinian truths, but because Wittgenstein has a subjective grasp on them as readers; each 'discovery' is but a manifestation of their particular 'cure'. Reading Wittgenstein rightly leads to diverse convictions because maladies differ; each author champions the 'Wittgenstein theory' that most reflects the way that he or she has escaped his or her own fly-bottle.
>
> (Kallenberg 2001:13)

Half a century after his death, commentators are still deeply divided over Wittgenstein's legacy for Western thought. This book has been an attempt to show the difficulties of trying to 'pin down' such a *lebendig* philosopher as Wittgenstein. I hope to have demonstrated that we untangle the heady mix of biography, thought, passion and action that he produced at our peril and we must do so with extreme caution. Early attempts by 'the founding mothers and fathers' of Wittgensteinian scholarship to make Wittgenstein another analytic philosopher of religion have had middling success and, in some writer's opinions, failure. As such, the co-opting of Wittgenstein into the ranks of 'philosophers of religion' has meant that some of the *passion* and *awe* with which he approaches the subject has been necessarily lost.

Wittgenstein's approach, then, may be characterized as a 'transformational epistemology' which has as its goal the transformation of the interlocutor through participation in the linguistic strategies of performative discourse. He is not simply concerned with acquiring knowledge of ourselves, the world or others, but rather that our engagement with the task presented will transform us ontologically 'in our sensibilities, in the things we notice and are sensitive to, the things we seek and desire' (Shotter 1997:1).[2] In this respect, I have argued, he shares a common aim with a mystical writer such as Teresa of Avila in her own 'transformational strategies'. For Shotter, Wittgenstein's 'transformational methods' are practical, not utopian, they are embodied and 'lay'.[3] What we are left with is a much more active transformational mode of understanding that is not built upon 'occult ontological entities'. Our 'mystical strategies' are simply this – strategies to be explored, to 'make connections' (*Zwischengliedern*) rather than referring to ontological entities – whether supposed 'mystical states', 'mystical phenomena' or 'mysticism' itself.[4]

As we saw earlier, it is possible to interpret Wittgenstein as encouraging a move from the Cartesian 'I' to a more embodied self. Fergus Kerr in his *Theology after Wittgenstein* (Kerr 1997) spells out, perhaps more than most, the consequences of this approach for Christian theology and spirituality. Wittgenstein's dethroning of the Cartesian 'I' presents a spirit 'unlike anything I know in Western thought and in many ways opposed to the aims and methods of traditional philosophy' (Malcolm quoted in Kerr 1997:187). What Malcolm is suggesting, Kerr observes,

2 See also Kerr (1997:158) where he states that Wittgenstein in his later work 'strives to show that neither feeling nor reason but *action* is the foundational thing'. In his latest work (Kerr 2008), Kerr reiterates his view that Wittgenstein's later philosophy is to be seen as a call to 'work upon oneself'.

3 'In being multidimensional, indeterminate, fluid, flexible, unfinished, contested, changeable, and still developing, the kind of knowledge involved must, in itself, be amenable to disciplinary confines: that is, these practices must be continuous with, and work from within, our ordinary everyday practices, without it being necessary, so to speak, to step outside them. Hence, theoretical explanations are not only unnecessary, but inimical to what is required' (Shotter 1997:7).

4 This is the 'moment of apophasis' that has run like a thread throughout the narrative. Space has not permitted a more detailed analysis and it is hoped to pick this up at a future date. In the meantime I refer the interested reader to my full doctoral thesis (Tyler 2009).

'is a radical questioning of the whole way of thinking about the self, and hence of others, of the world and of the divine, which has captivated Western Christian culture for a long time'. In essence, Wittgenstein's later project is about 'subverting the entire metaphysical tradition which is constituted by rancour against the *physical and historical conditions of human life*' (Kerr 1997:188, my emphasis). It has been the argument throughout this book that this Wittgensteinian 'anti-metaphysic', so well described by Kerr, was preserved through the Middle Ages in the performative discourse of *theologia mystica* especially in its deconstructive embodiment, or in Wittgensteinian terms, in the move from saying to showing to acting.

Thus, the Wittgensteinian move from *Weltanschauung* to *Weltbild* under the *Übersichtliche Darstellung* – from mind/body Cartesian dualism to a post-enlightenment suspicion of the Cartesian 'I' – mirrors the strategies of 'mystical discourse'. The mystical strategies we have already identified – those of unknowing and affectivity – are held alike by the contemporary post-enlightenment discourse of Wittgenstein and the pre-enlightenment discourse of *theologia mystica*. That is, with the 'postmodern' critique of Cartesian dualism we return to a 'pre-modern' notion of self. Both discourses share similar strategies and, as we have seen, for both 'style' is as important as 'content'.

Both Teresa and Wittgenstein, I suggest, are in their own ways inviting their readers to move 'out of the head' into embodied practices. This, I conclude, is the key 'transformational strategy' of both Ludwig Wittgenstein and the writers of the Christian tradition of *theologia mystica*:

A religious question is either a 'life question' or (empty) chatter. This language game, we could say, only deals with 'life questions'.
                                          (Wittgenstein BEE 183:202)[5]

---

5   *Eine religiöse Frage ist nur entweder Lebensfrage oder sie ist (leeres) Geschwätz. Dieses Sprachspiel – könnte man sagt – wird nur mit Lebensfragen gespielt.*

Bibliography

PRIMARY TEXTS

Ludwig Wittgenstein

AS   'Some Remarks on Logical Form' in *Proceedings of the Aristotelian Society*. Supp. Vol 9, 1929

BB   *The Blue and Brown Books*. Oxford: Blackwell, 1958

BEE   *Wittgenstein's Nachlass: The Bergen Electronic Edition*. Oxford: Oxford University Press, 2000

BT   *The Big Typescript – TS213: German-English Scholar's Edition*, ed. C. Grant-Luckhardt and M.E. Aue. London: Wiley Blackwell, 2005

BW   *Briefe, Briefwechsel mit B. Russell, G.E. Moore, J.M. Keynes, F.P. Ramsey, W. Eccles, P. Engelmann and L. von Ficker*, ed. B. McGuinness and G.H. von Wright. Frankfurt am Main: Suhrkamp, 1980

CLA   *Wittgenstein's Lectures: Cambridge 1932–1935, from the Notes of Alice Ambrose and Margaret Macdonald*, ed. A. Ambrose. Chicago: Chicago University Press, 1979

CLL   *Wittgenstein's Lectures: Cambridge 1930–1932, from the Notes of John King and Desmond Lee*, ed. D. Lee. Oxford: Blackwell, 1980

CV   *Culture and Value*, ed. G.H. von Wright and H. Nyman. Oxford: Blackwell, 1980

GT   *Geheime Tagebücher 1914–1916*, ed. W. Baum. Vienna: Turia and Kant, 1992

LC   *Lectures and Conversations on Aesthetics, Psychology and Religious Belief*, ed. C. Barrett. Oxford: Blackwell, 1989

LF   *Letters to Ludwig von Ficker* in 'Wittgenstein: Sources and Perspectives', ed. C.G. Luckhardt. London: Harvester, 1979

LO   *Letters to E.K. Ogden with an Appendix of Letters by Frank Plumpton Ramsey*, ed. G.H. von Wright. Oxford: Blackwell, 1973

LPE   *Letters from Ludwig Wittgenstein with a Memoir by Paul Engelmann*, ed. B. McGuinness. Oxford: Blackwell, 1967

LPP   *Lectures on Philosophical Psychology 1946–47. From the Notes of P. Geach, K.Shah and A. Jackson*, ed. P. Geach. London: Harvester, 1988

LR   *Letters to Russell, Keynes and Moore*, ed. G.H. von Wright and B. McGuinness. Oxford: Blackwell, 1974

NB   *Notebooks 1914–1916*, trans. G.E.M. Anscombe and G.H. von Wright. Oxford: Blackwell, 1984

OC   *On Certainty*, ed. G.E.M. Anscombe and G.H. von Wright. Oxford: Blackwell, 1969

PG   *Philosophical Grammar*, ed. R. Rhees. Oxford: Blackwell, 1974

PI   *Philosophical Investigations*, ed. G.E.M. Anscombe and R. Rhees. Oxford: Blackwell, 1958

PO   *Philosophical Occasions 1912–1951*, ed. J. C. Klagge and A. Nordmann. Cambridge: Hackett, 1993

PR   *Philosophical Remarks*, ed. R. Rhees. Oxford: Blackwell, 1975

RC   *Remarks on Colour*, ed. G.E.M. Anscombe; trans. L. McAlister and M. Schättle. Oxford: Blackwell, 1977

RFGB   *Remarks on Frazer's Golden Bough*, reprinted in *Philosophical Occasions 1912–1951*, ed. J.C. Klagge and A. Nordmann. Cambridge: Hackett, 1993

RPP1   *Last Writings on the Philosophy of Psychology, Vol I*, ed. G.E.M. Anscombe and G.H. von Wright. Oxford: Blackwell, 1982

RPP2   *Remarks on the Philosophy of Psychology, Vol II*, ed. G.H. von Wright and H. Nyman. Oxford: Blackwell, 1980

T   *Tractatus Logico-Philosophicus*, trans. D.F. Pears and B. McGuinness. London: Routledge & Kegan Paul, 1961

VB   *Vermischte Bemerkungen* in Volume 8: *Werkausgabe in 8 Bände*. Frankfurt am Main: Suhrkamp, 1993

W   *Werkausgabe in 8 Bände*. Frankfurt am Main: Suhrkamp, 1993

WA   *Wiener Ausgabe*, ed. M. Nedo. Vienna: Springer Verlag, 1993

WB   *Wörterbuch für Volks- und Bürgerschulen*. Vienna: Hölder-Pichler-Tempsky, 1926.

Z   *Zettel*, ed. G.E.M. Anscombe and G.H. von Wright. Oxford: Blackwell, 1967

Teresa of Avila

The Collected Works of St. Teresa of Avila, trans. K. Kavanaugh and O. Rodriguez, 3 Vols. Vol. 1:2nd edn; Vols 2 and 3:1st edn. Washington: Institute of Carmelite Studies, 1980–1987 (Kavanaugh and Rodriguez CW)

The Complete Works of St. Teresa of Jesus, trans. E. Allison Peers, 3 vols. London: Sheed and Ward, 1946 (Allison Peers CW)

The Interior Castle or The Mansions, trans. Benedictine of Stanbrook. London: Thomas Baker, 1930

Obras Completas de Santa Teresa de Jésus, ed. Efrén de la Madre de Dios and Otger Steggink, 9th edn. Madrid: Biblioteca de Autores Cristianos, 1997

Santa Teresa Obras Completas, ed. T Alvarez, 10th edn. Burgos: Editorial Monte Carmelo, 1998

The Way of Perfection, trans. Benedictines of Stanbrook. London: Thomas Baker, 1925

Abbreviations
C=	*Meditaciones Sobre Los Cantares*
CE=	*El Camino de Perfección,* Escorial Codex
CV=	*El Camino de Perfección,* Valladolid Codex
CT=	*El Camino de Perfección,* Toledo Codex
Exc=	*Exclamaciones*
F=	*El Libro de las Fundaciones de Su Reformacion*
M=	*Las Moradas*
V=	*El Libro de La Vida*

OTHER PRIMARY TEXTS

Abbreviations
AM=	*Ascent of Mount Sion,* Bernardino de Laredo
CH=	*Celestial Hierarchy,* Dionysius
Dion=	*Dionysiaca*
DN=	*On the Divine Names,* Dionysius
DS=	*Dictionnaire de Spiritualité Ascétique et Mystique Doctrine et Histoire,* eds. M. Viller, F. Cavallera, J. de Guibert, A. Rayez, A. Derville, P. Lamarche and A. Solignac. 1932–1995. Paris: Beauchesne.

EH=   *Ecclesiastical Hierarchy,* Dionysius
Ep=   *Epistles,* Dionysius
GMT= *De Mistica Theologia,* Jean Gerson
MT=   *De Mistica Theologia,* Dionysius
PG=   *Patrologiae Cursus Completus:* Series Graeca, ed. J.-P. Migne. Paris, 1857–1866, 161 volumes
PL=   *Patrologiae Cursus Completus.* Series Latina, ed. J.-P. Migne, Paris, 1844–1864, 221 volumes
TA=   *Tercer Abecedario Espiritual,* Francisco de Osuna
VSL=   *Viae Sion Lugent,* Hugh of Balma

Bernardino de Laredo

The Ascent of Mount Sion, trans. E. Allison Peers. London: Faber and Faber, 1952

Subida de monte Sión in *Misticos Franciscanos Españoles,* Vol. 2, ed. J. Gomis. Madrid: Biblioteca de Autores Cristianos, 1948

Dionysius

Corpus Dionysiacum, ed. B.R. Suchla, G. Heil and A. M. Ritter. Berlin: De Gruyter, 1990–1991

Dionysiaca: Recueil donnat L'ensemble des traditions latines des ouvrages attributes au Denys de l'Aréopage, ed. M. Chevalier. Paris: Desclée de Brouwer, 1937–1950

Dionysius the Areopagite on the Divine Names and Mystical Theology and *Denis Hid Divinity,* ed. McCann. London: Burns and Oates, 1924

Mystical Theology: The Glosses by Thomas Gallus and the Commentary of Robert Grosseteste on De Mystica Theologia, ed. and trans. J. McEvoy. Paris: Peeters, 2003

Opera Veteris ac novae translationis cum Hugonis, Alberti, Thomae et aliorum. Strassbourg 1502 (Salisbury Cathedral A 5.8, 1502)

Pseudo-Dionysius: The Complete Works, trans. C. Luibheid and P. Rorem. New York: Paulist, 1987

A Thirteenth-Century Textbook of Mystical Theology at the University of Paris. The Mystical Theology *of Dionysius the Areopagite in Eriugena's Latin Translation with the Scholia translated by Anastasius the Librarian and Excerpts from Eriugena's Periphyseon*, ed. and trans. L.M. Harrington. Paris: Peeters, 2004

Francisco de Osuna
Francisco de Osuna: The Third Spiritual Alphabet, trans. M. Giles. New York: Paulist, 1981

Tercer Abecedario Espiritual de Francisco de Osuna, ed. S. López Santidrián. Madrid: Biblioteca de Autores Cristianos, 1998

Jean Gerson
Ioannis Carlerii de Gerson De Mystica Theologia, ed. A Combes. Lugano: Thesaurus Mundi, 1958

Jean Gerson: Early Works, trans. B McGuire. New York: Paulist, 1998

De Theologia mystica, unpublished translation by B. McGuire. Made available by permission of the translator

Hugh of Balma
De Balma, Hugues, Théologie Mystique, trans. F. Ruello. Paris: Editions du Cerf, 1995

The Roads to Zion Mourn, trans. D. Martin in *Carthusian Spirituality: The Writings of Hugh of Balma and Guigo de Ponte*. Mahwah, NY: Paulist, 1997

Others
Scripture quotations from the *New Revised Standard Version*. London: Harper, 2007

The Cloud of Unknowing, Anonymous, ed. J.J. Walsh. New York: Paulist, 1981

The Cloud of Unknowing: together with The epistle of privy counsel by an English mystic of the XIVth century, ed. J. McCann. London: Burn & Oates, 1964

D. Martin Luthers Werke, Kritische Gesamtausgabe. Weimar Edition, 60 volumes, ed. G. Ebeling and H. Schilling. Weimar: Hermann Böhlaus Nachfolger, 1980

Denis Hid Divinity by the Anonymous Author of the Cloud of Unknowing, ed. J.J. Walsh in *The Pursuit of Wisdom.* New York: Paulist, 1988

SECONDARY WORKS

Ahlgren, G.   (1996) *Teresa of Avila and the Politics of Sanctity.*
                     Ithaca, NY: Cornell University Press

Allison Peers, E.   (1930) *Studies of the Spanish Mystics* (2 vols).
                     London: Sheldon Press
                     (1952) *The Ascent of Mount Sion by Bernardino
                     de Laredo,* trans. E. Allison Peers. London: Faber
                     and Faber
                     (1953) 'Saint Teresa's Style: A Tentative Appraisal'
                     in *Saint Teresa of Jesus and Other Essays and
                     Addresses.* London: Faber and Faber

Andrés Martín,   (1975) *Los Recogidos: Nueva Vision de la Mistica
M.   Española (1500–1700).* Madrid: Fundacion
                     Universitaria Española, Seminario 'Suarez'
                     (1976) *La teología española en el siglo XVI.*
                     Madrid: Biblioteca de autores cristianos
                     (1982) *Osuna (François de)* in *DS,* pp. 1037–1051

Antonio Marco, J. — (1997) 'Recurrencias y Concatenadores: La Cohesión en el Discurso Teresiano' in *La Recepción de los Místicos Teresa de Jesús y Juan de la Cruz*' Ed. R. Gancia. Salamanca: Ediciones Universidad Pontificia

Armstrong, C.J.R. — (1975) *Evelyn Underhill (1875–1941). An Introduction to Her Life and Writings*. London: Mowbrays

Astigarraga, J.L. — (2000) *Concordancias de los Escritos de Santa Teresa de Jesus*. Rome: Editoriales OCD

Barnard, G.W. and Kripal, J.J. — (ed.) (2002) *Crossing Boundaries: Essays on the Ethical Status of Mysticism*. New York: Seven Bridges

Barrett, C. — (1991) *Wittgenstein on Ethics and Religious Belief*. Oxford: Blackwell

Bataillon, M. — (1982) *Erasmo y España*. Mexico: Fondo de cultura económica

Baum, W. — (ed.) (1992) Wittgenstein's *Geheime Tagebücher 1914–1916*. Vienna: Turia and Kant

Bell, D.N. — (1978) 'Love and Charity in the Commentary on the *Song of Songs* of Thomas the Cistercian' in *Citeaux* 29 (1978)

Blount, T.   (1656) *Glossographia: Or, A Dictionary,*
                    Interpreting All Such Hard Words, Whether
                    Hebrew, Greek, Latin, Italian, Spanish, French,
                    Teutonick, Belgick, British or Saxon; As Are Now
                    Used in Our Refined English Tongue. Also the
                    Terms of Divinity, Law, Physick, Mathematicks,
                    Heraldy, Anatomy, War, Musick, Architecture; and
                    of Several Other Arts and Sciences Explicated,
                    with Etymologies, Definitions, and Historical
                    Observations on the Same. London: Newcomb

Bonnard, F.   (1907) *Histoire de L'abbaye Royale et de L'ordre*
                    Des Chanoines Régulaires de St-Victor de Paris.
                    Paris: A. Savaète

Bouveresse, J.   (1995) *Wittgenstein Reads Freud: The Myth of*
                    the Unconscious, trans. C. Cosman. Princeton, NJ:
                    Princeton University Press

Bouyer, L.   (1981) 'Mysticism: A History of the Word' in
                    R.Woods (ed.) *Understanding Mysticism.*
                    New York: Image

Butler, C.   (1926) *Western Mysticism. The Teaching*
                    of Augustine, Gregory and Bernard on
                    Contemplation and the Contemplative Life, 2nd
                    edition with Afterthoughts, republished in 2001.
                    Oregon: Wipf and Stock

Callus, D.A.   (1947) 'The Date of Grosseteste's Translations
                    and Commentaries on Pseudo-Dionysius and the
                    Nichomachean Ethics' in *Recherches de théologie*
                    ancienne et médiévale 14 (1947), pp. 186–209

Carlson, T.A.   (1991) 'Transcending Negation: The Causal Nothing and Ecstatic Being in Pseudo-Dionysius's Theology' in *Indiscretion: Finitude and the Naming of God*. Chicago: University of Chicago Press

Cavell, S.   (1976) *Must We Mean What We Say?* Oxford: Oxford University Press
(1979) *The Claim of Reason: Wittgenstein, Skepticism, Morality and Tragedy*. Oxford: Oxford University Press

Chambers, E.   (1751–1752) *Cyclopeadia: Or, An Universal Dictionary of Arts and Sciences*, 2 vols. London: Innys

Chase, S.   (2003) *Contemplation and Compassion: The Victorine Tradition*. London: Darton Longman Todd

Chatterjee, R.   (2005) *Wittgenstein and Judaism: A Triumph of Concealment*. New York: Peter Lang

Chevallier, P.   (1957) 'Influence du Pseudo-Denys en Occident' in DS III, pp. 318–323

Chorpenning, J.   (1979) 'The Literary and Theological Method of *The Interior Castle*' in *Journal of Hispanic Philology* 3 (1979) pp. 121–133

Cioffi, F.   (1969) 'Wittgenstein's Freud' in *Studies in the Philosophy of Wittgenstein*, ed. P. Winch. London: Routledge

Clack, B. (1999a) *An Introduction to Wittgenstein's Philosophy of Religion*. Edinburgh: Edinburgh University Press
(1999b) *Wittgenstein, Frazer and Religion*. London: Macmillan

Coakley, S. and C. Stang (2009) *Re-Thinking Dionysius the Areopagite*. Chichester: Wiley-Blackwell

Coolman, B.T. (2009) *The Medieval Affective Dionysian Tradition* in Coakley, S. and C. Stang (2009) *Re-Thinking Dionysius the Areopagite*. Chichester: Wiley-Blackwell

Coventry, H. (1761) *Philemon to Hydapses: Or, the History of False Religion in the Earlier Pagan World, Related in a Series of Conversations*. Glasgow: Urie

Crary, A. and Read, R. (2000) *The New Wittgenstein*. London: Routledge

Cropper, M. (1958) *Evelyn Underhill: with a memoir of Lucy Menzies by Lumsden Barkway*. London: Longmans

Cupitt, D. (1987) *The Long Legged Fly: A Theology of Language and Desire*. London: SCM
(1998) *Mysticism after Modernity*. Oxford: Blackwell

de Bujanda, J. (ed.) (1984) *Index de L'Inquisition Espagnole 1551, 1554, 1559/Index des Livres Interdit*, Vol. 6. Québec: Éditions de l'Université de Sherbrooke

de Certeau, M. (1992) *The Mystic Fable: Vol One, The Sixteenth and Seventeenth Centuries* (trans. Smith). Chicago: University of Chicago Press

Delaporte, M. (2006) 'He Darkens Me with Brightness: The Theology of Pseudo-Dionysius in Hilduin's *Vita* of Saint Denis' in *Religion and Theology*, 13, 2006

Diamond, C. (2001) *The Realistic Spirit: Wittgenstein, Philosophy and the Mind.* Cambridge, MA: MIT Press

Dolejšová, I. (2001) *Accounts of Hope: A Problem of Method in Postmodern Apologia.* Oxford: Peter Lang

Dondaine, H. (1953) *Le Corpus dionysien de l'université de Paris au XIIIe siècle.* Rome: Edizioni di Storia et Letteratura

Drury, M. (1973) *The Danger of Words.* London: Routledge

Dubourg, P. (1927) 'La Date de la *Theologia Mystica*' in *Revue d'ascetique et de mystique* 8 (1927), pp. 156–161

Dumeige, G. (1952) *Richard de Saint-Victor et l'idée chrétienne de l'amour.* Paris

Dummett, M. (1991) *The Logical Basis of Metaphysics.* Cambridge, MA: Harvard University Press

Encyclopaedia Brittanica (1797) 'Mystics', vol. 12:598, Edinburgh: A. Bell and C. Macfarquhar
(1858) 'Mysticism', vol. 15:755–758. Boston, MA: Little, Brown

Efrén de la Madre de Dios y Otger Steggink (1977) *Tiempo y vida de Santa Teresa.* Madrid: Católica

Endean, P. (2004) *Karl Rahner and Ignatian Spirituality.* Oxford: Oxford University Press

Evans, D.   (1989) 'Can Philosophers Limit what Mystics
                       can do? A Critique of Steven Katz' in *Religious
                       Studies,* 25.1

Fann, K.T.   (1969) *Wittgenstein's Conception of Philosophy.*
                       Oxford: Blackwell

Fanning, S.   (2002) *Mystics of the Christian Tradition.* London:
                       Routledge

Ferrer, J.N.   (2001) 'Toward a Participatory Vision of Human
                       Spirituality' in *ReVision,* 24:2
                       (2002) *Revisioning Transpersonal Theory –
                       A Participatory Vision of Human Spirituality.*
                       New York: SUNY
                       (2003) 'Integral Transformative Practice:
                       A Participatory Perspective' in *The Journal of
                       Transpersonal Psychology.* 35:1

Flasche, H.   (1983) 'El Problema de la Certeza en el "Castillo
                       Interior" ' in *Actas de Congreso Internacional
                       Teresiano,* ed. T. Egido Martínez, V. García de la
                       Concha and O. Gonzalez de Caredal. Salamanca:
                       Universidad de Salamanca

Forman, R.   (1990) *The Problem of Pure Consciousness.*
                       Oxford: Oxford University Press
                       (ed.) (1998) *The Innate Capacity: Mysticism,
                       Psychology and Philosophy.* Oxford: Oxford
                       University Press

Fox, A.   (1960) *Dean Inge.* London: Murray

Francisco de   (1644–1655) *Reforma de los descalzos de Nuestra
Santa María   Senora del Carmen de la primitiva observancia,
                       hecha por Santa Teresa de Jesús.* Madrid

Frothingham, O.   (1891) *Recollections and Impressions.* New York:
                   Putnam's Sons

Gadamer, H-G.   (1990) *Truth and Method* (2nd edn), trans.
                   Weinsheimer and Marshall. New York: Crossroad

García de la   (1978) *El arte literario de Santa Teresa.*
Concha, V.   Barcelona: Ariel

Genova, J.   (1995) *Wittgenstein: A Way of Seeing.* London:
                   Routledge

Gimello, R.M.   (1983) 'Mysticism in its Contexts' in Katz, S. (ed.),
                   Mysticism and Religious Traditions. Oxford:
                   Oxford University Press
                   (1990) 'Remarks on the Future Study of Mysticism',
                   unpublished manuscript presented at the annual
                   meeting of the American Academy of Religion,
                   November 1990, cited in Herman 2000:99

Golitzin, A.   (2003) ' "Suddenly" Christ: The Place of Negative
                   Theology in the Mystagogy of Dionysius
                   Areopagites' in *Mystics: Aporia and Presence,* ed.
                   M. Kessler and C. Shepherd. Chicago: University
                   of Chicago Press

Green, D.   (1989) *Gold in the Crucible: Teresa of Avila and the
                   Western Mystical Tradition.* Shaftesbury: Element

Greene, D.   (1991) *Evelyn Underhill: Artist of the Infinite Life.*
                   London: Darton Longman Todd
                   (1988) *Evelyn Underhill: Modern Guide to the
                   Ancient Quest for the Holy.* Ed. with introduction.
                   New York: SUNY
                   (2004) 'Evelyn Underhill' in *The Dictionary of
                   National Biography.* Oxford: Oxford University
                   Press

Grimley, M.   (2004) 'William Ralph Inge' in *The Dictionary of
                       National Biography*. Oxford: Oxford University
                       Press

Guinan, P.A.   (1994) *Carthusian Prayer and Hugh of Balma's
                       Viae Sion Lugent*. San Francisco: Catholic
                       Scholar's Press

Habermas, J.   (1971) *Knowledge and Human Interest*, trans.
                       Shapiro. Boston: Beacon Press

Hacker, P.M.S.   (2001) *Wittgenstein: Connections and
                       Controversies*. Oxford: Clarendon Press

Hamilton, A.   (1992) *Heresy and Mysticism in Sixteenth Century
                       Spain: The Alumbrados*. Cambridge: James Clarke

Harrington, L.   (2004) *The Mystical Theology of Dionysius the
                       Areopagite in Eriugena's Latin Translation with
                       the Scholia translated by Anastasius the Librarian
                       and Excerpts from Eriugena's Periphyseon*. Paris:
                       Peeters

Harris, H. and   (2005) *Faith and Philosophical Analysis: The
Insole, C.   Impact of Analytical Philosophy on the Philosophy
                       of Religion*. Aldershot: Ashgate

Hartley, T.   (1764) *Paradise Restored: Or, a Testimony to the
                       Doctrine of the Blessed Millennium with Some
                       Considerations on its Approaching Advent from
                       the Signs of the Times to which is added, A Short
                       Defence of the Mystical*. London, Richardson

Haskins, C.H.   (1957) *The Renaissance of the 12th Century*. New
                       York: Meridian

Hauerwas, S.

(1983) *The Peaceable Kingdom: A Primer in Christian Ethics.* Notre Dame, IN: University of Notre Dame Press
(2004) 'Aquinas, Preller, Wittgenstein and Hopkins' in *Grammar and Grace: Reformulations of Aquinas and Wittgenstein,* ed. J. Stout and R. MacSwain. London: SCM

Heiler, F.

(1932) *Prayer: A Study in the History and Psychology of Religion,* trans. McComb. London: Oxford University Press

Herman, J.R.

(2000) 'The Contextual Illusion: Comparative Mysticism and Postmodernism' in Patton, K.C. and Ray, B.C. (eds) *A Magic Still Dwells: Comparative Religion in a Postmodern Age.* Berkeley: University of California Press

Hertz, H.

(1956) *Principles of Mechanics,* trans. D. Jones and J. Walley. New York: Dover Press

Hosseini, M.

(2007) *Wittgenstein und Weisheit.* Stuttgart: Kohlhammer

Howells, E.

(2002) *John of the Cross and Teresa of Avila: Mystical Knowing and Selfhood.* New York: Herder and Herder

Howells, E. and Tyler, P.M.

(eds) (2010) *Sources of Transformation: Revitilizing Traditions of Christian Spirituality.* New York: Continuum

Hutto, D.

(2003) *Wittgenstein and the End of Philosophy: Neither Theory nor Therapy.* London: Macmillan

Huxley, A.

(1946) *The Perennial Philosophy*. London: Chatto & Windus

Incandela, J.M.

(1985) 'The Appropriation of Wittgenstein's Work by Philosophers of Religion. Towards a Re-evaluation and an End.' In *Religious Studies*, 21:457–474

Inge, W.R.

(1899) *Christian Mysticism*. London: Methuen and Co
(1926) *The Platonic Tradition in English Religious Thought, the Hulsean Lectures at Cambridge, 1925–1926*. London: Longman, Green.
(1929) *The Philosophy of Plotinus*. London: Longman.

Insole, C.

(2006) *The Realist Hope: A Critique of Anti-Realist Approaches in Contemporary Philosophical Theology*. Aldershot: Ashgate

James, W.

(1897) *The Will to Believe and other Essays in Popular Philosophy*. London: Longmans, Green and Co
(1902) *The Varieties of Religious Experience: A Study in Human Nature*. London: Longmans, Green and Co

Jantzen, G.

(1995) *Power, Gender and Christian Mysticism*. Cambridge: Cambridge University Press

Jarman, D.

(1993) *This is not a Film of Ludwig Wittgenstein* in *Wittgenstein: The Terry Eagleton Script, The Derek Jarman Film*. London: British Film Institute

Javelet, R.

(1962) 'Thomas Gallus et Richard de Saint-Victor Mystiques.' In *Recherches de théologie ancienne et médiévale*, 29/30

Kallenberg, B.   (2001) *Ethics as Grammar: Changing the Postmodern Subject*. Notre Dame, Ind: University of Notre Dame Press

Kamen, H.   (1997) *The Spanish Inquisition*. London: Weidenfeld & Nicolson

Katz, S.   (1978) 'Language, Epistemology and Mysticism' in *Mysticism and Philosophical Analysis*, ed. Katz. London: Sheldon
(ed.) (1978) *Mysticism and Philosophical Analysis*. London: Sheldon
(1983) *Mysticism and Religious Traditions*. Oxford: Oxford University Press
(1992) *Mysticism and Language*. Oxford: Oxford University Press

Kenny, A.   (1959) 'Aquinas and Wittgenstein' in *The Downside Review*, 77

Kerr, F.   (1982) 'Wittgenstein and Theological Studies' in *New Blackfriars*, 63
(1983) 'Stories of the Soul' in *New Blackfriars*, 64
(1984) 'The Need for Philosophy in Theology Today' in *New Blackfriars*, 65
(1986, 1997) *Theology after Wittgenstein*. Oxford: Blackwell
(1987) 'Charity as Friendship' in *Language, Meaning and God: Essays in Honour of Herbert McCabe OP*, ed. B. Davies. London: Chapman
(2008) *Work on Oneself: Wittgenstein's Philosophical Psychology*. Arlington, VA: The Institute for Psychological Sciences Press

Kierkegaard, S.   (1992) *Concluding Unscientific Postscript to the Philosophical Fragments*, trans. H. and E. Hong. Princeton, NJ: Princeton University Press

King, R.   (1999) *Orientalism and Religion: Postcolonial
                      Theory, India and the 'Mystic East'.*
                      London: Routledge

King, U.   (1985) 'Indian Spirituality and Western
                      Materialism', in *Ideas For Action*, 1. Delhi: India
                      Social Institute

Klagge, J.   (2001) *Wittgenstein: Biography and Philosophy.*
                      Cambridge: Cambridge University Press

Knowles, M.D.   (1962) *The Evolution of Medieval Thought.*
                      London: Longmans
                      (1975) 'The Influence of Pseudo-Dionysios on
                      Western Mysticism' in *Christian Spirituality:
                      Essays in Honour of Gordon Rupp,* ed. P. Brooks.
                      London: SCM

Koch, A.   (1895) 'Proklus als Quelle des Ps-Dionysius
                      Areopagita in der Lehre von Bösen' in *Philologus,*
                      54/1, pp. 438–454

Kottman, K.   (1972) *Law and Apocalypse: The Moral Thought
                      of Luis de León.* The Hague: Nijhoff

Kripal, J.J.   (1995) *Kali's Child: The Mystical and the Erotic in
                      the Life and Teachings of Ramakrishna.* Chicago:
                      The University of Chicago Press
                      (2001) *Roads of Excess, Palaces of Wisdom:
                      Eroticism and Reflexivity in the Study of
                      Mysticism.* Chicago: University of Chicago Press
                      (2004) 'Comparative Mystics: Scholars as Gnostic
                      Diplomats' in *Common Knowledge*, 10 (3)

Laguardia, G.   (1980) 'Santa Teresa and the Problem of Desire' in
                      Hispania, 63, p.3

Lash, N.   (1988) *Easter in Ordinary: Reflections on Human Experience and the Knowledge of God.* London: University of Notre Dame Press

Levinson, H.S.   (1981) *The Religious Investigations of William James.* Chapel Hill, NC: University of North Carolina Press

Levy, D.   (1996) *Freud Among the Philosophers.* New Haven, CT: Yale University Press

Llamas-Martínez, E.   (1972) *Santa Teresa de Jesús y la Inquisicion española.* Madrid: CSIC

Llorca, B.   (1980) *La Inquisición española y los alumbrados (1509–1667).* Salamanca: Universidad Pontíficia

López Santidrián, S.   (1998) Introduction to *Tercer Abecedario* of *Francisco de Osuna.* Madrid: Biblioteca de Autores Christianos

Louth, A.   (1989) *Denys the Areopagite.* London: Geoffrey Chapman
(2009) *The Reception of Dionysius up to Maximus the Confessor* in S. Coakley and C. Stang *Re-Thinking Dionysius the Areopagite.* Chichester: Wiley-Blackwell

Malcolm, N.   (1993) *Wittgenstein: A Religious Point of View?* London: Routledge
(2001) *Ludwig Wittgenstein: A Memoir.* Oxford: Clarendon Press

Malysz, P.   (2009) *Luther and Dionysius: Beyond Mere Negations* in S. Coakley and C. Stang *Re-Thinking Dionysius the Areopagite.* Chichester: Wiley-Blackwell

Márquez, A.   (1980) *Los alumbrados: orígenes y filosofía*
                     (1525–1559). Madrid: Taurus

Martin, D.   (1997) *Carthusian Spirituality: The Writings of*
                     Hugh of Balma and Guigo de Ponte. Mahwah,
                     NY: Paulist.

Matter, E.A.   (1990) *The Voice of My Beloved: The Song*
                     of Songs in Western Medieval Christianity.
                     Pennsylvania: University of Pennsylvania Press.

McCutcheon, F.   (2001) *Religion Within the Limits of Language*
                     Alone: Wittgenstein on Philosophy and Religion.
                     Aldershot: Ashgate

McEvoy, J.   (2000) *Robert Grosseteste*. Oxford: Oxford
                     University Press
                     (2003) *Mystical Theology: The Glosses of Thomas*
                     Gallus and the Commentary of Robert Grosseteste
                     on De Mystica Theologia, ed. with introduction.
                     Paris: Peeters

McGinn, B.   (1989) 'Love, Knowledge and *Unio Mystica* in the
                     Western Christian Tradition' in *Mystical Union in*
                     Judaism, Christianity and Islam: An Ecumenical
                     Dialogue. Ed. Idel and McGinn. New York:
                     Continuum
                     (1991) *The Presence of God: A History of Western*
                     Christian Mysticism. Vol I: The Foundations of
                     Mysticism. London: SCM
                     (1993) 'The Letter and the Spirit: Spirituality as
                     an Academic Discipline', *Christian Spirituality*
                     Bulletin. 1(2):1–10
                     (1994) *The Presence of God: A History of Western*
                     Christian Mysticism. Volume 2: Gregory the Great
                     through to the Twelfth Century. London: SCM

(1995) 'God as Eros: Metaphysical Foundations of Christian Mysticism' in *New Perspectives on Historical Theology: Essays in Memory of John Meyendorff*, ed. B. Nassif. Grand Rapids: Eerdmans

(1998a) *The Presence of God: A History of Western Christian Mysticism. Volume 3: The Flowering of Mysticism: Men and Women in the New Mysticism, 1200–1350*. London: SCM

(1998b) 'Quo Vadis? Reflections on the Current Study of Mysticism' in *Christian Spirituality Bulletin*, 6 (1):13–21

(1998c) 'Thomas Gallus and Dionysian Mysticism' in *Studies in Spirituality*, 8

(2005a) *The Presence of God: A History of Western Christian Mysticism. Volume 4: The Harvest of Mysticism in Medieval Germany.* New York: Herder and Herder

(2005b) *Mysticism* in *The New SCM Dictionary of Christian Spirituality*, ed. P. Sheldrake. London: SCM

McGuinness, B.   (1988) *Wittgenstein: A Life. The Young Ludwig (1889–1921)*. London: Penguin

(2001) 'Wittgenstein and the Idea of Jewishness' in J. Klagge (ed.) *Wittgenstein: Biography and Philosophy*. Cambridge: Cambridge University Press

(2002) *Approaches to Wittgenstein*. London: Routledge

McIntosh, M.   (1998) *Mystical Theology: The Integrity of Spirituality and Theology.* Oxford: Blackwell

Menéndez
Pidal, R.   (1942) 'El estilo de Santa Teresa' in *La lengua de Cristobál Colón*. Buenos Aires: Espasa

Monk, R.   (1990) *Ludwig Wittgenstein – The Duty of Genius*. London: Jonathon Cape

Morrall, J.   (1960) *Gerson and the Great Schism*. Manchester: Manchester University Press

Morris, C.   (1972) *The Discovery of the Individual 1050–1200*. London: SPCK

Moyal-Sharrock, D.   (ed.) (2004) *The Third Wittgenstein: The Post-Investigations Works*. London: Ashgate

Nedo, M., Moreton, G. and Finlay, A.   (2005) *Ludwig Wittgenstein: There Where You Are Not*. London: Black Dog

Neil, B.   (1998) *Anastasius Bibliothecarius' Latin Translation of Greek Documents Pertaining to the Life of Maximus the Confessor*. Ann Arbor: UMI

Nelstrop, L., Magill, K. and Onishi, B. de   (2009) *Christian Mysticism: An Introduction to Contemporary Theoretical Approaches*. Farnham: Ashgate

Nygren, A.   (1957) *Agape and Eros: A Study of the Christian Idea of Love*, trans. P. Watson. London: SPCK

Otto, R.   (1957) *Mysticism East and West*. New York: Kessinger

Pears, D.F.   (1988) *The False Prison: A Study of the Development of Wittgenstein's Philosophy*, 2 Vols. Oxford: Clarendon Press

Perczel, I.   (2009) *The Earliest Syriac Reception of Dionysius* in S. Coakley and C. Stang (2009) *Re-Thinking Dionysius the Areopagite*. Chichester: Wiley-Blackwell

Peterman, J.   (1992) *Philosophy as Therapy: An Interpretation and Defense of Wittgenstein's Later Philosophical Project.* New York: SUNY Press

Rhees, R. (ed.)   (1981) *Ludwig Wittgenstein: Personal Recollections.* Totowa: Rowman & Littlefield
(1987) *Recollections of Wittgenstein.* Oxford: Oxford Paperbacks

Rivers, E.   (1984) 'The Vernacular Mind of St. Teresa' in *Carmelite Studies.* Washington: ICS

Rorem, P.   (1982) 'Iamblichus and the Anagogical Method in Pseudo-Dionysian Liturgical Theology' in *Studia Patristica*, vol 18 ed. Livingstone. Oxford: Pergamon
(1993) *Pseudo-Dionysius. A Commentary on the Texts and an Introduction to their Influence.* Oxford: Oxford University Press
(1998) with J. Lamoreaux, *John of Scythopolis and the Dionysian Corpus: Annotating the Areopagite.* Oxford: Oxford University Press
(2009) *The Early Latin Dionysius: Eriugena and Hugh of St. Victor* in S. Coakley and C. Stang *Re-Thinking Dionysius the Areopagite.* Chichester: Wiley-Blackwell

Rorty, R.   (1979) *Philosophy and the Mirror of Nature.* Princeton: Princeton University Press
(1982) *Consequences of Pragmatism (Essays 1972–1980).* Brighton: Harvester

Ros, Fidèle de, P.   (1936) *Un maître de Sainte Thérèse: Le père François d'Osuna.* Paris
(1948) *Un Inspirateur de Sainte Thérèse: Le Frère Bernardin de Larede.* Paris

Rothberg, D.   (1986) 'Philosophical Foundations of
                      Transpersonal Psychology: An Introduction to
                      Some Basic Issues' in *The Journal of Transpersonal
                      Psychology*, 18(1)
                      (1994) 'Spiritual Inquiry' in *ReVision*, 17(2)
                      (1996) 'Ken Wilber and Contemporary
                      Transpersonal Inquiry: An Introduction to the
                      ReVision Conversation' in *ReVision*, 18:4

Ruello, R.   (1981) 'Statut et rôle de l'intellectus et de l'affectus
                      dans la Théologie Mystique de Hughes de Balma'
                      in *Kartäusermystik u mystiker*, Vol. 1, Analecta
                      Cartusiana, 55.1. Salzburg: Institut für Anglistik u
                      Amerikanistik.

Saffrey, H.D.   (1979) 'Nouveaux liens objectifs entre le Ps-Denys
                      et Proclus' in *Revue des sciences philosophiques et
                      théologiques*, 63:3–16

Said, E.   (1978) *Orientalism: Western Conceptions of the
                      Orient*. Reprinted 1995. London: Penguin

Sass, L.   (2001) 'Deep Disquietudes: Reflections on
                      Wittgenstein as Antiphilosopher' in *Wittgenstein,
                      Biography and Philosophy* ed. J.C. Klagge.
                      Cambridge: Cambridge University Press

Savickey, B.   (1998) 'Wittgenstein's *Nachlass*' in *Philosophical
                      Investigations*, 21(4)

Schmidt, L.E.   (2003) 'The Making of Modern "Mysticism" ' in
                      Journal of the American Academy of Religion,
                      71(2):273–302

Sedgwick, M.   (2004) *Against the Modern World: Traditionalism
                      and the Secret Intellectual History of the Twentieth
                      Century*. Oxford: Oxford University Press

Sells, M.A.   (1993) 'From a History of Mysticism to a
Theology of Mysticism' in *The Journal of Religion*,
73(3). Chicago: University of Chicago Press
(1994) *Mystical Languages of Unsaying*. Chicago:
University of Chicago Press

Sheldrake, P.   (1991) *Spirituality and History: Questions of
Interpretation and Method*. London: SPCK

Shotter, J.   (1996) 'Now I Can Go On: Wittgenstein and Our
Embodied Embeddedness in the Hurly-Burly of
Life' in *Human Studies*, 19:385–407
(1997) 'Wittgenstein in Practice: From "The Way
of Theory" to a "Social Poetics" ' in Tolman,
Cherry, van Hezewijk and Lubek (eds.), *Problems of
Theoretical Psychology*. York, Ontario: Captus Press

Smart, N.   (1958) *Reasons and Faiths. An Investigation of
Religious Discourse: Christian and Non-Christian*.
London: Routledge
(1962) 'Mystical Experience' in *Sophia*, 1:19–25
(1967) 'Mystical Experience' in *Art, Mind and
Religion* ed. Capitan and Merrill. Pittsburgh
(1978) 'Understanding Religious Experience' in
Mysticism and Philosophical Analysis ed. S. Katz.
London: Sheldon

Smith, J.E.   (1983) 'William James's Account of Mysticism;
A Critical Appraisal' in *Mysticism and Religious
Traditions* ed. S. Katz. Oxford: Oxford University
Press

Smitheran, L.H.   (1997) 'Santa Teresa y la Noche Oscura del Alma'
in *La Recepción de los Místicos Teresa de Jesús
y Juan de la Cruz* ed. R. Gancia. Salamanca:
Ediciones Universidad Pontificia

Solignac, A.   (1988) 'Sarrazin (Jean), traducteur du Pseudo-Denys' in DS, Fas XCI, pp.351–355

Sontag, F.   (2000) *Wittgenstein and the Mystical: Philosophy as an Ascetic Practice*. Atlanta, Georgia: Scholars Press

Sorell, T.   (1991) *Scientism*. New York: Routledge

Spengler, O.   (1923) *Der Untergang des Abendlandes: Umrisse einer Morphologie der Weltgeschichte*. Munich: C.H. Beck'sche Verlag
(1926) *The Decline of the West: Form and Actuality*, trans. C.F. Atkinson. London: George Allen and Unwin

Stace, W.T.   (1960) *Mysticism and Philosophy*. Philadelphia, PA: J.B. Lippincott

Stang, C.   (2009) *Dionysius, Paul and the Significance of Pseudonym* in S. Coakley and C. Stang *Re-Thinking Dionysius the Areopagite*. Chichester: Wiley-Blackwell

Stern, D.   (1996) 'The Availability of Wittgenstein's Philosophy' in *The Cambridge Companion to Wittgenstein*, ed. H. Sluga and D. Stern. Cambridge: Cambridge University Press
(2001) 'Was Wittgenstein a Jew?' in Klagge (ed.) *Wittgenstein: Biography and Philosophy*. Cambridge: Cambridge University Press

Stiglmayr, J.   (1895) 'Der Neuplatoniker Proclus als Vorlage des sog. Dionysius Areopagita in der Lehre vom Übel' in *Historisches Jahrbuch*, 16:253–273

Stoelen, A.   (1969) 'Hughes de Balma' in DS Vol. 7. Paris: Beauchesne

Stout, J. and MacSwain, R. — (2004) *Grammar and Grace: Reformulations of Aquinas and Wittgenstein*. London: SCM

Suchla, B.R. — (1980) 'Die sogenannten Maximus-Scholien des Corpus Dionysiacum Areopagiticum' in *Nachrichten der Akademie der Wissenschaften in Göttingen, Philologisch-historische Klasse*, 3:33–66

Suzuki, D.T. — (1957) *Mysticism Christian and Buddhist*. London: Allen and Unwin

Swinburne, R. — (1979) *The Existence of God*. Oxford: Oxford University Press

Tanesini, A. — (2004) *Wittgenstein: A Feminist Interpretation*. Cambridge: Polity Press

Tellechea Idígoras, J.I. — (1962) 'Textos inéditos sobre el fenómeno de los alumbrados' in *Ephemerides Carmeliticae*,13:768–774
(1968) *El arzobispo Carranza y su tiempo*, 2 vols. Madrid

Théry, G. — (1950–1951) 'Documents concernant Jean Sarrazin réviseur de la traduction érigénienne du "Corpus Dionysiacum" ' in DS, Fas XCI:.351–355

Thompson, C. — (2000) 'Wittgenstein's Confessions' in *Philosophical Investigations*, 23:1

Tolstoy, L. — (1895) *The Four Gospels*. Croydon: The Brotherhood Publishing Company

Turner, D. — (1995a) *The Darkness of God: Negativity in Christian Mysticism*. Cambridge: Cambridge University Press
(1995b) *Eros and Allegory: Medieval Exegesis of the Song of Songs*. Kalamazoo: Cistercian Publications

Tyler, P.M.   (1993) *Realism and Anti-Realism in
                       Wittgensteinian Understandings of Religion.*
                       MA Dissertation presented at University of London
                       for completion of MTh in Philosophy of Religion
                       (1997) *The Way of Ecstasy: Praying with St.
                       Teresa of Avila.* Norwich: Canterbury Press
                       (1999) *Wittgenstein, Frazer and Superstition.*
                       Research Paper given at Sarum/STETS Research
                       Seminar, Sarum College, Salisbury, October 1999
                       (2005) '*Alumbrados*' in P. Sheldrake (ed.) *The New
                       SCM Dictionary of Christian Spirituality.* London:
                       SCM/Canterbury Press
                       (2009) *Mystical strategies and performative
                       discourse in the theologia mystica of Teresa of Avila:
                       A Wittgensteinian analysis.* Thesis submitted in
                       fulfilment of the PhD degree at University of Durham
                       (2010a) *John of the Cross: Outstanding Christian
                       Thinker.* London: Continuum
                       (2010b) '*Miguel de Molinos*' in *The Cambridge
                       Dictionary of Christianity,* ed. D. Patte.
                       Cambridge: Cambridge University Press
                       (2010c) 'Teresa of Avila's Transformative Strategies
                       of Embodiment in *Meditations on the Song of
                       Songs*' in *Sources of Transformation: Revitilizing
                       Christian Spirituality,* ed. E. Howells and
                       P.M.Tyler. London: Continuum

Underhill, E.   (1907) 'A Defence of Magic' in *The Fortnightly
                       Review,* LXXXII. London: Chapman and Hall
                       (1910) *Mysticism: The Nature and Development
                       of Spiritual Consciousness.* Reprinted 1993.
                       Oxford: Oneworld
                       (1943) *The Letters of Evelyn Underhill,* ed. with
                       introduction by C. Williams. London: Longman,
                       Green and Co

Vaughan, R.A.   (1856) *Hours with the Mystics: A Contribution to the History of Religious Opinion* (3rd edn 1895). London: Gibbings and Co
(1858) *Essays and Remains of the Revd Robert Alfred Vaughan edited with a memoir by the Revd Robert Vaughan*. London: John W Parker and Son

von Balthasar,   (1961–1969) *Herrlichkeit: Eine theologische*
H.U.   *Ästhetik*. (Einsiedeln: Johannes Verlag) trans. 'The Glory of the Lord: A Theological Aesthetic'(1982–1989) ed. J. Fessio and J. Riches, trans. O. Davies, A. Louth, J. Sayward, M. Simon, B. McNeil, F. McDonagh, J. Riches, E. Leiva-Merikakis and R. Williams. Edinburgh: T and T Clarke

von Hügel,   (1908) *The Mystical Element of Religion as*
Baron F.   *Studied in Saint Catherine of Genoa and her Friends*. London: Dent

von Ivánka, E.   (1964) *Plato Christianus: Übernahme und Umgestaltung des Platonismus durch die Väter*. Einsiedeln: Johannes-Verlag

von Wright, G.H. (1971) *Explanation and Understanding*. London: Routledge
(1982) *Wittgenstein*. Oxford: Blackwell

Waismann, F.   (1965) *The Principles of Linguistic Philosophy*, ed. R Harre. London: Macmillan

Walach, H.   (1994) *Notitia experimentalis Dei – Erfahrungserkenntnis Gottes: Studien zu Hugo de Balmas Text 'Viae Sion lugent' und deutsche Übersetzung*. Analecta Cartusiana, 98.1. Salzburg: Institut für Englische Sprache und Literatur

Walsh, J.J.   (1957) *Sapientia Christianorum: The Doctrine*
                   of Thomas Gallus, Abbot of Vercelli on
                   Contemplation. Dissertatio ad Lauream in
                   Facultate Theologica, Pontifical Gregorian
                   University, Rome

Weber, A.   (1990) *Teresa of Avila and the Rhetoric of*
                   Femininity, Princeton, NJ: Princeton University Press

Webster, N.   (1828) *American Dictionary of the English*
                   Language, 2 vols. New York: Converse

Weeks, A.   (1993) *German Mysticism from Hildegard of*
                   Bingen to Ludwig Wittgenstein: A Literary and
                   Intellectual History. New York: SUNY Press

Williams, R.   (1983) 'The Prophetic and the Mystical: Heiler
                   Revisited' in *New Blackfriars,* 64:330–347
                   (1984) 'Butler's *Western Mysticism*: Towards an
                   Assessment' in *The Downside Review,* 102:197–215
                   (1991) *Teresa of Avila.* London: Continuum

Winch, P.   (1958) *The Idea of a Social Science.* London:
                   Routledge
                   (1987) *Trying to Make Sense.* Oxford: Blackwell

Woods, R.   (1981) *Understanding Mysticism.* New York: Image

Zaehner, R.C.   (1957) *Mysticism Sacred and Profound.* Oxford:
                   Galaxy
                   (1970) *Concordant Discord. The Interdependence*
                   of Faiths being the Gifford Lectures on Natural
                   Religion Delivered at St. Andrews in 1967–1969.
                   Oxford: Clarendon Press

Zinn, G.A.   (1979) *Richard of St. Victor: The Twelve*
                   Patriarchs, The Mystical Ark, Book Three of the
                   Trinity, trans. with introduction. London: SPCK

Index